In Forme of Speche Is Chaunge

Readings
in the History of the English Language

JOHN H. FISHER
University of Tennessee

DIANE BORNSTEIN
Queens College, City University of New York

PRENTICE-HALL, INC., *Englewood Cliffs, New Jersey*

Library of Congress Cataloging in Publication Data

FISHER, JOHN H. comp.
  In forme of speche is chaunge.

  Bibliography: p.
  1. English language—Dialects—Texts.
2. English literature (Collections)
I. BORNSTEIN, DIANE, joint comp.
II. Title.
PE1702.A2   427'.008   73–15829
ISBN 0–13–464594–4
ISBN 0–13–464586–3 (pbk.)

Printed in the United States of America

10   9   8   7   6   5   4   3   2   1

PRENTICE-HALL INTERNATIONAL, INC., London
PRENTICE-HALL OF AUSTRALIA, PTY. LTD., Sydney
PRENTICE-HALL OF CANADA, LTD., Toronto
PRENTICE-HALL OF INDIA PRIVATE LIMITED, New Delhi
PRENTICE-HALL OF JAPAN, INC., Tokyo

CONTENTS

iii

LITERARY REPRESENTATIONS OF DIALECT

APPENDIX

LIST OF FACSIMILES

PREFACE

This book grows out of mimeographed materials which John Fisher has accumulated over the years for his course in the History of the English Language. Diane Bornstein has provided them with an introduction, headnotes, and exercises, verified them, and supplemented them with materials used in her course. Our purpose in assembling these selections has been to illustrate the development of the language by as many styles and levels of discourse as possible. Only through comparison and contrast do we come to recognize our own linguistic behavior or that of any other period. We hope that the appendices present in convenient form details concerning phonology, morphology, and syntax that the students would otherwise have to work out for themselves.

We express our gratitude to our students for what they have taught us about the way the history of the language should be presented. Especially we thank Mary M. Lynch and Leonora Sherman of Queens College for reading and reacting to parts of the text while it was in preparation, and our colleagues S. Robert Greenberg of Queens College and Robert R. Raymo of New York University for reading the manuscript and making helpful suggestions.

J. H. F.

D. B.

INTRODUCTION

"Ye knowe ek that in forme of speche is chaunge
Withinne a thousand yer, and wordes tho
That hadden prys now wonder nyce and straunge
Us thenketh hem, and yet they spake hem so."

(*Troylus and Criseyde,* II, 22–25)

The best way to perceive the development of the English language is to study its appearance in poetry and prose over the centuries. Writings have survived in a variety of regional, stylistic, and social forms. The purpose of this collection is to provide samples of many of these categories as a supplement to the usual textbooks for courses in the history of the English language. Authors may not consciously adhere to the principles of a particular style; yet in composing a letter, a journal, a will, a petition, a chronicle, an essay, a homily, or a poem, a sensitive writer (or speaker) unconsciously follows the rules of that particular genre or style.

We are all aware of functional variety in contemporary language, and each of us has a range of styles extending from intimate to formal. We use different styles to address members of our families, friends, neighbors, strangers, fellow workers, bosses, business associates, and public officials. Each style has its own vocabulary, syntax, and phonology. Martin Joos has presented the classic discussion of functional variety in *The Five Clocks* (New York: Harcourt, Brace and World, 1961). The same sort of variety existed in the past, but we cannot recapture all of it since only the written record survives. In the case of Old English, even that is meager. Nevertheless, we can perceive at least some of the range by examining historical samples of different kinds.

STYLE

During all periods, poetry has been further from colloquial speech than prose. It observes additional rules or restrictions (such as alliteration, rhyme, metrical patterns) that distinguish it from prose. These formal devices create

1

mnemonics or formulas by which the language is remembered. Poetry therefore tends to be more archaic, to preserve more old words, inflections, and
pronunciations. The alliterative poems of the Old English and Middle English
periods contain words and pronunciations that do not appear in the prose.
Chaucer used final unstressed "e" and various dialectal forms in his poetry but
not in his prose.

Besides comparing poetry and prose, we can follow the development of
two styles in English prose, the plain and the ornate: in Old English the plain
styles of the *Anglo-Saxon Chronicle,* Alfred, and Aelfric contrast with the ornate
alliterative prose of Wulfstan; in Middle English the conversational styles of
the *Ancrene Riwle* and John Wyclif with the rhetorical style of Richard Rolle;
in Late Middle English the native style of Sir Thomas Malory with the Frenchi-
fied prose of William Caxton; in Early Modern English the colloquial phrasing
of Hugh Latimer with the Ciceronian periods of Richard Hooker; in Colonial
American English the plain style of William Bradford with the rousing rhetoric
of Jonathan Edwards. For all periods we have some documents that are fairly
close to the spoken language, such as wills (in Old English), journals, and
letters. These materials provide a spectrum that enables us to study the language
both diachronically, or historically, and synchronically, or at different levels
during the same period of time.

Style has an especially marked effect on vocabulary. Alliterative poetry in
Old and Middle English made use of a highly specialized vocabulary with
many synonyms. Chaucer and Caxton, whose styles were strongly influenced
by French literature, introduced many French words into the language. In the
Prologue to the *Eneydos*, Caxton discusses the controversy that developed
regarding the borrowing of words, with some authors preferring to use a
native vocabulary and others wishing to "augment" it with foreign words.
Such borrowings came to be called "ink-horn terms" by disapproving Renaissance critics. Foreign words became a feature of the ornate style, as in the
Latinate prose of Richard Hooker.

SYNTAX

Style also affects the larger aspects of syntax, such as word order. For
example, modern scholarship has discredited traditional assumptions about
the syntactic freedom of Old English. In *La structure de la phrase verbale à l'époque
alfrédienne* (Paris: Les Belles Lettres, 1962), Paul Bacquet argues that Old
English word order is unpredictable only if one fails to recognize the funda-
mental distinction between normal word order (*ordre de base*) and word order
that calls attention to itself rhetorically (*ordre marqué*). While variation in word
order was possible, it was usually employed for a rhetorical or stylistic purpose.
In *A History of English Syntax* (New York: Holt, Rinehart and Winston, 1972),
Elizabeth Closs Traugott states that there is "a clear continuity of language

development from Old English on; most importantly from the syntactic point of view, most of the differences, like the use of inflection and a variety of word order patterns, turn out to be chiefly surface differences. The basic structure is very similar to that of Modern English—in fact, identical in most cases" (p. 66).

Two charts in the Appendix exhibit some of the basic sentence patterns of Old English and Middle English. The subject + verb + object order of Modern English was already dominant during the Old English period, but different orders were used for object pronouns, negative sentences, interrogatives, sentences beginning with adverbs, and subordinate clauses. These patterns became recessive during the late Old English period, and most of them disappeared in late Middle English. Yet relics of Old English surface structures survived. Sir Thomas Malory still used the adverb + verb + subject order so often found in Old English narrative prose. In Middle English the word order for negative and interrogative sentences frequently differed from that of Modern English, particularly when an auxiliary verb was not present; but the Modern English patterns already existed and gradually became dominant. In studying the selections that follow, we may observe the evolution of the basic patterns and see how they are varied for stylistic purposes.

MORPHOLOGY

Style has little effect on the morphological forms of the language, such as inflections and conjugations. These features are determined mainly by when and where a work was composed rather than by its stylistic level (yet even here a stylistic dimension is suggested by the disappearance of the final "e" and syncope of the final "ed" and "es" earlier in prose than in poetry). We can see how English changed from a synthetic language that used many inflections (for case, number, gender, mood, tense) to an analytic one that relies mainly on prepositions, auxiliaries, and word order. This change was actually one of degree. Old English already used analytic structures, such as the auxiliaries "habban" and "beon" for the perfect, and prepositions along with endings to indicate cases. In Middle English there was extensive generalization of an already existing system. In fact, it was probably their redundancy in many contexts that allowed the inflections to be reduced. Elements in a language that are simplified tend to be those that are not fully functional. The reduction of endings produced a cycle: as inflectional distinctions were lost, word order had to become more rigid; when case endings no longer identified the subject and the object of a sentence, the subject + verb + object order was required to signify the functions of subjects and predicates.

Together with the loss of inflections went an increasing reliance on segmentalization or the use of prepositions and auxiliaries. New auxiliaries were developed: "will" and "shall" came to be used mainly as future auxiliaries rather than as verbs of volition and obligation; "gin" and "do" emerged as new tense-carriers. The use of "gin" was short-lived, but "do" came to play a major role in Modern English as the tense carrier in negative and interrogative sentences that do not have another auxiliary. "Do" occasionally appeared as a tense-carrier in Middle English, but it was not used extensively until the Early Modern period, when it began to occur in all types of sentences. By the seventeenth century, its use began to decline in affirmative declarative sentences but increase in negative and interrogative sentences. In Modern English, "do" functions as a tense-carrier only in negative and interrogative sentences. When it appears in affirmative statements, it is a sign of emphasis. Alongside its function as an auxiliary, "do" has maintained an existence as a main verb and as a substitute verb (in sentences such as, "John came and so did I").

Modern English is still not totally analytic. The inflections that have survived already existed in Old English and were generalized by the process of analogy. Words with less common declensions or conjugations were assimilated to the patterns of the majority. For example, most nouns have taken on the "s" inflection for the plural and genitive singular, which is derived from the masculine declension in Old English. Most verbs form their past tense with a dental preterit (a "t" or "d" ending) including many that originally used vowel gradation to indicate past tense (such as "creep," "help," "sleep").

In comparing Old and Middle English inflectional patterns, we can see how the language has been simplified. Simplification is a common linguistic process because of the way in which language is learned. A child learns a language partly by imitation but mainly by forming inductive rules that will account for the utterances he hears and allow him to produce new utterances on the same models. The set of rules will be as simple and general as possible. This is the way children come up with analogical forms that are not part of the standard language (such as "foots" or "rided"). The rules created by different speakers vary. When many speakers abandon a rule, a feature becomes recessive; when all abandon it, it disappears. Features of Old English that were lost in Middle English include grammatical gender and all but the genitive and plural case endings for nouns, the accompanying endings on adjectives and demonstratives, and the dual person pronouns.

But language does not always move in the direction of simplification. Sometimes rules are created that contribute new complexities. In Old English the second person pronouns "þu" and "ge" were used purely on the basis of number. In Middle English "ye" began to be used in the singular to address a social superior or for polite address, whereas "thou" was often reserved for social inferiors or familiar address. This feature may have developed in imitation of the French use of "*tu*" and "*vous*." The selection from Malory shows how effective it could be as a literary device. The Quakers and Puritans objected to making a distinction on the basis of rank or politeness since this seemed to deny the equality of all men. John Winthrop used "thou" for the singular and "you" for the plural. Modern English has moved further toward democracy and simplification by using "you" as the only form for the second person pronoun.

In comparing Middle English with Modern English, we can see that the verbal endings were greatly simplified (although the use of auxiliaries grew much more complicated). We have lost all distinctions (except "was-were") for number and person in the past tense. In the present tense, the only inflection we use is an "s" for the third person singular. Of course, the same inflections were not lost by all individuals or on all words at the same time. For example, there was great variation in the third person singular ending in Middle and Early Modern English. During the Middle English period, different endings were features of regional dialects. By the Early Modern period, when the London dialect had come to serve as a written standard, "s" (the Northern form) was beginning to replace "th" (the original form in this dialect). In the selection by Hugh Latimer, the third person singular ending for all verbs is "th." A "th" inflection is more common in the prose of Hooker and Hakluyt, but "s" is used for some words. Individuals had different usages for different words, just as in Modern English there are special rules for plurals like "feet" and "men." Most writers maintained a "th" inflection on "hath" and "doth" for the third person singular until the latter part of the eighteenth century.

ORTHOGRAPHY AND PRONUNCIATION

Middle English texts dramatically demonstrate how individuals living at the same time but in different regions use diverse linguistic forms. Even within the major dialect areas of the North, East Midland, West Midland, Southwest, and Southeast, there was great variation. Practices differed from county to county and even from writer to writer. Linguistic variation became so apparent because of the absence of a uniform orthography.

During the Old English period, the West Saxon dialect functioned as a literary *koiné* or written standard. Informal documents, such as Aelfgar's will, show that this *koiné* was already very different from the language spoken during the late Old English period. After the Norman Conquest, this written standard was replaced by written standards in Latin and French. When English was written down, regional usages were followed. Texts produced in different areas of the country differed widely in their morphology and spelling.

Although we can't always be sure of what sounds were intended by orthographic symbols, they often provide some clues to pronunciation since the sounds of Latin remained the universal criteria for the sounds of the Roman alphabet (of course, Latin pronunciation varied from region to region, and the sounds and spelling of Latin were never entirely satisfactory for transcribing any of the vernacular dialects). Even when we are doubtful about the phonological equivalents of Middle English spellings, they help to localize texts. Since the identity of the manuscript in which a piece is found is an important factor in dealing with Old English and Middle English documents, this information is given in the headnotes. The citations give the location of the manuscript, the collection, and the classification number (for example, the *Beowulf* manuscript is British Museum, Cotton Vitellius A xv). Very occasionally we have an autograph manuscript to work with, such as Dan Michel's *Aȝenbite of Inwyt* written at Canterbury in 1340. Usually we are dealing with copies made by scribes. The earlier and later versions of *Cursor Mundi* show how scribes altered texts. They often modernized them, eliminating unfamiliar words or spellings; they sometimes acted as editors and tried to improve the writing; their own dialects would sometimes lead them unconsciously to alter the manuscripts they were copying. Consequently, in examining Middle English works, we are usually dealing with the linguistic forms of both the author and his scribes.

During the late Middle English period, a new written standard developed based on the London dialect. Since London was the economic and political center of England, it was natural that this dialect should become dominant. In *An Introduction to Middle English* (pp. 50–51), Charles Jones discusses the emergence of the Chancery Standard, so called because most of the manuscripts composed in it belong to the collection known as the Early Chancery Proceedings, at the Public Record Office in London. After about 1430, manuscripts produced in the London area tend to follow the orthographic conventions of the Chancery Standard, which is based on the Central East Midland dialect with the addition of features from London. This standard gradually gained acceptance as a national orthographic system. Letters addressed to the Lord Chancellor in London often used the Chancery Standard rather than the spelling characteristic of the region in which they were written.

Printing played a major role in standardizing the language. The first English printing press was set up by William Caxton at Westminster in 1476. Although he was born in Kent and spent many years in the Low Countries, he wrote and published works that were written in the London dialect. He was conservative in his spelling and followed the practices of the Middle English manuscripts he set in type. Since later printers followed his example, many spellings that have come to be standard in Modern English reflect Middle English pronunciations.

The conservative spelling of Caxton contrasts with the phonetic forms found in the letters and informal documents of the fifteenth century. There were many writers in the growing middle class unaffected either by scribal tradition or the evolving Chancery Standard. The spelling in the chronicle of William Gregory, the Paston letters, and the Cely letters tells us a great deal about the pronunciations of the writers. The Cely letters illustrate the dialect of the middle class in London during the latter part of the fifteenth century. Some of the same forms are found in the diary of Henry Machyn, a merchant tailor of London during the sixteenth century. In this work we have the dialect of an Elizabethan Cockney. Although some of the non-standard features of his writing occur in that of upper class individuals, they do not appear in such profusion. Henry Cecil Wyld discusses regional and class dialects and the development of a spoken standard in *A History of Modern Colloquial English* (London: Unwin and Fisher, 1920). The cultivated standard that emerged in England was based on the aristocratic speech of London and Westminster.

The speech of the American colonists ranged from the urban cultivated standard to the regional and rural. It was in large measure that of London and the southeastern counties of England. John Smith, a leader in the Jamestown settlement, came from Lincolnshire. John Winthrop, first Governor of the Massachusetts Bay Colony, came from Suffolk, and his wife from Essex. The dialects of New England and the tidewater Virginia area were originally very similar, and they still share many features (see the Appendix for Characteristic Regional Pronunciations of American English). Detailed information on early American pronunciation can be found in George Philip Krapp's *The English Language in America* (New York: The Century Company, 1925), and on later developments in Hans Kurath and R. McDavid, *The Pronunciation of English in the Atlantic States* (Ann Arbor: University of Michigan Press, 1961).

Informal records, letters, and journals are important sources of information on early American pronunciation. The local records of New England town meetings contain many phonetic spellings, since they were written by people with little formal training who often recorded words as they sounded to their ears (see the Plymouth Records). The letters of Margaret Winthrop are more phonetic than those of her husband John, since she was a less educated writer. The journal of Amos Farsworth, a soldier during the Revolutionary War, is written very phonetically and in a colorful, colloquial style. He frequently uses idioms, metaphors, and hyperbole, said to be characteristic of American speech.

During all periods the informal, colloquial documents, such as Aelfgar's will, the Paston letters, the Cely letters, Machyn's diary, the Winthrop letters, and Farsworth's journal, are closest to the spoken language. There is always a significant correlation between stylistic level and the kind of linguistic data that can be found in a text.

LITERARY DIALECT

Historical dialects both resemble and differ from those that appear in literary works. Real dialects are elusive and hard to define, whereas literary dialects must be readily recognizable. They tend to be simplified and exaggerated. Colloquialisms not confined to a region or class are mingled with genuine regional and social features. Authors have used literary dialect for humor and for a variety of social or political messages. Its first use in English literature appears in Chaucer's *Reeve's Tale*, where it suggests the social standing of the students. In the *Second Shepherds' Play*, dialect provides social commentary and humor. In Shakespeare's *Henry* plays, it contributes humor and local color. In Tyler's *The Contrast,* it signifies Yankee innocence and shrewdness. Lowell and Harris had a real respect for their local dialects and tried to provide genuine phonetic transcriptions. Yet since they were addressing readers rather than listeners, they used more eye dialect than the other authors.

From the early period of American history, an interest in American English was associated with patriotism. Nevertheless, this did not preclude an interest in English literature or in the earlier stages of the language. Lowell carefully investigated Middle English and Early Modern texts in order to trace the features of the New England dialect. Thomas Jefferson was the first American to advocate the study of Anglo-Saxon as a regular branch of academic education. In his *Essay Towards Facilitating Instruction in the Anglo-Saxon,* he discusses the continuity of the English language and sets forth a program for normalizing texts that resembles the one used in many modern editions. We thus come full circle with Thomas Jefferson, like King Alfred of Wessex, recommending the study of Anglo-Saxon.

EDITORIAL METHOD

Not only have the conventions of orthography and punctuation varied over the centuries (as illustrated by the facsimiles included with some of the selections), but modern editors vary as to the closeness of their transcriptions and the extent and nature of their expansion of abbreviations and modernization of spelling, capitalization, and punctuation. For example, many modern editors keep þ (thorn, *th*), but none keeps ƿ (wynn, *w*), and practice varies with regard to ȝ (yogh, *g, gh, y*). All editors expand "þͭ" to "that" and "ꝑͭ" to "part," but some keep 7 or & for "and." Most modern editors capitalize the first word in a sentence, but practice with regard to capitalization within sentences varies widely. Long vowels are not marked in medieval manuscripts, and all modern punctuation is editorial.

Since a primary objective of historical study of the language is to enable one to penetrate beneath the surface conventions of orthography and punctuation to the underlying sounds and structures, it is important to learn to recognize and to cope with these variations in editorial practice. Hence, the following selections have not been normalized or regularized, but present faithfully the practices of the editors identified in each piece in regard to punctuation, capitalization, and marking of vowels. Once the reader understands this, the variations present no obstacle to comprehension; the editorial variations are themselves a part of the history of the English language.

Old English

BEOWULF

Beowulf, the only extant Old English secular heroic epic, was probably composed during the first half of the eighth century and survives in a manuscript written about 1000 (British Museum, Cotton Vitellius A xv) in the late West Saxon literary *koiné*. Behind the poem lies a long oral tradition developed while the Germanic tribes still inhabited the European continent. The subject matter of the poem is not British but Scandinavian, revealing the close cultural ties between the Angles and Saxons who came to England in the fifth century, the Danes who followed them in the eighth, and the Scandinavian and Germanic peoples who remained on the continent. The same alliterative verse form was used in Old English, Old Icelandic, Old Saxon, and Old High German poetry. This poetic technique is based on a common linguistic phenomenon, the Germanic placement of stress on initial syllables. Each half line was composed of two stressed and a varying number of unstressed syllables. Half lines were separated by caesural pauses and linked by alliteration.

Since the poetry was originally oral, it could be composed and remembered only through formulas that were handed down from generation to generation. Formulas are syntactically related collocations of words that recur in regular rhythmic patterns. The poet could substitute individual words within the formulaic phrases to suit his contextual and alliterative requirements. Examples of formulas in this passage are "we . . . gefrunon" (lines 1–2), "wuldres Wealdend" (l. 17), "wine Scyldinga" (l. 30), "beaga bryttan" (l. 35), and "haeleð under heofenum" (l. 52). The existence of a stock of traditional formulas led to the device of variation, or the statement of the same idea in several ways. This technique is employed in the opening sentence, where "Gar-Dena," "þeodcyninga" and "aeþelingas" all point to the same referent. Another popular device was the kenning, a periphrastic expression that identifies a person or object with something it is only in a very special sense. An example occurs at line 10, where the ocean is called a "hron-rade" (whale road).

Because of the requirements of alliterative verse, word order in Old English poetry is further from Modern English than that of Old English prose. Examples of convoluted word order occur at lines 1–3, 4–5, 22–24, 26–27, 40–42. On the other hand, word order can be straightforward, as in line 11. Objects appear before the verb more often in the poetry than in the prose (lines 2, 3, 5, 7, 8, 11, 17, 30, 43). As in the prose, object pronouns usually precede the verb (lines 9, 16, 22, 28, 40, 43, 45, 47, 49). Prepositional phrases occur somewhat less frequently in the poetry; however, even here we find prepositions along with case endings at lines 1, 8, 10, 13, 19, 21, 25, 27, 37, 40, 52.

Archaic words or pronunciations are sometimes preserved in Old English poetry. At lines 16 and 25, the metrical pattern requires an additional syllable in the words "Liffrea" and "geþeon"; these expanded forms point to earlier pronunciations.

Beowulf

Lo   we   of the Spear-Danes   in former days
HWÆT, WĒ GĀR-DEna   in gēardagum

of the people's kings   glory have heard
þēodcyninga   þrym gefrūnon,

how the noblemen   noble deeds did
hū ðā æþelingas   ellen fremedon!

      often   from the enemy's troops
      Oft Scyld Scēfing   sceaþena þrēatum,

from many   tribes   mead benches took away
monegum mǣgþum   meodosetla oftēah,   5

terrified the warriors   after   first   was
egsode eorl[as],   syððan ǣrest wearð

destitute   found   he therefore comfort experienced
fēasceaft funden;   hē þæs frōfre gebād

waxed   heavens   in honors   throve
wēox under wolcnum   weorðmyndum þāh

until   each   of the neighboring peoples
oð þæt him ǣghwylc   ymbsittendra

Reprinted by permission of the publisher, from F. Klaeber, *Beowulf,* 3rd Edition (Lexington, Mass.: D.C. Heath and Company, 1950), pp. 1–3.

10   *whale road   obey   had to*
      ofer hronrāde   hȳran scolde,

      tribute   yield   good   king
      gomban gyldan;   þæt wæs gōd cyning!

      an   heir   born
      Þǣm eafera wæs   æfter cenned

      young one   courts   whom   sent
      geong in geardum,   þone God sende

      people   help   grievous distress perceived
      folce tō frōfre;   fyrenðearfe ongeat,

15   *that they before endured   lordless*
      þē hīe ǣr drugon   aldor(lē)ase

      long   him therefore Lord of life
      lange hwīle;   him þǣs Līffrēa

      of glory   Ruler   worldly honor   gave
      wuldres Wealdend   woroldāre forgeaf,

      famous   fame   widely   sprang
      Bēowulf wæs brēme   —blǣd wīde sprang—

      heir   Scandinavian lands
      Scyldes eafera   Scedelandum in.

      so   shall   young   man   work
20   Swā sceal (geong g)uma   gōde gewyrcean,

      with generous gifts of property   in father's   protection (bosom)
      fromum feohgiftum   on fæder (bea)rme,

      him in old age   afterwards may remain
      þæt hine on ylde   eft gewunigen

willing retainers   when   war   comes
wilgesīþas,   þonne wīg cume,

people   may follow   by praiseworthy deeds shall
lēode gelǣsten;   lofdǣdum sceal

    tribes   everywhere   thrive
in mǣgþa gehwǣre   man geþēon.   25

      then   departed   destined time
   Him ðā Scyld gewāt   to gescæphwīle

very strong   going   God's protection
felahrōr fēran   on Frēan wǣre;

they him   then carried   sea's   current
hī hyne þā ætbǣron   tō brimes faroðe,

dear   comrades   as   himself commanded
swǣse gesīþas,   swā hē selfa bæd,

while   wielded   leader
þenden wordum wēold   wine Scyldinga—   30

beloved lord   possessed (reigned)
lēof landfruma   lange āhte.

there   haven   ring-prowed
Þǣr æt hȳðe stōd   hringedstefna

icy   eager to go   prince's   ship
īsig ond ūtfūs   æþelinges fær;

laid   then   beloved   prince
ālēdon þā   lēofne þēoden,

of rings   giver   bosom   of the ship
bēaga bryttan   on bearm scipes,   35

glorious one by   mast   *of treasures many*
mærne be mæste.   Þǣr wæs mādma fela

    distant lands   ornaments brought
of feorwegum   frætwa gelǣded;

    heard   more beautiful   ship   adorned
ne hȳrde ic cȳmlīcor   cēol gegyrwan

war weapons   battle garments
hildewǣpnum   ond heaðowǣdum

swords   corslets   bosom   laid
40   billum ond byrnum;   him on bearme læg

of treasures many   with   should
mādma mænigo,   þā him mid scoldon

   sea's   power   far   travel
on flōdes ǣht   feor gewītan.

not at all they him   less   gifts   provide
Nalæs hī hine lǣssan   lācum tēodan,

people's treasures   than   those did
þēodgestrēonum,   þon þā dydon,

who him   in the beginning   forth   sent
45   þē hine æt frumsceafte   forð onsendon

alone   waves   child   being
ǣnne ofer ȳðe   umborwesende.

then yet   they   set   banner   golden
Þā gȳt hīe him āsetton   segen g(yl)denne

high   head   let   sea
hēah ofer hēafod,   lēton holm beran,

gave   *sea (spearman-Neptune?)*   *sad*   *mind*
gēafon on gārsecg;   him wæs geōmor sefa,

mourning   *spirit*   *know*
murnende mōd.   Men ne cunnon   50

tell   *truth*   *hall-counsellor*
secgan tō sōðe,   selerædende,

warrior   *heavens*   *who*   *cargo*   *received*
hæleð under heofenum,   hwā þæm hlæste onfēng.

KING ALFRED'S PREFACE TO
POPE GREGORY'S PASTORAL CARE

King Alfred's writings occupy an important position in the development of English prose. He sponsored an educational program and translated various Latin works into English so that free-born youths could read them in their native language. His translations include Pope Gregory's *Pastoral Care,* Boethius' *Consolation of Philosophy,* Orosius' *Compendious History of the World,* and Saint Augustine's *Soliloquies*; he probably commissioned a version of Bede's *Ecclesiastical History of the English People* and directed the compilation of the *Anglo-Saxon Chronicle.* The only works of Alfred that are preserved in ninth-century manuscripts are the Orosius and the *Pastoral Care.*

In the Preface to the *Pastoral Care,* he discusses his educational program and his reasons for writing (the text here is taken from British Museum, Cotton Tiberius B xi). It begins with a formal greeting but then falls into a natural, conversational manner. Rhetorical emphasis is achieved by parallel structure and repetition of "hu" (how) in lines 4–11. We find the subject + object + verb word order typical of subordinate clauses in Old English in lines 5–6, 7, 8, 11, 18–19, 22, 23, 24, 25–26. Lines 28–29 and 39–40 exhibit the two types of word order that could occur with "þa", depending on its meaning: the subordinating conjunction "þa" (when) initiates the subject + object + verb order; the adverb "þa" (then) introduces the verb + subject word order. Object pronouns precede the verb (lines 2, 8, 12, 13, 21, 24, 25, 32, 35, 45, 48, 50, 71, 72, 73, 80). Titles, which may be reduced relative clauses, occur after names (lines 1, 69, 70, 71). Negative sentences are formed by placing "ne" before the auxiliary or main verb, as in lines 18, 36, 38; multiple negatives, common in Old and Middle English, appear at lines 17, 26, 32, 42, 76. The verbs "willan" (will) and "sculan" (shall) are used primarily as main verbs, "willan" for volition (lines 22, 42, 45, 62, 74, 79, 80), and "sculan" for obligation (lines 11, 12); but "sculan" is extended to a predictive function in lines 13 and 44.

Analytic structures appear together with synthetic ones. The prefix "ge" is used to indicate perfective aspect, as in "geseah" (l. 29) and "geleornode" (l. 69); but the segmentalized perfect with "habban" appears at lines 41, 71–72. Nominal functions are indicated by case, but prepositions often occur together

18

with case endings (lines 9, 10, 14, 16, 25, 35, 39, 46, 56, 69, 70, 73, 74). Natural gender sometimes replaces grammatical gender, particularly with pronouns separated from their respective nouns: "þone wisdom" (masc.) is referred to as "hine" (masc.) at line 24, but as "hit" (neuter) at line 25.

Some of the vowels in this passage reveal that it is written in early West Saxon. The vowel "a" before "l," as in "anwald" (lines 5, 7), becomes "ea" in late West Saxon. Examples of the diphthong "io" instead of the later "eo" appear in almost every line: "gio" (l. 3), "hiora" (lines 6, 7, etc.), "gehioldan" (l. 7), "hioldan" (l. 34), "hio" (l. 13), "behionan" (l. 14), "sio" (l. 44), "geþiode" (lines 42, 46), "gioguþ" (l. 57), "friora" (l. 58), "bibiode" (l. 75).

King Alfred's Preface to
Pope Gregory's Pastoral Care

king   bids   greet   lovingly
Alfred kyning hateð gretan . . . his wordum luflice

with friendship   to thee make known   very   often   mind
& freondlice; & ðe   kyðan hate þæt me com suiðe oft on gemynd,

what   wise men formerly   throughout   both   of religious
hwelce witan gio wæron geond Angelkynn, ægðer ge godcundra

vocations and secular   how happy   times then   throughout
hada ge woruldcundra; & hu gesæliglica tida þa wæron geond

*   kings   who   power   had   (over) the people*
5   Angelcynn; & hu þa kyningas þe ðone anwald hæfdon ðaes folces

*   ministers   obeyed   they both   their*
Gode & his ærendwrecum hirsumedon; & hu hi ægðer ge hiora

peace   customs   power   at home   preserved
sibbe ge hiora sido ge hiora anwald innanbordes gehioldon,

*   also outwards   territory extended   to them   prospered both*
& eac ut hiora oeðel rymdon; & hu him ða speow ægðer ge

From *King Alfred's West Saxon Version of Gregory's Pastoral Care,* ed. Henry Sweet (London: The Early English Text Society, 1871), pp. 1–8. Reprinted by permission of The Council of the Early English Text Society.

with   war   also   religious   vocations   zealous
mid wige ge mid wisdome; & eac ða godcundan hadas hu georne

    both   about   teaching   learning
hie wæron ægðer ge ymb lare ge ymb leornunga, & ymb ealle   10

    services   do   should   from abroad
þa ðeowutdomas þe hie Gode don sceoldon; & hu mon utanbordes

    learning here   sought   these
wisdom & lare   hider on lond sohte, & hu we hi nu sceoldon

from abroad get   if   so   entirely   it (learning)
ute   begietan gif we hie habban sceoldon. Swa clæne hio wæs

declined   very   few   on this side
oðfeallen nu on Angelkynne ðætte swiðe feawe wæron behionan

    their   services   could
Humbre þe hiora ðenunga cuðen understandan on Englisc,   15

or   even   letter   Latin   translate
oððe furðum an ærendgewrit of Lædene on Englisc areccan; &

 believe   not   many   beyond   were not   so
ﻪic wene ðætte nauht monige begeondan Humbre næren. Swa

few   of them   even   a single one   may
feawe hiora wæron ðaette ic furðum anne anlepne ne mæg

remember   south of   Thames   when   to the throne came
geðencean besuðan Temese ða ða ic to rice feng. Gode

almighty   be thanked   any   supply
ælmiehtegum si ðonc ðætte we nu ænigne onstal habbað   20

of teachers   therefore   command   as   believe
lareowa.ﻪ Forðam ic ðe bebeode ðæt ðu doo swa ic gelife ðæt

of these worldly matters   *disengage*
ðu wille, ðæt ðu ðe þissa woruldðinga to þæm geæmettige

as often as you   may   *which   gave   where*
swa ðu oftost mæge, ðæt ðu ðone wisdom þe ðe God sealde ðær

it   entrust   may   entrust   consider   what   punishment
ðær ðu hine befæstan mæge, befæste. Geðenc hwelc witu

because   it (wisdom) neither
25 us þa becomon for ðisse worulde, þa þa we hit   nohwæðer ne

ourselves   loved   also other   men   permitted
selfe ne lufedon ne eac oðrum monnum ne lifdon: ðone naman

alone   very   few   (of) the
anne we hæfdon ðætte we Cristene wæron, & swiðe feawe þa

virtues   when   considered   then   also
ðeawas. Þa ic þa ðis eall gemunde ða gemunde ic eac hu ic

had seen   before   ravaged   burned
geseah, ærþæmþe hit ealle forheregod wære & forbærned, hu

churches   treasures   books filled
30 þe cirican geond eall Angelkynn stodon maðma & boca gefylda

also great   many   servants   those very   use   of the
& eac micel menigu Godes ðeowa & þa swiðe lytle feorme ðara

books knew   because   of them nothing   understand
boca wiston, forþæmþe hie heora nan-wuht ongietan ne meahton,

because   were not   their   own   language   written   thus
forþæmþe hie næron on hiora ægen geðeode awritene. Swelce

they might say   ancestors who   those places   before held
hie cwæden: Ure ieldran, ða þe ðas stowa ær hioldon, hie

loved   through it   obtained   wealth   to us left
lufedon wisdom & ðurh ðone hi begeaton welan & us læfdon.   35

*   yet   see   track   but   them cannot*
Her mon mæg giet gesion hiora swæð, ac we him ne cunnon

follow   therefore   both   lost
æfterspyrigan, forðæm we habbað nu ægðer forlæten ge

*   wealth   because   would not   track*
þone welan ge þone wisdom, forðamþe we noldon to ðæm spore

with   spirit   incline   when   considered   then wondered
mid ure mode onlutan| Þa ic þa ðis eall gemunde, þa wundrode

*   exceedingly   good   wise men   formerly   throughout*
ic swiðe swiðe þara godena witena þe giu wæron geond   40

*   books completely   learned   had*
Angelcynn, & þa bec befullan ealla geleornod hæfdon, þæt hi

of them   no   portion would not   own   language   translate
hiora þa nanne dæl noldon on hiora ægen geðiode wendan. Ac

*   afterwards   answered   said   did not believe*
ic þa sona eft me selfum andwyrde & cwæð: Hie ne wendon

*   ever   so   careless   become   the learning*
þætte æfre men sceoldon swa reccelease weorðan & sio lar swa

decline   desire   they   omitted
oðfeallan; for ðære wilnunga hi hit forleton, & woldon ðæt   45

*   the more   would be the   more languages   knew*
her þy mara wisdom on londe wære ðy we ma geðioda cuðon| Þa

considered   the law   first   Hebrew   language   found
gemunde ic hu sio æ wæs ærest on Ebreisc geðiode funden,

afterwards　　　it　　Greeks　　had learned　　　　　translated　　they it
& eft, þa þa hie Crecas geleornodon, þa wendon hi hie on

　　　own　　language　　　　also　　　other　books
hiora ægen geðiode ealle, & eac ealle oðre bec. And eft

Romans　　　　　　　when　　they it　had learned　　　　　translated
50　Lædenware swa same, siððan hi hie geleornodon, hi hie wendon

　　through　　translators　　　　own　language
ealla ðurh wise wealhstodas on hiora agen geðeode. & eac ealla

other　　　peoples　some　portion of it　　　own　language
oðra Cristena ðioda sumne dæl　hiora on hiora agen geðiode

translated　therefore　seems　　if to you　so　seems
wendon. Forðy me ðyncð betre, gif iow swa ðyncð, þæt we eac

　books　　most needful　be　to all　people　　know
suma bec, ða þe nidbeðyrfesta sien eallum monnum to witanne,

　　　　　　language　translate　　　know　may
55　þæt we þa on ðæt geðeode wenden þe we ealle gecnawan mægen,

　　　　　very　easily may　with　help
& ge don swa we swiðe eaðe magon mid Godes fultume, gif we þa

tranquillity　　　　　youth
stilnesse habbað, ðætte eal sio gioguð þe nu is on Angelkynne

of free　men　　　support　have　　to that
friora monna, þara þe þa speda hæbben þaet hie ðæm

apply　may　be　learning　set
befeolan mægen, sien to leornunga oðfæste, þa hwile þe hi to

no　other　occupation　until　　　can
60　nanre oðerre note ne mægen, oð ðonne first þe hie wel cunnen

writing   read   teach   one   then   further   Latin language
Englisc gewrit arædan: lære mon siððan furður on Lædengeðeode

those who   teach   higher   vocation
þa þe mon furður læran wille & to hierran hade don wille.

considered   knowledge of Latin   before this   declined
Þa ic þa gemunde hu sio lar   Lædengeðeodes ær ðysum oðfeallen

throughout   yet   many   could   writing
wæs geond Angelkynn, & ðeah monege cuðon Englisc gewrit

read   began   among   various   manyfold
arædan, þa ongan ic ongemang oðrum mislicum & monigfaldum   65

cares   of this   kingdom   translate
bisgum ðisses kynerices þa boc wendan on Englisc þe is

named   Latin   Shepherd's Book sometimes
genemned on Læden Pastoralis & on Englisc Hirdeboc, hwilum

by   sometimes   sense for sense   as   it
word be worde, hwilum ondgit of andgite, swæ swæ ic hie

had learned   from   my   archbishop
geleornode æt Plegmunde minum ærcebiscepe & æt Asserie

my   bishop   my   mass-priest
minum biscepe & æt Grimbolde minum mæssepreoste & æt   70

when   it   learned
Iohanne minum mæssepreoste. Siððan ic hie þa geleornod

had   so   that   it understood   most intelligibly
hæfde, swæ swæ ic hie forstod, & swæ ic hie andgitfullicost

interpret   might   translated   each
areccean mæhte, ic hie on Englisc awende; & to ælcum

bishopric   *kingdom*   *one*   *send*   *each*   *is*

biscepstole on minum rice wille ane onsendan; & on ælcre bið an

clasp   *which is (worth) fifty*   *mancuses (one mancus = thirty pence)*

75   æstel, se   bið on fiftegum moncessa.   Ond ic

command   *name*   *the*   *clasp*   *book*

bibiode on Godes noman þæt nan mon ðone æstel from þære bec

take   *church*   *unknown*   *such*

ne doe, ne þa boc from þæm mynstre: uncuð hu longe þær swæ

learned   *bishops*   *may be as*   *now*   *be thanked nearly everywhere*

gelærede biscopas sien, swæ swæ nu Gode ðonc well hwær

are   *therefore*   *they (the books) always*   *at*   *the*   *place*

sindon; forðy ic wolde ðætte hie   ealneg æt ðære stowe

should be   *unless*   *with*   *or*   *it*

80   wæren, buton se biscep hie mid him habban wille, oððe hio

somewhere   *lent*   *be*   *or*   *someone another should copy*

hwær to læne sie, oððe hwa oðre bewrite.

AELFRIC'S HOMILY

ON ST. GREGORY THE GREAT

Aelfric, monk of Cerne and Abbot of Eynsham, was the outstanding scholar of the late Old English period. In the face of increased Viking activity during the tenth century and a decay of discipline within the Church, he tried to strengthen the English people through learning. His program resembled Alfred's, but it was devoted to a religious cause. In order to maintain the Latin tradition of the Church, he compiled a Latin *Grammar,* and a *Glossary.* His *Colloquy* is an interesting example of the "conversational" method of language teaching. In order to help those who did not know Latin, he composed or translated into English homilies, saints' lives, a portion of the Old Testament, and missives designed for the guidance of the clergy.

Aelfric was aware of the three styles of Latin rhetoric: *tenue* (plain), *medium* (middle), and *grande* (elevated). However, instead of imitating the stylistic devices of Latin, he used the resources of English. His plain and middle styles follow the rhythm and syntax of the spoken language, with occasional rhetorical inversions. His elevated style uses the rhythms of Old English poetry, systematically linking two-stress phrases in pairs by the use of alliteration. Alliteration and balance appear in his plain style also, but in no set pattern.

Aelfric's Homily on St. Gregory the Great is in the plain style. It is based on Bede's *Ecclesiastical History of the English People* and bears witness to the tradition that King Alfred translated this work (the text is taken from Cambridge University Library, MS. Gg. 3. 28). The homily opens with a periodic sentence (one in which the meaning is suspended until the end). Syntactic balance and semantic contrast are used at lines 5–6, 34, 42–43. Other rhetorical ornaments include word pairs (lines 2–3, 4–5, 6–7, 17, 26), and alliteration (lines 5 and 19).

The subordinate word order of subject + object + verb appears at lines 4–6, 7–8, 10–11, 18–19, 37–39, 42–43. Introductory adverbs of time initiate a verb + subject word order at lines 9, 18, 21–22, 25, 29, 36. Object pronouns precede the verb (lines 5, 9–10, 20, 21, 32, 35, 40, 44). Titles occur after names at lines 1 and 7 but before at line 12. At line 9, the verb "wylle" indicates volition but has a predictive function at the same time. Prepositions occur together with case endings at lines 4–5, 8, 9, 12, 16–17, 18, 20, 21, 22, 24, 28,

29, 38, 42–43, 46, 47. At lines 12–13, we find a split coordinate adjective ("æðelborenre mǣgðe and eawfæstre"). In Old English complex sentence elements were sometimes broken up, whereas in Modern English they are arranged according to syntactic grouping (nobly born kin and religious = nobly born, religious kin).

Aelfric's Homily
on St. Gregory the Great

holy   Pope   people

Grēgōrius sē hālga pāpa, Engliscre ðēode apostol, on

this   present   day   many   labors

ðisum andwerdan dæge, æfter menigfealdum gedeorfum and

holy   studies   kingdom happily   ascended

hālgum gecnyrdnyssum, Godes rīce   gesæliglīce āstāh. Hē is

truly   people   because   through   advice

rihtlīce Engliscre ðēode apostol, for ðan ðe hē þurh his rǣd

mission   devil's   worship   released

and sande ūs fram dēofles biggengum ætbrǣd, and tō Godes   5

faith   converted   many   holy   books make known   conduct

gelēafan gebīgde. Manega hālige bēc cȳðað his drohtnunge and

holy   also   which

his hālige līf, and ēac Historia Anglōrum, ðā ðe Aelfrēd cyning

Latin   translated   speaks enough clearly

of Lēdene on Englisc āwende. Sēo bōc sprecð genōh swutelīce

From *Bright's Anglo-Saxon Reader*, ed. James R. Hulbert (New York: Holt, Rinehart and Winston, Inc., 1935), pp. 86–89. Reprinted by permission of the publisher.

           man   *shortly*   *to you*
be ðisum hālgan were. Nū wylle wē sum ðing scortlīce ēow be

     relate   *because*   *is not to you all*
10   him gereccan, for ðan ðe sēo foresæde bōc nis   ēow eallum

known though   *it*   *translated is*
cūð, þēah ðe hēo on Englisc āwend sȳ.

      blessed   *pope*   *nobly born*   *kin*
Þēs ēadīga pāpa Grēgōrius wæs of æðelborenre mægðe

   religious   *descended*   *senators*   *kinsmen*
and ēawfæstre ācenned; Rōmānisce witan wæron his māgas;

        was called   *religious*   *pope*
his fæder hātte Gordiānus, and Fēlix, sē ēawfæsta pāpa,

   great-great-grandfather   *as*   *said*
15   wæs his fīfta fæder. Hē wæs—swā swā wē cwædon—for

      nobly born   *but*   *surpassed*   *noble birth*   *with*
worulde æðelboren, ac hē oferstāh his æðelborennysse mid

holy   *virtues*   *works*   *adorned*
hālgum ðēawum and mid gōdum weorcum geglengde. . . .

   then perceived   *who*
Þā undergeat sē pāpa, þe on þām tīman þæt apostolīce

seat   *sat*   *blessed*   *holy*   *virtues*   *thriving*
setl gesæt, hū sē ēadiga Grēgōrius on hālgum mægnum ðēonde

             monastic   *life*   *took*
20   wæs, and hē ðā hine of ðære munuclīcan drohtnunge genam and

     helper   *appointed*   *office of a deacon*   *ordained*
him tō gefylstan gesette, on dīaconhāde geendebyrdne. Þā

happened   it   one   time   as   still   does
gelamp hit æt sumum sǣle, swā swā gȳt for oft dēð, þæt

merchants   their   wares   Rome
Englisce cȳpmenn brōhton heora ware tō Rōmānabyrig, and

went   street
Grēgōrius ēode be þǣre strǣt tō ðām Engliscum mannum, heora

things showing   saw   wares   boy slaves
ðing scēawigende. Þā geseah hē betwux ðām warum cȳpecnihtas   25

set (for sale)   of white   body   of fair   countenance
gesette, þā wǣron hwītes līchaman and fægeres andwlitan

nobly   haired
menn, and æðellīce gefexode. Grēgōrius ðā behēold þǣra

boys'   beauty   inquired   which   nation   brought
cnapena wlite, and befrān of hwilcere þēode hī gebrōhte

wǣron. Þā sǣde him man þæt hī of Englalande wǣron, and

nation   human   beautiful   afterwards
þæt ðǣre ðēode mennisc swā wlitig wǣre. Eft ðā Grēgōrius   30

inquired   whether   or heathen
befrān, hwæðer þæs landes folc crīsten wǣre ðe hǣðen.

heathen   within
Him man sǣde þæt hī hǣðene wǣron. Grēgōrius ðā of innweardre

long   sigh   drew   said   Alas
heortan langsume siccetunge tēah, and cwæð, "Wālāwā, þæt swā

of fair   hew   should be   black   devil   subject to
fægeres hīwes menn sindon ðām sweartan dēofle underðēodde!"

   asked   *nation*

35 Eft hē āxode, hū ðǣre ðēode nama wǣre þe hī of cōmon. Him

    answered   *named*

 wæs geandwyrd, þæt hī Angle genemnode wǣron. Þā cwæð hē,

  rightly   *are*   *called* *because*   *of angels' beauty*

 "Rihtlīce hī sind Angle gehātene, for ðan ðe hī engla wlite

     likewise *befits*   *angels'*

 habbað, and swilcum gedafenað þæt hī on heofonum engla

 companions be   *inquired*   *shire*

 gefēran bēon." Gȳt ðā Grēgōrius befrān, hū ðǣre scīre nama

    boys   *led*

40 wǣre þe ðā cnapan of ālǣdde wǣron. Him man sǣde, þæt ðā

 shire-men   *Deirians called*   *answered*

 scīrmen wǣron Dēre gehātene. Grēgōrius andwyrde, "Wel hī

 are   *called*   *are* *wrath* *saved*

 sind Dēre gehātene, for ðan ðe hī sind fram graman generode,

    mercy   *called*

 and tō Crīstes mildheortnysse gecȳgede." Gȳt ðā hē befrān,

   nation *king* *called*   *answered*

 "Hū is ðǣre lēode cyning gehāten?" Him wæs geandswarod,

     called

45 þæt sē cyning Aelle gehāten wǣre. Hwæt ðā Grēgōrius

 played

 gamenode mid his wordum tō ðām naman, and cwæð,

   it *befits*

  "Hit gedafenað

be   sung   *praise   almighty*

þæt Allēlūia sȳ gesungen on ðām lande, tō lofe þæs ælmihtigan

Creator

Scyppendes."

AELFRIC'S COLLOQUY

Aelfric's *Colloquy*, a dialogue between a teacher and his pupils, is one of the earliest extant English educational documents. Like the "direct method" in recent years, colloquies were used in the monastic schools of Western Europe to teach boys conversational Latin. Since Latin was the language of the schools both for educational and domestic purposes, students needed a vocabulary that would enable them to discuss everyday things. Aelfric tried to teach such a vocabulary by assigning the boys various roles to act out, such as monks, ploughmen, shepherds, herdsmen, and hunters. The following selection, containing the replies of the "monk" and the "ploughman," is taken from British Museum, MS. Tiberius A III, the only surviving version that has a continuous interlinear gloss in Old English. The Latin text was definitely composed by Aelfric. The glosses may have been his work, or they may have been added later by someone else.

The *Colloquy* is written in a simple, colloquial style, but the syntax of the Old English is conditioned by the Latin original. In lines 16–17, an absolute construction is used to correspond to the ablative absolute of the Latin. The Latin word order is preserved in "weorc þin" (l. 12) and "hlafordes mines" (l. 16), with the possessive pronoun following the noun. However, Old English sentence patterns are often maintained. We find the usual word order of interrogative sentences in Old English, with the verb preceding the subject (lines 1, 2, 7, 12). Subject pronouns are used in the English version even though they do not appear in the Latin: "þu" (lines 1, 2), "ic" (lines 1, 3, 4, 5, 13, 15, 16).

PLATE I: THE COTTON MANUSCRIPT
OF AELFRIC'S COLLOQUY

The copy of Aelfric's *Colloquy* found in British Museum, MS. Cotton Tiberius A III, is the only one with a continuous interlinear gloss in Old English. It was probably written during the second quarter of the eleventh century. The Latin text begins on folio 60^V with the large capital *N* of "Nos" (the selection in this reader begins with "Interrogo te" or "ic axie," line 7).

The text exhibits two different forms of writing. The Latin is in Caroline miniscule, developed in the scriptoria of France and brought to England in the tenth century. The Old English is in the native Insular script, based on the Irish modification of the Roman alphabet. The national hand, which came primarily from the script introduced by Irish missionaries, was used for English vernacular writings until about 1200. Note particularly the different forms in the Latin and English for *g, a, r, d*.

Letters used only in Insular script included wynn (*ƿ*) for *w* and thorn (*þ*) for *th*, both of which came from the Germanic runic alphabet; eth (ð), a modification of *d*, for *th* (it does not appear in this selection); ash (æ—the name came from the runic alphabet but the symbol from the Roman); yogh (ȝ) for *g*. Of these letters, thorn had the longest life, occurring in vernacular documents until the sixteenth century.

Some letters have unfamiliar forms. A long *s* was used (ſ), which looks very much like *f* except that there may be no horizontal stroke, or if there is it does not cross the vertical. This form of *s* was employed until the end of the eighteenth century. Long *r* had a descending stroke below the line. Small *f, d,* and *t* had no ascenders. The letter *y* was dotted to distinguish it from thorn (see line 11 for examples); *i* was not dotted.

Abbreviations included a line above a vowel to indicate omission of a following *n* or *m*, as in "ȝebroþrū" (l. 8); "7" for "and" (l. 8); and þt for "that" (l. 16). Punctuation marks used in the manuscript are (⸵) for a question, (:) or (.) for a full stop, and (.) for a comma.

þe cildra biddaþ þe eala lareow þæt þu tæce us sprecan

Nos pueri rogamus te magister   ut   doceas   nos loqui

36

Aelfric's Colloquy

I   ask   you   what   say   you

Ic axie þe, hwæt sprycst þu?

Interrogo te, quid mihi loqueris?

what   have   you   of work

Hwæt hæfst þu weorkes?

Quid habes operis?

I am   fluent of speech   monk   and   sing   each   day   seven

Ic eom ȝeanwyrde monuc, 7 ic sincȝe ælce dæȝ seofon

Professus sum monachus, et psallam omni die septem

times   brothers   am   occupied   in reading   in

tida mid ȝebroþrum, 7 ic eom bysȝod _____ 7 on

sinaxes cum fratribus, et occupatus sum lectionibus et

singing   but nevertheless   I would   between (times) learn   to speak

sanȝe, ac þeahhwæþere ic wolde betwenan leornian sprecan   5

cantu, sed tamen uellem interim discere sermocinari

Latin language

on leden ȝereorde.

latina lingua.

From *Aelfric's Colloquy,* ed. G. N. Garmonsway (London: Methuen & Co. Ltd., 1939), pp. 19–20. Reprinted by permission of Methuen & Co. and Appleton-Century-Crofts.

    know   *these your companions*

Hwæt cunnon þas þine ʒeferan?

Quid sciunt isti tui socii?

    are   *ploughmen*   *shepherds*   *herdsmen*

Sume synt yrþlincʒas, sume scephyrdas, sume oxanhyrdas,

Alii sunt aratores, alii opiliones, quidam bubulci

    also   *hunters*   *fishermen*   *fowlers*

sume eac swylce huntan, sume fisceras, sume fuʒeleras,

quidam etiam venatores, alii piscatores, alii aucupes,

    merchants   *tailors*   *dealers in salt*

10   sume cypmenn, sume scewyrhtan, sealteras,

quidam mercatores, quidam sutores, quidam salinatores,

    bakers   *cooks*

bæceras.   _____

quidam pistores, coci.

    what   *say*   *you*   *ploughman*   *how*   *do*   *you work*   *your*

Hwæt sæʒest þu, yrþlinʒc? Hu beʒæst þu weorc þin?

Quid dicis tu, arator? Quomodo exerces opus tuum?

    Alas   *dear*   *lord*   *hard*   *I*   *labor*   *I*   *go out*

Eala, leof hlaford, þearle ic deorfe. Ic ʒa ut

O, mi domine, nimium laboro.   *Exeo*

    daybreak   *driving*   *oxen*   *yoke*   *them*   *plow*

on dæʒræd þywende oxon to felda, 7 iuʒie hiʒ to syl;

diluculo minando boues ad campum, et iungo eos ad aratrum:

    it is not   *stark*   *I*   *dare*   *lurk*   *home*

15   nys hit swa stearc winter þæt ic durre lutian æt ham

non est tam aspera hiems ut audeam latere domi

    fear   *of lord*   *my*   *but*   *yoked*   *oxen*   *fastened*

for eʒe hlafordes mines, ac ʒeiukodan oxan, 7 ʒefæstnodon

pro timore domini mei, sed iunctis bobus, et confirmato

ploughshare coulter   plow each   day   must   plow

sceare 7 cultre mit þære syl, ælce dæȝ ic sceal erian

uomere et cultro aratro, omni die debeo arare

full   acre   or   more

fulne æcer oþþe mare.

integrum agrum aut plus.

WULFSTAN'S SERMO AD ANGLOS

Wulfstan was an important administrator, legislator, and homilist of the late Old English period. During the reigns of Ethelred, Edmund, and Cnut, he was an influential counsellor. Even after the Norman Conquest he continued to serve as Bishop of Worcester and to provide a refuge for Anglo-Saxon culture. Many of the surviving manuscripts of Anglo-Saxon homilies were transcribed at Worcester under Wulfstan. His own sermons were preached in the eleventh century and read in the twelfth and thirteenth. Together with those of Aelfric, they form an important link in the development of English prose.

Although Wulfstan wrote in the plain, middle, and elevated styles, he is most noted for his highly rhetorical ornate style. He rarely used figures of thought, such as simile and metaphor, but concentrated on figures of sound, such as alliteration, assonance, rhyme, rhythm, repetition, and parallelism of word and clause. His rhythmic prose is based on the four-stress line of heroic poetry. It can often be analyzed into a series of two-stress phrases, each a separate syntactic unit.

The *Sermo Ad Anglos* (talk to the English), Wulfstan's most topical sermon, deals with the Viking invasions of the late tenth and early eleventh centuries. It was composed in 1014 (the text is that of MS. Corpus Christi College, Cambridge, 201). The theme is that the invasions and calamities afflicting the English are God's punishment for the sins of the people. The phrase "leofan men" was Wulfstan's characteristic opening. Rhetorical ornaments include alliteration (lines 5, 5–6, 7, 11–12, 13, 14, 16), parallelism and duplication of parts of speech (lines 11–12, 13, 16–17), and intensifying adjectives and adverbs (lines 4, 7, 9, 10, 12, 13, 16, 17).

The adverb "þonne" initiates a verb + subject word order at line 14. The subordinate order of subject + object + verb occurs at line 14. A double negative appears at line 9. An object pronoun precedes the verb at line 16. The verb "willan" is used for volition at line 5, where it also has a predictive function; "sculan" indicates obligation at lines 3 and 10 but prediction at lines 14 and 18. The prefix "ge" is used for the perfect at lines 6 and 16; at line 13 it appears along with the auxiliary "habban." Prepositions occur together with case endings at lines 2, 4, 8, 9, 12, 15, 16, 17.

Wulfstan's Sermo Ad Anglos

beloved   *know*   *true*   *in*
Leofan men, gecnawað þæt soð is: þeos world is on

haste   *and it*   *approaches*   *therefore*   *always the*
ofste, 7 hit nealæð þam ende, 7 þi hit is on worlde a   swa

longer   *the*   *worser*   *must necessarily before*   *coming*
lengc swa wirse; 7 swa hit sceal nyde ær Anticristes tocyme

grow worse exceedingly   *days*   *composed*
yfelian swiðe. Þis wæs on Aeðelredes cyninges dagum gediht,

four   *years'*   *time*   *before*   *died*   *pay heed*   *who*
feower geara fæce ær he forðferde. Gime se ðe wille hu   5

then   *since*   *has happened*   *also*
hit þa wære 7 hwæt siððan gewurde. Understandað eac

well   *devil*   *nation*   *many years*   *misled*   *much*
georne þæt deofol þas þeode nu fela geara dwelode to swiðe,

truths   *with*   *though they*
7 þæt litle getreowða wæron mid mannum, þeah hi wel

spoke   *injustices*   *many prevailed*   *was not never*
spræcon, 7 unrihta to fela ricsode on lande. And næs na

From *The Homilies of Wulfstan,* ed. Dorothy Bethurum (Oxford: Oxford University Press, 1957), p. 261. Reprinted by permission of The Clarendon Press, Oxford.

many   who thought   about   remedy as   eagerly   as   should
10 fela manna þe hogode ymbe þa bote swa georne swa man scolde,

but daily   added evil   others   injustice
ac dæghwamlice man ihte yfel æfter oðrum, 7 unriht

began   violations of law many   all   too widely throughout   nation
arærde 7 unlaga   manega ealles to wide geond ealle þas ðeode.

also therefore   many injuries   insults   experienced
And we eac forðam habbað fela bersta 7 bismra gebiden,

if   any   remedy obtain   shall   then   must
7 gif we ænige bote gebidan sculon, þonne mote we þæt

deserve   better   before   therefore
15 to Gode earnian bet þonne we ær ðisum didon. Forðam

with   great   deserts   have earned   miseries   oppress
mid micclum earnungum we geearnodon þa yrmða þe us onsittað,

very   great   merit   remedy   from
7 mid swiðe micelan earnungan we þa bote motan æt Gode

obtain   if   it shall henceforth   better   become
geræcan gif hit sceal heonanforð godigende wurðan.

THE WILL OF AELFGAR

Anglo-Saxon wills are of great importance for the study of Old English because of their informal language. Following Germanic custom, the individual making his will spoke his words in the presence of witnesses. Wills came to be recorded under clerical influence. But the oral act created the legal obligation. The writing was merely the documentation of the spoken will.

The following will is that of Aelfgar, an alderman who owned lands in Essex and Suffolk. His daughter Aethelflæd was the wife of King Edmund. His younger daughter Aelfflæd married Brihtnoth, the hero of the Battle of Maldon, which is commemorated in a heroic poem and reported in the *Anglo-Saxon Chronicle* entry for 991 (Brihtnoth is mentioned in the will at lines 25, 32, 43). Aelfgar's will, dated between 946 and 951, is preserved in two fourteenth-century cartularies, British Museum Additional MS. 14847, and Cambridge University Library, MS. Ff. 2. 33 (the basis for the following text).

The document has the loose, repetitious style of speech. It is made up of a series of simple declarative statements linked by coordination (usually by the conjunction "and") or parataxis (juxtaposition in which linking words are absent). The subordinate word order of subject + object + verb occurs at lines 17–18, 19, 22, 26, 27, 30–31; however, the subject + verb + object word order of main clauses appears in a subordinate clause in lines 4–5. The adverb "þanne" initiates the verb + subject word order at lines 23, 26, 27; the same order occurs without an adverb at line 19, and with an adverbial phrase at line 44. Object pronouns precede the verb in lines 4, 5, 18, 54, but follow it in lines 26, 27 (probably because of the verb + subject word order). Titles come after names (lines 4, 5). We find double negatives in lines 19, 27, 51, 54. The verb "willan" signifies both volition and prediction in lines 49, 57. The segmentalized perfect with "habban" occurs at lines 52, 54. Prepositions appear together with case endings in lines 2–3, 6, 11, 14–15, 23–24, 29–30, 33, 38, 41, 54–55. The subject pronoun "ic" (I) is omitted at line 31, and the verb "an" (grant) at line 46.

In an informal document such as this, the standard written forms of Old English were not followed as carefully as in literary texts. Some constructions preserve archaic inflections, such as the dual person ("vnker bother," l. 48), and the uninflected genitive ("hire moder soule," "hire brother soule," l. 11). Others show simplification of inflections, such as the "es" plural for "stedes," "scheldes" (l. 3), and the "en" ending for "buten" (l. 8), "bidden" (l. 49). Loss of aspiration occurs in "louerd" (for "hlaford," line 1), and in the omission of "h" on "hit" (lines 23, 27, 52). An intrusive "h" is attached to "ic" at line 47. Several words appear in reduced form, such as "wo" for "hwa" (l. 52). The vowels in a number of words are typical of the Northumbrian and Mercian dialects: "a" for "æ" in "þat" (lines 1, 5, etc.), "þam" (l. 6); "a" for "ea" in "aldre" (l. 12), "alderman" (l. 4); "e" for "æ" in "nefre" (lines 4, 51, 54), "red" (l. 10), "er" (l. 55); "e" for "eo" in "werken" (lines 50, 51). Since Mercian is the ancestor of Modern English, it is not surprising that these forms are more familiar than the corresponding ones in West Saxon.

The Will of Aelfgar

        will   *first*   *grant*   *lord*
Þis is Alfgares quide þat is erst þat ic an mine louerd

two   *swords*   *harnessed*   *two*   *armlets each*   *of (worth)*
tueye suerde fetelsade and tueye bege ayther of

      (one mancus = thirty pence)
      fifti mancusas

of gold   *three stallions*   *three shields*   *three spears*
goldes. and þre stedes. and þre scheldes. and þre speren.

     made known   *bishop*   *when*   *gave*
And me kidde Þeodred bisscop and Edric Alderman þa ic selde

    mine

lord   *sword*   *gave worth one-hundred-twenty*
louerd þat suerd þat Eadmund king me selde on hundtuelftian   5

      of gold   *pounds* *of silver*   *harness*
mancusas goldes. and four pund silueres on þam fetelse þat ic

might   *petition my*   *of will*   *establish*   *never*   *did wrong*   *nor have*
moste ben   mine quides wirde. And ic nefre forwrouht ne habbe

From *Anglo-Saxon Wills,* ed. Dorothy Whitelock (Cambridge: Cambridge University Press, 1930), pp. 6–8. Reprinted by permission of Cambridge University Press.

opposed   *lord*   *if*   *I could help it*   *grant*

on godes witnesse wið mine louerd buten ic so mote. And ic an

my   *daughter*   *land*   *Cockfield*

Athelflede mine douhter þe lond at Cokefeld. and at Dittone.

       after   *my*   *lifetime*   *condition*   *she*   *be the more zealous*

10   and þat at Lauenham. ouer min day. on þe red þat heo be þe bet

my   *soul*   *mother's*   *and*   *brother's*

for mine soule. and hire moder soule 7 for hire brother soule.

   herself   *after*   *our*   *lifetime*   *grant*

7 for hire seluen. And þanne ouer vre aldre day ic an þat lond

Cockfield   *Bedericesworth*   *Bury St. Edmunds*   *foundation*

at Cokefeld into Beodricheswrthe to seynt Eadmundes stowe.

         grant   *after*   *lifetime those lands*

And ic wille þat Athelfled vnne ouer hire day þo londes at

       whatever holy   *foundation*   *that*   *to her most advisable may seem*

15   Dittone into suilke halegen stowe.   suilk hire redlikest þinge

our   *ancestors' souls*   *after*   *our*   *lifetime*   *grant*

for vre aldre soule. And ouer vre aldreday. ic an þat lond at

     to my   *daughter's*   *child*   *she*

Lauenham mine douhter childe gif þat god wille þat heo ani

   unless   *wishes to him of it grant (before)*   *if*   *she*

haueð. buten Atelfled her wille him his vnnen. and gif heo

           go   *our*   *ancestors' souls*   *I*

non ne habbe. gange it into Stoke for vre aldre soule. and ic

grant   *Baythorn*   *to Athelflede*

20   an þat lond at Babingþirne Atelflede mine douhter. And after

lifetime *lifetime* *after* *their* *both*
hire day. min other douhter hire day. And ouer here bothre

lifetime *child* *if* *she* *child* *should have* *she* *child*
day. mine douhter berne gif heo bern habbe. And gif heo bern

does not have *St.* *foundation* *Barking*
ne habbe. þanne go it into sc̄e Marie Stowe at Berkynge for

our *ancestors' souls* *I* *grant* *younger*
vre aldre soule. And ic an þat lond at Illeye mine ginger

after *if*
douhter hire day. and ouer hire day. Berthnoðe his day gif he 25

longer *live* *she* *children* *grant I (it) to them*
leng libbe þanne heo. gif he bern habben þanne an ic hem.

grant I
gif he non ne habbeþ. þanne an ic it Athelfleð mine douhter.

Christchurch
ouer here day. and after hire day. into Cristes kirke at

Canterbury *for the community* *use*
Caunterbiri þen hirde   to brice. And þe lond at Colne and at

Tey *I* *grant* *younger* *if* *she*
Tigan ic an min gingere douhter. and ouer hire day gif heo 30

child *to her child* *if* *she* *child does not have* *bequeath*
bern habbe. hire bern. and gif heo bern ne habbe. bequeðe it

after *our* *ancestors'*
Bernothe his day. and ouer his day. into Stoke for vre aldre

souls *I* *grant* *Peldon* *Mersea*
soule. And ic an þat lond at Piltendone and at Mereseye into

   I grant   *use*   *as long as (it)* *to her*
Stoke. And ic an þat Athelfled bruke þe lond þer wile þe hire

agreeable is on *condition she*   *rightly hold*   *the condition* *she*
35 lef beth one raða heo it on riht helde. and on þe red þat heo

does for the community *the best* *she*   *can* *at*
do þan hirde so wel so heo best may into Stoke for mine soule

    our ancestors' *I grant*   *Greenstead*
and for ure aldre. And ic an þat lond at Grenstede into Stoke

                       I (grant)
for mine soule 7 for Athelwardes 7 for Wiswiðe. And ic

     the *use* *while* *her* *life lasts*   *condition*
Athelfled þere brice wille hire lif beth on þe red þat heo do

   those souls *the best* *she*   *can* *now of it may*   *grant*
40 for þa saule so wel so heo best may. nu his me god uþe 7 min

lord   *I grant*   *after*
lauerd. And ic an þat lond at Tidwoldingtone Alfwold ouer

     if he (pay) a food-rent each year to the community
mine day þe he   formige ilke ihere þen hird at Paulesbiri for

   ancestors
vre aldre soule. And ic an þat lond at Totham Berchnoðe and

   younger   *their*   *go*
mine gingere douhter here day. and after here day wende lond

   Mersea *(for) Athelfled*   *I grant* *woodland*
45 into Mereseye Athelfled mine douhter. And ic an þat wudelond

  Ashfield to   *as*   *himself here bought*   *I (grant)*
at Aisfeld into Stoke also Eakild self it her bouhte. And ic

my   mother   Rushbrooke   if   she   longer   live   I
mine moder þat lond at Ryssebroc gif heo leng liuið þan hic.

then   our   both   lives   I   grant   if   she
þanne after vnker bother day ic an it Winelme gif heo Athelfled

loyally   serve   beseech   whatever lord   may then
on richte hird. And ic wille Bidden suilc louerd so þanne

be   love   saints   do   my
beth for godes luuen and for alle hise halegen. werken min   50

children what they may do   never   may   set aside   my
bern þat he werken þat he nefre ne mugen forwerken mine

will   that I   declared   have   if   anyone
quide þe ic for mine soule cueden habbe. and gif it wo

alter   may he have   reckoning   holy   saints
awende. habbe him wið god gemæne and wið þe holi scas

whom I   it (my property) bequeathed   have   so that   never   may repent except   in
þe   ic it to   becueþen habbe. þat he it nefre ne bete buten on

hell's   torment whoever this will   may alter   unless   myself   alter   before
helle wite se   þis quide awende boten it me seluen wende er   55

my   death   grant a   hide   of land which
min ende. And ic Athelgar an an hide lond þes þe Aeulf

had   of one-hundred-twenty   acres   dispose of as   he wishes
hauede be hundtuelti   acren ateo   so he wille.

THE LORD'S PRAYER (MATTHEW 6.9-13)

A continuity may be perceived in biblical prose from the Old English period on. Since translators were dealing with the same text, their syntax and vocabulary were influenced by that of the original. The Old English and Middle English translations were based on the Latin Vulgate. The King James version, much indebted to William Tyndale's sixteenth-century translation, went back to Greek manuscripts of the New Testament and Hebrew manuscripts of the Old (the sources for the Latin). Later modern editions have been strongly influenced by the King James Bible. The following versions of the Lord's Prayer show the differences in phonology, morphology, and syntax of Old, Middle, and Modern English translations.

The word order of the four Old English versions closely follows that of the Latin original. The two West Saxon versions were composed as separate translations, whereas the Northumbrian and Mercian were written as glosses above a Latin text. That is why two different equivalents appear for some words (lines 17, 25). Yet the glosses are no more literal than the translations. The first West Saxon version is written in the standard *koiné* of late Old English. All inflections and vowel sounds are fully represented even though they were already undergoing change in the spoken language. This change can be perceived in the later West Saxon version: "æ" in "fæder" appears as "a," "ea" in "eart" as "e." Many endings are reduced: "heofonum" occurs as "heofene" (l. 12) and "heofenan" (l. 14), "nama" as "name" (l. 12), "gehalgod" as "gehalged" (l. 12), "gyltendum" as "geltenden" (l. 15), "urne" as "ure" (l. 14). Similar characteristics can be observed in the Northumbrian version even though it is the earliest of the four. The vowel "a" appears in "fader" and "arð" (l. 17). Syllables are reduced in "heofnum" or "heofnas" (l. 17—note the analogical "s" plural in the second form), "heofne" (l. 19), "eorðo" (l. 19), and "ric" (l. 18). The final syllables are reduced in "heofune" and "eorþe" (l. 25) in the Mercian version. Changes in the morphology and phonology of Old English occurred earliest in Northumbrian and Mercian, and it is from these dialects that Modern English was eventually derived.

Word order and inflections are more modern in the Middle English version. Most endings have disappeared or have been reduced to "e." An analogical "s" plural appears for "heuenes" (l. 29) and "dettouris" (l. 32). A Latin influence in the vocabulary can be seen in the use of "substaunce" (l. 31), and in the replacement of "costnung" by "temptacioun" (1. 33) and "gyltas" or "scylda" by "dettis" (1. 32).

The King James Bible, written in the Early Modern period, became the version known by English speaking peoples for more than two and a half centuries. No other authorized translation was made until 1881. The only archaic features that appear in the Lord's Prayer are the use of the relative pronoun "which" for a person (1. 35), the verb form "art" for the second person singular (1. 35), and the second person singular pronouns "thy" (1. 36) and "thine" (1. 39). The final sentence was added by sixteenth-century translators from the the Greek manuscripts of the New Testament.

The Lord's Prayer (Matthew 6.9-13)

LATIN (c. 4th Century)

father   our   who is   heavens   be hallowed   name   your
Pater noster qui es in caelis, sanctificetur nomen tuum:

come   kingdom   your   be done will   your as   heaven   and
adueniat regnum tuum: fiat uoluntas tua sicut in caelo et in

earth   bread   our   necessary for life   give us   today   and
terra. Panem nostrum supersubstantialem da nobis hodie: et

dismiss   to us   debts   our   just as   we   dismiss (forgive)
dimitte nobis debita nostra, sicut et nos dimittimus

debtors   our   do not lead   us   temptation   but
5   debitoribus nostris, et ne inducas nos in temtationem: sed

liberate   us   evil
libera nos a malo.

From *Nouum Testamentum Latine*, ed. J. Wordsworth and H. J. White (Oxford: Oxford University Press, 1920), p. 13.

ANGLO-SAXON KOINÉ (before 1000)

are   heavens   be   hallowed
Fæder ure þu þe eart on heofonum; Si þin nama gehalgod.

kingdom become   earth   as
to-becume þin rice. gewurþe ðin willa on eorðan swa swa on

our   daily   loaf   give   and
heofonum. urne gedæghwamlican hlaf syle us to dæg. 7

guilts (sins)   *sinners*
forgyf us ure gyltas swa swa we forgyfað urum gyltendum. 7   10

lead   temptation   release   evil   truly
ne gelæd þu us on costnunge ac alys us of yfele soþlice.

From *The Holy Gospels in Anglo-Saxon, Northumbrian, and Old Mercian Versions*, ed. W. W. Skeat (Cambridge: Cambridge University Press, 1871–87), pp. 54–55.

LATE WEST SAXON (after 1150)

Fader ure þu þe ert on heofene. sye þin name gehalged.

to-becume þin rice. Gewurðe þin gewille. on eorðan swa swa on

heofenan. ure dayghwamlice hlaf syle us to dayg. 7

forgyf us ure geltas swa swa we forgyfeð ure geltenden. 7   15

ne læd þu us on costnunge. ac ales us of yfele soðlice.

NORTHUMBRIAN (c. 8th Century)

Fader urer, ðu arð/ ðu bist in heofnum/ in heofnas

sie gehalgad noma ðin. to-cymeð ric ðin. sie willo ðin

suae is in heofne 7 in eorðo. hlaf userne ofer wistlic sel

us todæg. 7 forgef us scylda usra suae uoe forgefon   20

scyldgum usum. 7 ne inlæd usih in costunge ah gefrig

usich from yfle.

MERCIAN (*c. 9th Century*)

Fæder ure, þu þe in heofunum earð beo gehalgad þin

noma. cume to þin rice. weorþe þin willa swa swa on

25　heofune swilce on eorþe. hlaf userne/ ure dæghwæmlicu/

instondenlice sel us to dæge. 7 forlet us ure scylde swa swa

we ec forleten þæm þe scyldigat wið us. 7 ne gelæt us

gelæde in constungæ ah gelese us of yfle.

WYCLIFFITE BIBLE (*c. 1395*)

Oure fadir that art in heuenes, halewid be thi name;

30　thi kyngdoom come to; be thi wille don in erthe as in

heuene; ʒyue to vs this dai oure breed ouer othir substaunce;

/and forʒyue to vs oure dettis, as we forʒyuen to oure dettouris;/

and lede vs not in to temptacioun, but delyuere vs fro

yuel. Amen.

From *The Holy Bible, Containing the Old and New Testaments, with the Apocryphal Books, in the Earliest English Versions*, eds. J. Forshall and F. Madden (Oxford, 1850), IV, 14.

KING JAMES BIBLE (1611)

35　Our father which art in heauen, hallowed be thy name.

Thy kingdome come. Thy will be done, in earth, as it is in

heauen. Giue vs this day our daily bread. /And forgiue vs

our debts, as we forgiue our debters./And lead vs not into

temptation, but deliuer vs from euill. For thine is the

kingdome, and the power, and the glory, for euer. Amen.   40

From *The Holy Bible, Conteyning the Old Testament, and the New: Newly Translated out of the Originall Tongues* (London, 1611).

THE ANGLO-SAXON CHRONICLE

During the Middle Ages, historical and official documents were usually written in Latin. The *Anglo-Saxon Chronicle* was one of the few histories written in a vernacular; it contains the oldest historical prose in a Germanic language. The purpose of each entry was to summarize the main events of the year (the adverb of place "her" indicates "at this point of the series"). The seven surviving manuscripts of the *Chronicle* are based on four versions that go back to a common original, compiled during King Alfred's reign. Although local annals were kept before his time, Alfred supervised and directed the compilation of a national chronicle up to 892. Copies were sent to different religious houses; at some, scribes continued the record. The *Peterborough Chronicle* (Bodleian Library, Laud Misc. 636), from which the following extracts are taken, was kept up the longest. From 1080 until it ended in 1154, it is the only remaining version.

Being the work of many writers over more than three centuries, the *Chronicle* contains a variety of styles. The simplest is a bare statement of facts without interpretation or commentary, as in the reports for 449, 601, 991, and 1017. The entry for 1066, which exhibits more complex historical writing, describes a related series of events that led to the downfall of Harold at the Battle of Hastings. In the selection for 1137, the writer indulges in a great deal of editorializing.

In the Peterborough Chronicle, we can see the development of English syntax and morphology from Old English to Middle English. Since the writers usually were making factual statements, even the early passages follow normal declarative word order. Clauses are commonly linked by coordination (usually the conjunction "and" abbreviated as "7") or parataxis. Introductory adverbs or adverbial phrases of time initiate a verb + subject word order at lines 2, 10, 12, 16, 17, 20, 23, 32, 42, 49, 54, 65, 72, 74, 76; but such phrases appear with a subject + verb word order at lines 18, 24. Object pronouns precede the verb at lines 26, 29, 34, 35, 36, 37, 41, 47, 59, 62, but follow it at lines 4, 8, 33, 40, 47, 51–52, 67. Titles come after names at lines 12, 14, 17, 20, 28, 32–33, 37, 38, 42–43, 53; however, when a demonstrative is included, the word order is demonstrative + title + name (lines 4, 25, 38, 41, 49). Double negatives occur at lines 53, 58–59, 60, 68, 69–70, 75. The verb "sculan" (shall) indicates obligation in lines 5, 50; in the second example it also has a predictive function.

Coordinate verbs are separated at lines 51–52. In Old English, complex sentence elements were sometimes ordered according to their length, whereas in Modern English ordering is based on syntactic groupings. Prepositions occur together with case endings at lines 2, 3, 4–5, 9, 10–11, 13, 17–18, 20, 27, 32, 33, 34, 35, 40, 43; prepositional phrases appear without case endings on the nouns at lines 49, 55, 57, 72.

Inflections are greatly reduced in the selections from the twelfth century. The adverbial phrase "on þissum geare" appears as "þis geare" in the entry for 1137, and "þis gær" for 1154. The "es" ending has become the general plural form for all classes and cases of the noun: for example, "neues" at l. 56 was an n-declension noun in Old English, and "weorces" (l. 64) was an ending-less neuter; the dative plural ends with "es" rather than "um" in "weorces" (l. 64) and "deoules" (l. 65). Some endingless neuters survive, such as "wunder" at l. 59. The preterit plural ends with "en" more frequently than "on."

After 1137, we see the written forms of the language being respelled by Anglo-Norman scribes. Old English diphthongs and other orthographic symbols start to give way to what we use today. French words begin to enter the vocabulary. In these later passages we have the earliest examples of Middle English combined with surviving forms from the standard written language of late Old English.

The Anglo-Saxon Chronicle

            and   *seized*   *kingdom reigned*

449.   Her Martianus 7 Ualentinus onfengon rice. 7 rixadon

           invited   *Vortigern*   *race (kin)*

.vii. winter. 7 on þeora dagum gelaðode Wyrtgeorn Angel cin

here   *three ships*

hider. 7 hi þa coman on þrim ceolum hider to Brytene. on þam

harbor Ebbsfleet   *king*   *Vortigern*   *gave them*

stede Heopwines fleot. Se cyning Wyrtgeorn gef heom land on

south   *east*   *on condition that they*   *fight*   *against*

5   suðan eastan ðissum lande. wiððan þe hi sceoldon feohton wið

Picts   *fought*   *had*   *victory*   *wherever*

Pyhtas. Heo þa fuhton wið Pyhtas. 7 heofdon sige swa hwer swa

                ordered   *more* *aid*

heo comon. Hy ða sendon to Angle, heton sendon mara fultum.

ordered   *tell of* *Britons*   *worthlessness*   *virtues*

7 heton heom secgan Brytwalana nahtscipe. 7 þes landes cysta.

          army   *others*   *help*

He ða sona sendon hider mare weored þam oðrum to fultume.

From *Two of the Saxon Chronicles Parallel,* ed. Charles Plummer and John Earle (Oxford: The Clarendon Press, 1952), pp. 13, 21, 127, 155, 195–98, 263–64, 268. By permission of The Clarendon Press, Oxford.

three   tribes   *Old Saxons*

Þa comon þa men of þrim megðum Germanie. Of Ald Seaxum. of   10

Angles   Jutes

Anglum. of Iotum.

                sent   *Pope*   *Archbishop*

601.   Her sende Gregorius papa Augustine arcebiscope

pallium

pallium

                    religious   *teachers*   *help*

on Brytene. 7 wel manega godcunde larewas him to fultume.

             converted

7 Paulinus biscop gehwirfede Eadwine Norðhymbra cining to

baptism (Christianity)

fulluhte.   15

           Ipswich   *harried*

991.   Her wæs G[ypes]wic gehergod. 7 æfter þam swyðe

soon   *alderman*   *slain*   *Maldon*

raðe wæs Brihtnoð ealdorman ofslægen æt Mældune. 7 on þam

year   *it is agreed   that*   *payed   first   tribute*

geare man gerædde þt man geald ærest gafol Deniscan mannum.

      great   *terror*   *sea   coast*

for þam mycclan brogan þe hi worhtan be þam sæ riman.

          year   *succeeded*   *whole*

1017.   Her on þisum geare feng Cnut cyning to eall Angel   20

realm of England   divided   four
cynnes rice. 7 hit to dæld on fower. him sylfum West Seaxan.

Þurcylle East Englan. 7 Eadrice Myrcean. 7 Yrice Norðhymbran.

                                                        killed
7 on þisum geare wæs Eadric ealdormann ofslagen.

                    year   consecrated   church
      1066.   On þissum geare man halgode þet mynster æt

              Childermass   Day   died
25 Westmynster on Cilda mæsse dæg. 7 se cyng Eadward forðferde

        Twelfth Mass   eve   buried
on twelfta mæsse æfen. 7 hine mann bebyrgede on twelftan

                          consecrated   church
mæsse dæg. innan þære niwan halgodre circean on Westmynstre.

                  succeeded   kingdom   as
7 Harold eorl feng to Engla landes cyne rice. swa swa se cyng

          had granted   also   had chosen
hit him geuðe. 7 eac men hine þær to gecuron. 7 wæs

consecrated   *same   year*
30 gebletsod to cynge on twelftan mæsse dæg. 7 þy ilcan geare

                      went   fleet   against
þe he cyng wæs. he for ut mid scip here togeanes Willelme.

    meanwhile   *ships*
7 þa while com Tostig eorl into Humbran mid .lx. scipum.

      Eadwine

with   *army*   *drove him*   *out*   *boat*   *men (sailors)*
eorl com [mid] land fyrde. 7 draf hine ut. 7 þa butse carlas

deserted   *went*   *ships*
hine forsocan. 7 he for to Scotlande mid .xii. snaccum.

                    Norse   *ships*
7 hine gemette Harold se Norrena cyng mid .ccc. scipum.   35

            did homage   *both*   *went*   *Humber*   *until*
7 Tostig him tobeah. 7 hi bægen foran into Humbran. oð þet

          York   *fought*
hi coman to Eoferwic. 7 heom wið feaht Morkere eorl.

                              had   *of victory* *control*
7 Eadwine eorl. 7 se Norrena cyng ahte siges   geweald. 7 man

made known   *done*   *had happened*
cydde Harolde cyng hu hit wæs þær gedon 7 geworden. 7 he

with great   *army*
com mid mycclum here Engliscra manna. 7 gemette hine æt   40

Stamford   *Bridge*   *killed*
Stængfordes brycge. 7 hine ofsloh. 7 þone eorl Tostig.

            army *bravely*   *meanwhile*
7 eallne þone here ahtlice ofercom. 7 þa hwile com Willelm

          Hastings   *saint*
eorl upp æt Hestingan on sc̄e Michæles mæsse dæg. 7 Harold

      from the north   *before*   *army*
com norðan 7 him wið feaht ear þan þe his here come eall.

        fell   *two*   *brothers*
7 þær he feoll. 7 his twægen gebroðra Gyrð 7 Leofwine.   45

conquered
7 Willelm þis land geeode. 7 com to Westmynstre. 7 Ealdred

archbishop   *consecrated*   *yielded*   *gold*
arceƀ hine to cynge gehalgode. 7 menn guldon him gyld.

  hostages gave   *thus*   *bought (back)*
7 gislas sealdon. 7 syððan heora land bohtan.

               went   *sea*
   1137.   Þis gære for þe king Stephne ofer sæ to Normandi 7

     received   *because* *that* *thought*   *just*
50 ther wes underfangen for þi þt hi uuenden þt he sculde ben alsuic

as   *uncle*   *still*   *divided*
alse the eom wes. 7 for he hadde get his tresor. ac he todeld

     foolishly   *much*
it 7 scatered sotlice. Micel hadde Henri king gadered gold

    no good   *soul*
7 syluer. 7 na god ne dide me for his saule thar of.

  when   *made*
Þa þe king Stephne to Englalande com þa macod he his

council   *Oxford*   *arrested* *bishop*   *Salisbury*
55 gadering æt Oxeneford. 7 þar he nam þe ƀ Roger of Sereberi 7

      bishop Lincoln   *the chancellor*   *nephews*
Alexander ƀ of Lincol 7 te Canceler Roger hise neues. 7 dide

      they gave   *traitors*
ælle in prisun. til hi iafen up here castles. Þa the suikes

understood   *that*   *justice*
undergæton þt he milde man was 7 softe 7 god. 7 na iustise ne

horrors   *homage*
dide. þa diden hi alle wunder. Hi hadden him manred maked

oaths *sworn*   *but they no*   *troth*
7 athes suoren. ac hi nan treuthe ne heolden. alle he wæron   60

troths   *abandoned*   *every*   *powerful*
forsworen 7 here treothes forloren. for æuric rice man his

filled
castles makede 7 agænes him heolden. 7 fylden þe land ful of

oppressed   *greatly*   *wretched*
castles. Hi suencten suyðe þe uurecce men of þe land mid

works   *when*   *were*   *then filled*
castel weorces. þa þe castles uuaren maked þa fylden hi mid

devils   *evil*   *seized*   *thought*
deoules 7 yuele men. Þa namen hi þa men þe hi wenden þt ani   65

goods *had*   *men*
god hefden. bathe be nihtes 7 be dæies. carlmen 7 wimmen.

put   *tortured them*
7 diden heom in prisun efter gold 7 syluer. 7 pined heom

(with) indescribable torturing   *were*   *never*   *so*
untellendlice pining. for ne uuæren næure nan martyrs swa

tortured
pined alse hi wæron. . . . I ne can ne i ne mai tellen alle

horrors   *tortures that*   *wretched*
þe wunder ne alle þe pines þt hi diden wrecce men on þis land.   70

that
7 þt lastede þa .xix. wintre wile Stephne was king.

1154.　On þis gær wærd þe king Stephne ded 7 bebyried
                 became

                  buried   *Faversham*
þer his wif 7 his sune wæron bebyried æt Faures feld.

    church   *founded*
þæt minster hi makeden. Þa þe king was ded. þa was þe eorl

  over   *sea*
75　beionde sæ. 7 ne durste nan man don oþer bute god for þe

  great   *awe*
micel eie of him. Þa he to Engleland com. þa was he

  received   *great*   *honor*   *consecrated*
underfangen mid micel wurtscipe. 7 to king bletcæd in Lundene

         Sunday
on þe sunnen dæi be foren midwinter dæi. 7 held þær

  great   *court*
micel curt.

QUESTIONS AND ASSIGNMENTS

1. Old English becomes easier for the modern reader to understand once he becomes aware of the following correspondences:

Old English	Modern English
ꝥ, þ and ð	th
sc	sh
c	k
cw	qu
ci or ce	chi, che
gi or ge	y
cg	dg
hw	wh
hl, hn, hr	l, n, r
æ	a, e, ea
a	o
y	i
u	o
ȝ	y, gh

Many words can be identified more easily once they are stripped of prefixes (such as "a," "be," "ge") and suffixes (such as "an," "on," "um," "ena").

Rewrite some of the words that reveal such correspondences in the first four selections from the *Anglo-Saxon Chronicle*.

2. Study the charts on Old English inflectional patterns in the Appendix.

    a. Which inflections have survived in Modern English?

    b. Which ones have increased in importance and are living inflections that can be used with new words?

    c. Which ones have survived as relics and are used only with a small number of words?

3. Old English poetry used a special vocabulary that included archaic words (like "mece" for sword), metaphoric or metonymic expressions (like "ceol," literally "keel," for "ship"), kennings or metaphoric expressions that identify a referent with something it is only in a very special sense (like "hron-rade" [whale road] for "ocean"), and compounds consisting of nouns plus limiting genitives (like "sceaþena þreatum," "from troops of the enemy").

List all such examples of poetic diction that you can find in the selection from *Beowulf*.

Are similar poetic devices ever used in Modern English? If they are, give some examples.

4. Old English "scops" or poets composed their verse by joining together formulaic half-lines that were linked by alliteration or initial rhyme. With consonants and the combinations "sc," "sp," and "st," the alliteration was usually exact (although the palatal and guttural "c" and "g" could alliterate, as in "gar" and "gear" in the first line of *Beowulf*); any stressed syllables beginning with vowels were considered sufficiently alike to alliterate with each other. The poet could substitute words within his formulaic phrases to suit his meaning.

The following verse lines are taken from the conclusion of *Beowulf*, which provides an elegy for the hero. Fill in the blanks to write your own version, using the list of words that has been provided (the first word in each group is the one that was used by the *Beowulf* poet).

A. hlæw (mound)
    haga (enclosure)
    ham (home)
    heall (hall)
    hearg (temple)
    heorþ (hearth)

B. care (sorrow)
    camp (battle)
    ceap (business transaction)
    cynn (race, kin)
    cild (child)
    cniht (boy, knight)

C. wordgyd (dirge)
    wa (woe)
    wanscæft (misfortune)
    wanung (lament)
    wealdend (ruler)
    weard (guardian, warden)

D. wrecan (utter)
    wacian (keep watch)
    wadan (proceed)
    wanian (lament)
    wearnian (warn)
    weorþian (honor)

E. eorlscipe (nobility)
    are (mercy)
    agend (ruler)
    earnung (merit)
    eaþmoedu (humility)
    eafoþ (strength)

F. duguþum (excellence)
    dierling (dear one)
    dolwillen (rashness)
    drohtaþ (condition of life)
    dryhten (lord)
    dysig (folly, error)

G. freogan (love)
    fandian (try)
    faran (go)
    fealdan (fold)
    feohtan (fight)
    ferian (carry)

H. lichaman (body)
    lagu (law)
    land (land)
    langung (longing)
    leod (nation, people)
    leoht (light)

I. hryre (fall)
    had (condition)
    hata (enemy)
    heaf (grief)
    heafod (head)
    heap (troop)

J. mildust (mildest)
    meagol (impressive)
    meahtiȝ (mighty)
    mearu (tender)
    medwis (dull, stupid)
    medspoediȝ (unprosperous)

K. monþwærust (most gentle)
    medeme (small, middling)
    micel (great)
    modiȝ (noble minded)
    myrþe (murderous)
    myrȝe (merry)

L. liþost (kindest)
    læst (least)
    laþost (most hostile)
    lefost (weakest)
    leofost (most loved)
    leohtost (most agile)

M. lofgeornost (most eager for fame)
    leaslic (false)
    leodhwæt (courageous)
    liciend-lic (agreeable)
    lif-fæst (vigorous)
    list-hendiȝ (skillful)

	then around		*rode*	*brave in battle*
1	Þa ymbe	A	riodan	hildedeore

	of noblemen children	*all*
2	æþelinga bearn,	ealra twelfe

		lament	*king*	*mourn for*
3	woldon	B	cwiðan,	ond kyning mænan,

			about the man speak
4	C	D	, ond ymb wer sprecan;

	praised		*valiant deeds*
5	eahtodan	E	, ond his ellenweorc

		judged	*as*	*it*	*fitting is*
6	F	demdon,	swa hit gedefe bið

	friendly lord	*praise*
7	þæt mon his winedryhten	wordum herge

	in heart		*when*	*forth shall*
8	ferhðum	G	, þonne he forð scile

		led	*be*
9	of	H	læded weorðan.

	so	*mourned*	*people*
10	Swa begnornodon	Geata leode

	lord's	*hearth companions*
11	Hlafordes	I	, heorðgeneatas;

	said	*of worldly kings*
12	cwædon þæt he wære	wyruldcyninga

	of men		
13	manna	J	ond	K

	to the people		
14	leodum	L	ond	M .

From *Beowulf*, lines 3169–3182.

5. Do a literal, word-for-word translation of selections from King Alfred's Preface to Pope Gregory's *Pastoral Care* (written in the ninth century), Aelfric's

Homily on St. Gregory (written in the tenth century), and Aelfgar's Will (tenth century).

    a. Which work seems furthest from Modern English?
    b. Which one seems closest?
    c. Which differences seem to be due to the dates at which the works were written?
    d. Which ones seem to be due to the stylistic level?

6. Four principal dialects were spoken in Anglo-Saxon England: Kentish (part of Sussex and Kent), Northumbrian (north of the Humber), Mercian (from the Thames to the Humber, except for Wales), and West Saxon (south of the Thames, except for the Kentish area and Cornwall). Because of the cultural and political importance of the kingdom of Wessex, West Saxon came to function as a *koiné* or literary standard.

    Aelfric's Homily on St. Gregory and Aelfgar's Will both date from the tenth century; however, the homily is written in the literary standard, and the will is not. Compare the two works and make a list of words that are spelled differently (some differences in spellings may have occurred in later copying of the manuscripts rather than in the originals). Some examples are dæge/day, ræd/red, eallum/alle, weorc/werk.

    What do the variations suggest about the differences that existed between the West Saxon and Mercian dialects?

7. Go over the Old English selections, and copy some of the sentences that contain the auxiliary verbs "will" (forms you will find include "willan," "wille," "wylle," "wolde") and "shall" ("sculan," "sceal," "scolde").

    a. For "will," note whether the verb signifies volition, promise, or prediction.
    b. For "shall," note whether it indicates obligation, promise, or prediction.
    c. Which meanings seem to have been dominant in Old English?
    d. Does the predictive function of "will" and "shall" seem to have emerged from the other meanings?

8. Perfective aspect indicates that an event or action is completed. It does not specify a particular moment in the past, as the past tense does, but indicates that the action is completed at the time of utterance. In Modern English, perfective aspect is expressed by the auxiliary "have" plus the past participle of the following verb (such as "have learned," "has come"). In Old English, two methods were employed: the older was the use of the prefix "ge" (from Germanic "ga"), but we also find the segmentalized perfect with "habban" (the ancestor of "have") for most verbs, and a "be" verb ("beon," "wesan," "weorþan") for verbs denoting change of place or state (such as "hæfde geleornod," "wæs gecumen").

    Make a list of occurrences of perfective aspect in some of the Old English selections. Which method seems to be dominant? Does "ge" or "habban" always appear when the meaning calls for the past perfect tense?

9.   Sacred writings tend to preserve older forms of language. The Old English translations of the Lord's Prayer remained close to the word order of the Latin Vulgate. The King James Bible has strongly influenced Modern English versions. In the Revised Standard Version of 1901, the only changes made were the substitution of "who" for "which" and "on earth" for "in earth."

Rewrite the King James version of the Lord's Prayer in idiomatic Modern English, eliminating all archaisms in vocabulary, morphology, and spelling. What does your own reaction or that of other people to your version suggest about the reason for archaism in religious expression?

10.   Compare the earlier selections in the *Anglo-Saxon Chronicle* with those that date from the twelfth century, and make a list of words and phrases that appear in different form. Which differences indicate real changes that have occurred in the sounds or structure of the language? Which differences are due merely to spelling?

Middle English

ROBERT MANNYNG'S STORY OF ENGLANDE

Between the mid-twelfth and the mid-fourteenth centuries, historical writing in English disappeared because French and Latin were the languages of the court. At about the time the *Anglo-Saxon Chronicle* was discontinued at Peterborough, an Anglo-Norman poet named Geoffrey Gaimar was translating the *Chronicle* into French rhymed couplets. French verse became the medium for historical writing in England for about two centuries.

Robert Mannyng was one of the earliest to turn again to English for a chronicle. He was born in Bourn, Lincolnshire, and was a member of the Gilbertine Order, residing at the priory of Sixhill in Lincolnshire. His two extant works are *Handlyng Synne* (c. 1303), a treatise on the Seven Deadly Sins, and the *Story of Englande* (c. 1338), a chronicle based on Wace's *Brut* and Pierre de Langtoft's *Chronicle*. Mannyng followed the example of his Anglo-Norman sources in using verse rather than prose. His chronicle survives in two manuscripts, the Inner Temple Library, Petyt MS. 511, and one in the Lambeth Palace (the basis for the following selection).

Mannyng wrote to inform and entertain the unlearned common man who knew only English. In the following introduction to his *Story of Englande,* he defends English as the proper medium for his audience and criticizes difficult, ornate language because it will condemn a work to obscurity (ll. 29–46). He himself used a plain, colloquial style. Most of his lines fall into natural speech patterns. Clauses are usually linked by coordination, "and" or "for" being his favorite conjunctions. He occasionally repeats constructions for emphasis, as with "whilk" at lines 17–20 and "no" at lines 25–26. Word order is sometimes distorted because of the rhyme scheme, as at lines 4, 5, 22, 37, 40, 55–56. The vocabulary is simple with few words from French or Latin.

Mannyng wrote in the North-East Midland dialect of Lincolnshire. His ending for plural nouns is "s," as in "lordynges" (l. 1), "thynges" (l. 15), "dedis" (l. 16), "kynges" (l. 16). The present participle ends in "yng" as in "sayng" (l. 32), the past participle in "en" as in "wryten" (l. 4). In this selection the only form that appears for the third person singular present indicative is "s," as in "has" (l. 5) and "semes" (l. 32); the plural ends in "e," as in "wille" (l. 2), "wone" (l. 7), and "cone" (l. 8). The third person plural pronouns are "þai" (l. 10), "þam" (l. 18), and "þer" (l. 32) or "þare" (l.39). A Northern influence can be seen in the frequent use of the symbol "þ"; in the use of "s" for "sh" in lightly accented syllables, such as "Inglis" (l. 22) and "suld" (l. 56); in the use of "u" for "o" as in "gude" (l. 15); and in the use of "k" for "ch" as in "whilk" (l. 17), "suylk" (l. 42), "ilk" (l. 44).

Robert Mannyng's Story of Englande

lords
Lordynges that be now here,

you   *learn*
if ӡe wille listene & lere

All the story of Inglande

as   *found*
als Robert Mannyng wryten it fand,

showed
& on Inglysch has it schewed,   5

learned   *unlearned*
not for þe lerid bot for þe lewed,

those   *dwell*
ffor þo þat in þis lande wone

Latin or·French do not know
þat þe Latyn no Frankys cone,

amusement
ffor to haf solace & gamen

From *The Story of England by Robert Manning of Brunne,* ed. F. J. Furnivall, (London: Longmans, 1887), pp. 1–4.

together
10 In felawschip when þai sitt samen.

know
   And it is wisdom for to wytten

   þe state of þe land, & haf it wryten,

won
   what manere of folk first it wan,

race
   & of what kynde it first began;

15 And gude it is for many thynges

   for to here þe dedis of kynges,

which   *fools*
   whilk were foles, & whilk were wyse,

knew   *cunning*
   & whilk of þam couthe most quantyse

   and whilk did wrong, & whilk ryght,

20 & whilk maynten[e]d pes & fyght.

   · · · · · · · · · · · · ·

as
   Als þai haf wryten & sayd,

   haf I alle in myn Inglis layd,

could
   In symple speche as I couthe,

easiest
þat is lightest in mannes mouthe.

wrote   *minstrels*
I mad noght for no disours,   25

storytellers
ne for no seggers, no harpours,

Bot for þe luf of symple men

difficult   *understand*
þat strange Inglis can not ken.

. . . .

telling
I see in song, in sedgeyng tale

of Erceldoun & of Kendale,   30

none   *recites*   *composed*
Non þam says as þai þam wroght,

recitation   *seems to be nothing*
& in þer sayng it semes noght;

hear
þat may þou here in sir Tristrem;

heroic stories   *esteem*
ouer gestes it has þe steem,

Ouer alle that is or was,   35

recited as Thomas composed it
if men it sayd as made Thomas;

But I here it no man so say,

couplet

þat of som copple som is away;

fine narrative   before

So þare fayre sayng here beforn

effort   nearly lost

40 is þare trauayle nere forlorn;

honor

þai sayd it for pride & nobleye,

such

þat non were suylk as þei;

intended everywhere

And all þat þai wild ouerwhere,

same   perish

all þat ilk will now forfare.

spoke   strange

45 þai sayd in so quante Inglis

knows not

þat many one wate not what it is.

hesitated

þerfore [I] henyed wele þe more

work   hard

In strange ryme to trauayle sore;

intelligence
And my witte was oure thynne

work
So strange speche to trauayle in;   50

knew
And forsoth I couth[e] noght

so strange Inglis as þai wroght;

And men besoght me many a tyme

easy
to turne it bot in light[e] ryme;

complicated style
þai sayd, if I in strange it turne,   55

would scorn
to here it manyon suld skurne;

there are   *strange*
ffor it   ere names full selcouthe

þat ere not vsed now in mouthe;

common people
And þerfore for þe comonalte

would
þat blythely wild listen to me,   60

easy   *language*
On light[e] lange I it began,

unlearned

for luf of þe lewed man,

events

to telle þam þe chaunces bolde

þat here before was don & tolde.

DOCUMENTS IN LONDON ENGLISH

England had preceded the other nations of Western Europe in developing an official vernacular prose. During the Old English period, the West Saxon dialect of Wessex came to be used all over the country as a written standard. The Norman Conquest put an end to this. In the early post-Conquest years, many of the Conqueror's proclamations were in English. But during the following reigns, Latin and Anglo-Norman became the administrative languages. English rarely appeared in official documents in the twelfth and thirteenth centuries, began to be used in the fourteenth, and became dominant in the fifteenth. The dialect that came to serve as a new written standard was that of London, the political and economic center of the country. During the early Middle English period London English was mainly Southern or Southeastern, but by the fourteenth century it became mainly East Midland with some Southern influence.

The English Proclamation of Henry III (1258) is the earliest extant example of the London dialect in Middle English. It was issued to confirm the Provisions of Oxford, a charter of rights obtained from the King by the barons in 1258. Versions survive in French and English. The English probably reflects the nationalistic feelings of the barons.

The Proclamation is written in a formal administrative style, which shows the influence of the legal style of the chancellories of the Middle Ages, developed in Latin by clerks of the Roman curia and imitated in the vernacular in other countries. This style strongly influenced French prose and from French and Latin passed into English. It is characterized by the use of verbal formulas, such as the listing of titles at the beginning of the document (ll. 1–3) and the expression "ȝeare of vre cruninge" (l. 25) at the end; by repetition of set phrases, such as "þe moare dæl" (ll. 6, 14), "stedefæst and ilestinde" (ll. 10, 21); and by the use of terms of reference, such as "biforen iseid" (l. 15), "toforeniseide" (ll. 9, 14). Clauses are usually linked by subordination (ll. 4–10, 10–15, 18–20, 20–22). Doublets or word pairs are used extensively, both to cover all aspects of a situation and to provide rhetorical ornamentation (ll. 3–4, 5, 7, 8, 10, 12, 13, 17, 20).

The language of the Proclamation is mainly Southern with some East Midland influence. The spellings for many of the vowels reveal Southern pronunciations. Old English "æ" remains a front vowel, written as "æ" in "þæt" (ll. 4, 6), "rædesmen" (ll. 5, 14), "dæl" (ll. 6, 14), and as "e" in "ilestinde" (l. 10). Old English "ea" is preserved as "ea" as opposed to the Midland "o" or "a" in "healden" (ll. 12, 20). Old English "y" is preserved as a rounded front vowel written as "u" in "kuneriche" (ll. 7, 27). The frequently used "eo" indicates a rounded front vowel: "heom" (l. 6), "heo" (l. 11), "beo" (l. 10), "beon" (l. 13), "treowþe" (l. 8), "treowe" (l. 11). "Iwersed" (l. 18) is a Kentish form of the Old English "gewyrsed." The digraph "oa" ·is probably an early writing of Middle English "o" from Old English "a" (ll. 1, 2, 6), a change that occurred in the South and East Midlands. The East Midland "a" appears instead of "ea" in "alle" (l. 4) and "halden" (l. 23).

The inflections also show a strong Southern influence. The infinitive often ends with "ien," as in "swerien" (l. 12), "werien" (l. 13), "makien" (l. 13). The present participle ends with "inde" in "ilestinde" (l. 10), "lestinde" (l. 22). The past participle has an "i" prefix, as in "ilærde, ileawede" (ll. 3–4), "ichosen" (l. 6), "idon" (l. 7), "imakede" (l. 13), "iseid" (l. 15), "ilet" (l. 18), "isend" (l. 26). The present indicative plural sometimes ends in "þ," as in "beoþ" (l. 6) and "habbeþ" (l. 7). But the Midland "en" is more common: "willen, vnnen" (l. 5), "shullen" (l. 7), "hoaten" (l. 11), "oȝen" (l. 11), "cumen" (l. 19), "healden" (l. 20), "senden" (l. 22).

The language of the First Petition to Parliament in English (1386) is much closer to Modern English. There are fewer unfamiliar words and spellings. The diphthongs "ea" and "eo" and the digraphs "æ" and "oa" no longer appear. This document shows that by the end of the fourteenth century, the London dialect had become mainly East Midland. The Midland "en" is the only ending that appears in this passage for the present indicative plural ("compleynen," l. 2). Except for the form "ydo" (l. 5), an "i" or "y" prefix no longer appears on the past participle: "passed" (l. 5), "knowen" (lines 12, 19), "sompned" (lines 23, 24), "armed" (lines 27, 28), "laide" (l. 29), "breken" (l. 30).

The Petition concerns a series of feuds that took place in the 1380s between the Grocers and Fishmongers guilds, led by Nicholas Brembre, and the Mercers and Drapers, led by John Northampton. In 1386 petitions were submitted to Parliament by ten of the London guilds. The Mercers' Petition was the only document of the ten in English. It is written in the administrative language but is less formal than the proclamation of Henry III. Its author was probably a member of the Mercers Company, who would have been less influenced than a royal clerk by the legal style. Nevertheless, it has many characteristics of the legal style. It opens with a verbal formula (lines 1–2), uses terms of reference such as "bifore" (l. 13), "forsaid" (lines 15, 21), and employs many word pairs (lines 1–2, 4–5, 7–8, 9, 12, 22). The word order in the expression "wronges subtiles" (l. 4), with the adjective following the noun, shows the influence of Law French, which still survives in Modern English in "letters patent" and "lords chief justices." In lines 29–33 the style becomes more colloquial as the writer tells of the strong-arm tactics of Nicholas Brembre's retainers.

Documents in London English

THE ENGLISH PROCLAMATION OF HENRY III, 1258

through   *help*   *England*
Henri, þurȝ Godes fultume King on Engleneloande,

lord   *Ireland*
Lhoauerd on Yrloande, Duk on Normandi, on Aquitaine, and Eorl

   Anjou   *faithful*   *learned (clerical)*
on Aniow, send igretinge to alle hise holde, ilærde and

unlearned (lay)   *may know you*
ileawede, on Huntendoneschire. þæt witen ȝe wel alle þæt

             wish   *our*   *counsellors*   *or*
we willen and vnnen þæt, þæt vre rædesmen alle, oþer þe   5

greater   *part*   *them*
moare dæl of heom, þæt beoþ ichosen þurȝ us and þurȝ þæt

               kingdom
loandes folk on vre kuneriche, habbeþ idon and shullen don

                        our   *troth*   *profit*
in þe worþnesse of Gode and on vre treowþe, for þe freme of

From *Early Middle English Texts,* ed. Bruce Dickins and R. M. Wilson (New York: W. W. Norton & Company, Inc.; London: Bowes & Bowes Publishers Ltd., 1951), pp. 8–9. The transcription is from the Patent Rolls, 43 Henry III, M. 15.

        provision   *aforesaid*   *counsellors*

þe loande þurȝ þe besiȝte of þan toforeniseide redesmen,

            lasting   *without*   *end*

10   beo stedefæst and ilestinde in alle þinge a buten ænde.

         command   *subjects*   *loyalty*   *owe*

And we hoaten alle vre treowe in þe treowþe þæt heo vs oȝen,

þæt heo stedefæstliche healden and swerien to healden and

    defend   *statutes*

to werien þo isetnesses þæt beon imakede and beon to makien,

       aforesaid   *counsellors*   *greater*   *part*

þurȝ þan toforeniseide rædesmen, oþer þurȝ þe moare dæl of

                               each

15   heom, alswo alse hit is biforen iseid; and þæt æhc oþer

             same   *oath*

helpe þæt for to done bi þan ilche oþe aȝenes alle men riȝt

        receive   *none*   *take*

for to done and to foangen. And noan ne nime of loande ne

   property   *provision* *might*   *be*   *hindered*   *worsened*

of eȝte wherþurȝ þis besiȝte muȝe beon ilet oþer iwersed on

any   *manner*   *any man or*   *any men*   *against*

onie wise. And ȝif oni   oþer onie cumen her onȝenes, we

         command   *subjects*

20   willen and hoaten þæt alle vre treowe heom healden deadliche

foes   *because*

ifoan. And for þæt we willen þæt þis beo stedefæst and

lasting   *letter   patent   sealed (signed)*
lestinde, we senden ʒew þis writ open, iseined wiþ vre seel,

 hold *among*   *hoard (safekeeping)*
to halden amanges ʒew ine hord. Witnesse vsseluen æt Lundene

þane eʒtetenþe day on þe monþe of Octobre, in þe two and

   year   *crowning (reign)*   *each*
fowertiʒþe ʒeare of vre cruninge. . . . And al on þo ilche   25

      every   *shire*
worden is isend into æurihce oþre shcire ouer al þære

kingdom   *also*
kuneriche on Engleneloande, and ek in-tel Irelonde.

A PETITION OF THE FOLK OF MERCERYE, 1386

[T]o the moost noble & Worthiest Lordes, moost ryghtful

& wysest conseille to owre lige Lorde the Kyng, compleynen,

 please   *cloth merchants*
if it lyke to yow, the folk of the Mercerye of London, [as]

              secret
a membre of the same citee, of many wronges subtiles & also

      done
open oppressions, ydo to hem by longe tyme here bifore passed. 5

Of which oon was where the eleccion of Mairaltee is to

From *A Book of London English*, ed. R. W. Chambers and M. Daunt (Oxford: The Clarendon Press, 1931), pp. 33–34. By permission of The Clarendon Press, Oxford. The transcription is from the Public Record Office, Ancient Petitions, File 20, No. 997.

advice
be to the fre men of the Citee bi gode & paisible auys of the

one   *freely*
wysest & trewest at o day in the yere frelich, there,

nought-withstondyng the same fredam or fraunchise, Nichol

supporters   *put forward*   *himself*
10   Brembre wyth his vpberers purposed hym, the yere next after

John Northampton, Mair of the same Citee with stronge honde, as

dissension   *against*
it is ful knowen, & thourgh debate & strenger partye ayeins

peace   *provided*
the pees bifore purueyde was chosen Mair in destruccion of

many ryght.

15   For in the same yere the forsaid Nichol, with-outen

against   *armings*   *also*
nede, ayein the pees made dyuerse enarmynges bi day & eke bi

subjects
nyght & destruyd the kynges trewe lyges, som with open slaughtre,

some bi false emprisonementz, & some fledde the Citee for feere

openly
as it is openlich knowen.

20   And so ferthermore, for to susteyne thise wronges & many

othere, the next yere after, the same Nichol, ayeins the forsaide fredam & trewe comunes, did crye openlich that no man sholde

come to chese her Mair but such as were sompned, & tho that
choose *summoned*

were sompned were of his ordynaunce & after his auys. And in
summoned *party* *advice*

the nyght next after folwynge he did carye grete quantitee of   25

Armure to the Guyldehalle, with which as wel straungers of the

contree as othere of with-jnne were armed on the morwe, ayeins

his owne proclamacion that was such that no man shulde be armed;

& certein busshmentz were laide, that, when free men of the
ambushes

Citee come to chese her Mair, breken vp armed cryinge with   30
choose

loude voice "sle! sle!" folwyng hem; wherthourgh the peple

for feere fledde to houses & other [hidy]nges as in londe of
shelters

werre, adradde to be ded in comune.
war   *afraid*   *common*

GEOFFREY CHAUCER'S GENERAL PROLOGUE
TO THE CANTERBURY TALES

Many critics consider Geoffrey Chaucer the greatest English poet of the Middle Ages. He was born about 1340, the son of John Chaucer, a wealthy London wine merchant with good connections at court. Geoffrey became a page in the household of the Countess of Ulster and gradually advanced to responsible positions as a court official and diplomat. As Chaucer himself tells us in the *House of Fame* (II, 652–660), poetry was a part-time activity in his busy life. Yet his positions at court provided him with a sophisticated audience, Continental contacts, and a breadth of experience that greatly enriched his poetry.

Chaucer wrote in the London dialect, which already was becoming the chief form of English because of its social, economic, and political position. But Chaucer gave that dialect a new prestige as a literary medium. Before the time of Chaucer, aristocratic literature was written primarily in French. He adapted French genres and verse forms into English. He combined the syllabic French line with the accentual English line, bringing a new smoothness to English verse. The verse forms, themes, and phrases used by Chaucer dominated English poetry for the next hundred years.

The Canterbury Tales, Chaucer's most popular work, is preserved in eighty-three manuscripts. One of the best is the richly illuminated Ellesmere Manuscript, now at the Huntington Library in San Marino, California. It is the basis for the following selection from the General Prologue, which exhibits Chaucer's wide range of styles. The formal, rhetorical opening consists of a long periodic sentence, two parallel "when" clauses followed by a "then" clause (lines 1–14). Metrical requirements sometimes bring about a distorted word order: the object occurs before the verb at lines 2 and 17, and the verb before the subject at lines 12, 23–25, 58. Enjambment (the running on of a sentence from one line to the next) is frequently used to unify the verse paragraph (lines 1–14, 15–18, 20–22, etc.). The vocabulary varies with the level of style and the subject. A considerable number of French words occur in the first paragraph ("perced," "veyne," "vertu," "licour," "engendred," "flour"), and in the description of the Knight ("chivalrie," "honour," "curteisie," "degree," "noble," "armee," "batailles," "sovereyn"). Few French words appear in the description and speech of the Host. The Host's speech, an example of Chaucer's colloquial style, contains many idiomatic phrases (ll. 766, 768, 769, 774, 775, 781, 782).

Chaucer's language generally agrees with that of the official London documents of his day. It contains a mixture of Southern and East Midland features. The Midland "s" inflection is the usual plural form for nouns, as in "shoures" (l. 1), "croppes" (l. 7), "corages" (l. 11), "pilgrimages" (l. 12); an exception occurs with "eyen" (l. 753). The genitive form is commonly "es" as in "shires" (l. 15), "lordes" (l. 47); but an "r" form appears with "oure aller" (l. 799) and an uninflected genitive with "fader" (l. 781). The third person plural pronouns are "they" (l. 16), "hem" (l. 11), and "hir" (l. 32). The ending for the third person singular present indicative is "th" as in "hath" (l. 2), "priketh" (l. 11). The usual plural ending is the Midland "en" as in "maken" (l. 9), "slepen" (l. 10), "shapen" (l. 772); but the Southern "eth" appears in "herkneth" (l. 788).

Chaucer's poetry contains more conservative features than his prose. A major one is the retention of final unstressed "e"; it was disappearing from the spoken language in the late fourteenth century, but Chaucer used it for metrical purposes. Past participles with a "y" prefix are rare in his prose but common in his poetry; those found in the following selection are "yronne" (l. 8), "yfalle" (l. 25), "ycome" (l. 77), and "ytaught" (l. 755).

Chaucer used dialectal variants to increase the number of his rhymes and to vary his versification. "Ycome" appears at l. 77, but "come" at l. 23. The infinitive can end with either "en" as in "seken" (l. 13), "wenden" (l. 21), "riden" (l. 45), or "e", as in "seke" (l. 17), "telle" (l. 38). Both forms appear in l. 772 ("to talen and to pleye"). The Kentish form "leste" is used as a rhyme word at l. 787 ("liste" is the Midland form), and the Southern "mury" is used to rhyme with "Caunterbury" at l. 802 ("myrie" appears at ll. 757 and 782).

PLATE II: THE ELLESMERE MANUSCRIPT
OF THE CANTERBURY TALES

The Ellesmere Manuscript, copied before 1410, is the finest manuscript of *The Canterbury Tales*. It contains a series of twenty-three colored miniatures depicting the Pilgrims (including one of Chaucer), elaborately illuminated borders, and an excellent text of the poem.

It is written in a cursive bookhand known as Anglicana Formata, a calligraphic script used for copying large, deluxe volumes of vernacular texts. Among its characteristics are the use of broken strokes for the lobes of *d, q, g, a*, and for the ascenders of letters such as *l* and *h*. There are long and round forms for *s*: long *s* usually occurs medially, but it appears initially in "so," "semed" (l. 39). Two forms also exist for *r* (see "hir *corage*," line 11). The same form is used for *u* and *v, v* initially (as in "veyne," l. 3) and *u* in other positions. The letters *i, m, n*, and *u* are composed of detached minims or short downstrokes, and the intended grouping is sometimes not clearly marked (see "in," l. 3).

The Ellesmere scribe consistently dots his *y* to distinguish it from thorn and does not dot his *i*. He often uses abbreviations for *r* plus a following or preceding vowel (see lines 4, 12, 13, 27). Other abbreviations include the forms for "with" (l. 5), "that" (l. 18), "and" (l. 35).

Capital letters normally appear at the beginnings of lines. Large initials in gold and colors often introduce new paragraphs. Double *ff* is used for capital *F* ("fful," l. 47).

The virgule or slant bar in the middle of the line indicates a caesura or a brief pause in reading. It sometimes marks a syntactic division, as in line 7.

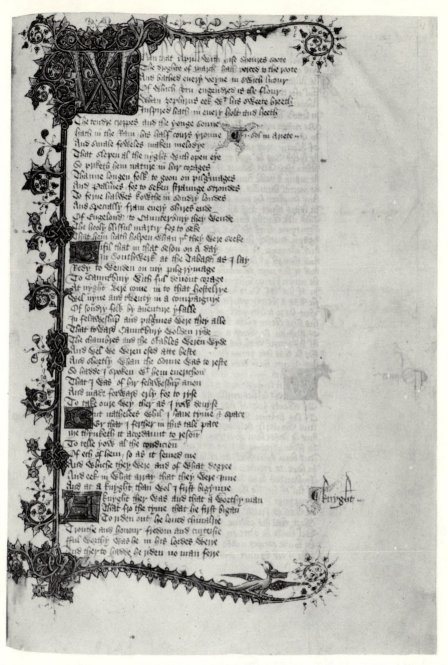

PLATE II: From Chaucer's General Prologue to *The Canterbury Tales* (Huntington Library, MS. Ellesmere Chaucer, Folio 1). Reproduced by permission of The Huntington Library, San Marino, California.

Whan that Aprill with his shoures soote

Geoffrey Chaucer's General Prologue
to The Canterbury Tales

showers   *gentle*
Whan that Aprill with his shoures soote

The droghte of March hath perced to the roote,

vein   *such*   *moisture*
And bathed every veyne in swich licour

power
Of which vertu engendred is the flour;

also
5   Whan Zephirus eek with his sweete breeth

breathed on
Inspired hath in every holt and heeth

leaves
The tendre croppes, and the yonge sonne

run
Hath in the Ram his halfe cours yronne,

And smale foweles maken melodye,

Text of *The Canterbury Tales* edited by John H. Fisher from the Ellesmere Manuscript, with corrections from the Hengwrt, and used with his permission.

sleep
That slepen al the nyght with open eye   10

                              hearts
So priketh hem nature in hir corages—

Thanne longen folk to goon on pilgrimages,

                              foreign   *shores*
And palmeres for to seken straunge strondes

distant shrines   known
To ferne halwes, kowthe in sondry londes;

And specially from every shires ende   15

                              go
Of Engelond to Caunterbury they wende

                              seek
The hooly blisful martir for to seke

                              sick
That hem hath holpen whan that they were seeke.

it befell
Bifil that in that seson on a day

In Southwerk at the Tabard as I lay   20

        go
Redy to wenden on my pilgrymage

                              heart
To Caunterbury with ful devout corage,

At nyght was come into that hostelrye

Wel nyne and twenty in a compaignye

chance   *fallen*
25   Of sondry folk, by aventure yfalle

In felaweship, and pilgrimes were they alle,

That toward Caunterbury wolden ryde.

The chambres and the stables weren wyde,

at the
And wel we weren esed atte beste.

30   And shortly, whan the sonne was to reste,

So hadde I spoken with hem everichon

That I was of hir felaweship anon,

agreement
And made forward erly for to ryse,

describe
To take oure wey ther as I yow devyse.

35   But nathelees, whil I have tyme and space,

before   *progress*
Er that I ferther in this tale pace,

seems
Me thynketh it acordaunt to resoun

situation in life
To telle yow al the condicioun

Of ech of hem, so as it semed me,

what profession   *rank*
And whiche they weren, and of what degree,   40

also   *dress*
And eek in what array that they were inne,

And at a knyght than wol I first bigynne.

brave
A KNYGHT ther was, and that a worthy man,

That fro the tyme that he first bigan

knightly combat
To riden out, he loved chivalrie,   45

loyalty   *generosity*
Trouthe and honour, fredom and curteisie.

Ful worthy was he in his lordes werre,

And therto hadde he riden, no man ferre,

heathendom
As wel in cristendom as in hethenesse,

And evere honoured for his worthynesse.   50

Alexandria
At Alisaundre he was whan it was wonne.

sat at the head of the table
Ful ofte tyme he hadde the bord bigonne

Prussia
Aboven alle nacions in Pruce.

Lithuania   *campaigned*   *Russia*
In Lettow hadde he reysed and in Ruce,

                  rank
55   No Cristen man so ofte of his degree.

Granada
In Gernade at the seege eek hadde he be

Algeciras   *Benmarin (Morocco)*
Of Algezir, and riden in Belmarye.

Ayas (Armenia)   *Attalia (Asia Minor)*
At Lyeys was he and at Satalye,

                Mediterranean Sea
Whan they were wonne, and in the Grete See

      armed expedition
60   At many a noble armee hadde he be.

    combats
At mortal batailles hadde he been fiftene,

             Tlemcen (Morocco)
And foughten for oure feith at Tramyssene

  the lists
In lystes thries, and ay slayn his foo.

  same
This ilke worthy knyght hadde been also

            Palatia (Asia Minor)
65   Somtyme with the lord of Palatye

Agayn another hethen in Turkye,

> *great*   *reputation*

And everemoore he hadde a sovereyn prys.

> *brave*   *prudent (wise)*

And though that he were worthy, he was wys,

> *behavior*

And of his port as meeke as is a mayde.

> *rude remark*

He nevere yet no vileynye ne sayde   70

> *person*

In al his lyf unto no maner wight.

> *true*   *perfect*   *noble*

He was a verray, parfit, gentil knyght.

> *dress*

But for to tellen yow of his array,

> *horses*

His hors weren goode, but he was nat gay.

> *thick cotton*   *tunic*

Of fustian he wered a gypoun   75

> *stained*   *coat of mail*

Al bismotered with his habergeoun,

> *expedition*

For he was late ycome from his viage,

And wente for to doon his pilgrymage.

. . . .

751   A semely man oure HOOSTE was withalle

marshal (main household official)
For to been a marchal in an halle.

eyes   *protruding*
A large man he was with eyen stepe—

Cheapside
A fairer burgeys was ther noon in Chepe—

755 Boold of his speche, and wys, and wel ytaught,

And of manhod hym lakked right naught.

merry
Eek therto he was right a myrie man,

Anf after soper pleyen he bigan,

And spak of myrthe amonges othere thynges,

paid   *bills*
760 Whan that we hadde maad our rekenynges,

And seyde thus: "Now, lordynges, trewely,

Ye been to me right welcome, hertely;

For by my trouthe, if that I shal nat lye,

I saugh nat this yeer so myrie a compaignye

at once   *inn*
765 Atones in this herberwe as is now.

gladly   *knew*
Fayn wolde I doon yow myrthe, wiste I how.

And of a myrthe I am right now bythoght,

To doon yow ese, and it shal coste noght.

⁻Ye goon to Caunterbury—God yow speede!

                requite   *reward*
The blisful martir quite yow youre meede!   770

            know
And wel I woot, as ye goon by the weye,

    intend   *talk*
Ye shapen yow to talen and to pleye.

For trewely, confort ne myrthe is noon

To ride by the weye doumb as a stoon.

                        diversion
And therefore wol I maken yow disport,   775

        before
As I seyde erst, and doon yow som confort.

                unanimous
And if yow liketh alle by oon assent

    agree to
For to stonden at my juggement,

And for to werken as I shal yow seye,

780 Tomorwe, whan ye riden by the weye, /

Now, by my fader soule that is deed,

unless   *give*   *head*
But ye be myrie, I wol yeve yow myn heed!

Hoold up youre hondes, withouten moore speche."

                                                seek
Oure conseil was nat longe for to seche

seemed   *worth while to deliberate*
785 Us thoughte it was noght worth to make it wys,

                                        consideration
And graunted hym withouten moore avys,

                          verdict   *pleased*
And bad him seye his voirdit as hym leste.

                                  listen
"Lordynges," quod he, "now herkneth for the beste,

But taak it nought, I prey yow, in desdeyn.

790 This is the poynt, to speken short and pleyn,

                        shorten
That ech of yow, to shorte with oure weye,

                        two
In this viage shal telle tales tweye

To Caunterbury-ward, I mene it so,

And homward he shal tellen othere two,

once   *have*
Of aventures that whilom han bifalle.   795

And which of yow that bereth hym best of alle,

That is to seyn, that telleth in this caas

instruction   *amusement*
Tales of best sentence and moost solaas,

of us all
Shal have a soper at oure aller cost

Heere in this place, sittynge by this post,   800

Whan that we come agayn fro Caunterbury.

And for to make yow the moore mury,

I wol myselven goodly with yow ryde,

Right at myn owene cost, and be youre gyde."

GEOFFREY CHAUCER'S
TREATISE ON THE ASTROLABE

Most of Chaucer's prose works, such as the "Tale of Melibee," the "Parson's Tale," and the *Consolation of Philosophy,* are translations from the French or the Latin. The Introduction to the *Treatise on the Astrolabe,* written for Chaucer's son Lewis, is the only extant piece of his original prose. The *Treatise* has survived in twenty-five manuscripts. Cambridge University Library, MS. Dd.3.53. is the basis for the following selection.

Although the Introduction is an original composition, its structure and vocabulary reveal the influence of French prose style upon Chaucer and upon English prose in general. Medieval French prose was characterized by a trailing sentence structure in which clauses were loosely joined by linking words and phrases, such as "car" (for), "cest a dire" (that is to say), "dont" (therefore), "lequel" (the which). Similar trailing sentences appear in the following selection at lines 4–11 and 22–28. A French influence can be seen in phrases such as "than for as mechel" (l. 4), "as for" (l. 7), "that is to sein" (l. 28), "for that" (l. 35). The noun + adjective word order in the expression "clerkes Grekes" (l. 24) follows French usage. French words occur throughout the selection; the first sentence alone has ten out of thirty-six ("aperceyve," "certeyne," "evydences," "abilite," "sciencez," "touching," "proporciouns," "considre," "special," "tretis"). Because of this French influence, Chaucer's prose appears less colloquial than his verse.

The language of Chaucer's prose is close to that of official London documents of the fourteenth century, which also exhibit French influence in their phrasing. As in these documents, his dialect is mainly East Midland. The plural ending for nouns is "s," as in "evydences" (l. 2), "noumbres" (l. 2), "preiers" (l. 6), "conclusions" (l. 10). The infinitive can end with "e," as in "lerne" (l. 2), or "en," as in "wryten" (l. 38). The third person singular present indicative ends with "th," as in "seith" (l. 5), "wrappeth" (l. 5), "condescendeth" (l. 6). The plural ends with the Midland "en," as in "performen" (l. 18), "leden" (l. 31). The present participle form is "ing": "touchinge" (l. 2), "apertenyng" (l. 10), "endyting" (l. 34). The past participle appears without the Southern "y" prefix: "geven" (l. 7), "fownde" (l. 13), "seyn" (l. 17), "divided" (l. 20), "lerned" (l. 30), "tawht" (l. 30).

Geoffrey Chaucer's
Treatise on the Astrolabe

Litell Lowis my sone, I have perceived well by certeyne

evidences thin abilite to lerne sciencez touchinge noumbres and

busy
proporciouns; and as wel considere I thy bisi preyere in special

much
to lerne the Tretis of the Astrolabie. Than for as mechel as

a philosofre seith, "He wrappeth him in his frend that   5

condescendeth to the rihtful preiers of his frend,"

given   *adequate*
therfor have I geven the a suffisaunt astrolabie as for owre

horizon   *computed*
orizonte, compowned after the latitude of Oxenforde, upon

means   *intend*
which by mediacion of this litel tretis I purpose to teche

the a certein nombre of conclusions apertenyng to the same   10

Edited by John H. Fisher from Cambridge University Library MS. Dd. 3. 53,
and used with his permission.

instrument. I seye a certein of conclusiouns for thre causes.

The furst cause is this: truste wel that alle the conclusiouns

that han ben fownde, or elles possibli myghten be fownde in so

noble an instrument as is an astralabie ben unknowe perfitly

15   to any mortal man in this regioun, as I suppose. Another cause

truly
is this: that sothly, in any tretis of the astrelabie that I

have seyn there be some conclusions that wole nat in alle

fulfill   *their promises*
thinges performen hir byhestes. And some of hem ben to harde

conceive (understand)
to thy tendre age of ten yeer to conseyve.

20   This tretis, divided in fyve parties, wole I shewe the

light   *plain*
under full lihte rewles and naked wordes in Englissh, for

know thou
Latyn ne kanstow yit but smal, my litel sone. But

natheles, suffise to the thise trewe conclusiouns in Englissh

as wel as suffisith to thise noble clerkes Grekes thise same

25   conclusiouns in Grek, and to Arabiens in Arabik, and to Jewes

in Ebrew, and to the Latyn folk in Latyn; whiche Latyn folk

han hem furst owt of othre diverse langages, and writen hem

language *knows*
in hir owne tonge, that is to sein in Latyn. And God wot

more
that in alle thise langages and in many mo han thise

conclusiouns ben suffisantly lerned and tawht, and yit by 30

diverse rewles, right as diverse pathes leden diverse folk

the righte way to Roome. Now wol I prey mekely every

discret persone that redeth or hereth this litel tretis, to

rude *composition*
have my rewde endyting for excused, and my superfluite of

erudite
wordes, for two causes. The firste cause is for that curious 35

writing *subject* *difficult* *such*
endyting and hard sentence is ful hevy at ones for swich a

truly
child to lerne. And the seconde cause is this, that sothly

me semeth betre to wryten unto a child twies a good

sentence than he forgete it ones.

JOHN WYCLIF'S
DE OFFICIO PASTORALI

The translation of the Bible into English was a major element in John Wyclif's program of religious reform. He believed that every man was God's "tenant-in-chief." No intermediary could come between a man and his God, and the individual was finally responsible to God alone. Therefore, each man had to be able to interpret God's law, which outweighed both civil and canon law. Wyclif wanted to make the Bible directly accessible to the common man, who knew only English. Although he himself did not translate the first English Bible (it was done by his followers, Nicholas Hereford and John Purvey), he translated portions of it for his sermons. He also wrote many English treatises defending his views. *De Officio Pastorali* (c. 1377) was based on a Latin tract of the same name. Chapter 15, on the translation of the Bible, was written especially for the English version. The entire chapter appears below. The text is given according to Ashburnham MS. xxvii, copied during the fifteenth century.

This selection demonstrates Wyclif's skill as a prose stylist. He employs a conversational plain style, using relatively short sentences made up of one or two clauses. Rhetorical inversion appears occasionally, as at line 42, where it signals a shift to the imperative mood. The syntax is compact, and the vocabulary is simple. There are few French or Latin words, and those that do occur are functional rather than ornamental.

Wyclif's language is Midland with no Southern features. The only present participle form that appears in this selection is "ing," as in "knowing" (lines 38, 61), "translating" (l. 40), "turnyng" (l. 41), "techinge" (l. 51). The past participle of strong verbs always appears with an "en" or "un" ending and without the "y" prefix characteristic of the South, as in "knowun" (lines 2, 7), "foundun" (l. 43), "seun" (l. 47). The third person present indicative singular ends in "iþ," as in "groundiþ" (l. 4), "semyþ" (l. 6), "seiþ" (l. 7). The plural ends in "en," as in "bringen" (l. 3), "shulen" (l. 9), "seyen" (l. 31), "knowen" (l. 33), "travelen" (l. 44). The third person plural pronouns are "þey" (lines 3, 44, 46, etc.), "þer" (lines 1, 37, 52), "her" (l. 48—less common), "hem" (lines 4, 56).

Wyclif's writing shows little trace of the Northern speech he must have used as a boy in Yorkshire, where he was born. But one northern feature is the appearance of "i" instead of "e" in suffixes, such as "is," "iþ," and "id." His language displays a few Western features, probably reflecting his many years at Oxford; these include the occasional use of "u" in unaccented syllables, as in "knowun" (lines 2, 7), and the rounding of "a" to "o" before a nasal, as in "vnderstondith" (l. 9). On the whole, it is much like that of London, showing the emergence of cultivated London English as a class dialect by the end of the fourteenth century.

John Wyclif's
De Officio Pastorali

    friars   *supporters*
Ant heere þe freris wiþ þer fautours seyn þat it is

heresye to write þus goddis lawe in english, & make it knowun

   unlearned (lay)
to lewid men. & fourty signes þat þey bringen forto shewe

                  repeat   *nothing* *supports*
an heretik ben not worþy to reherse, for nouȝt groundiþ hem

   conjuring
5 but nygromansye.

               meaning
It semyþ first þat þe wit of goddis lawe shulde be

      language   *meaning*
tauȝt in þat tunge þat is more knowun, for þis wit is goddis

word. whanne crist seiþ in þe gospel þat boþe heuene & erþe

shulen passe but his wordis shulen not passe, he vndirstondith

From *The English Works of Wyclif,* ed. F. D. Matthew (London: The Early English Text Society, 1880), pp. 429–30. Reprinted by permission of The Council of the Early English Text Society.

meaning
bi his woordis his wit. & þus goddis wit is hooly writ, þat   10

gave
may on no maner be fals. Also þe hooly gost ȝaf to apostlis

knowledge
wit at wit-sunday for to knowe al maner langagis to teche þe

people
puple goddis lawe þerby; & so god wolde þat þe puple were

languages
tauȝt goddis lawe in dyuerse tungis; but what man on goddis

behalf
half shulde reuerse goddis ordenaunse & his wille? & for   15

Saint   Jerome   studied
þis cause seynt ierom trauelide & translatide þe bible fro

dyuerse tungis into lateyn þat it myȝte be aftir translatid to

oþere tungis. & þus crist & his apostlis tauȝten þe puple in

þat tunge þat was moost knowun to þe puple; why shulden not

New Testament
men do nou so? & herfore autours of þe newe law, þat weren   20

apostlis of iesu crist, writen þer gospels in dyuerse tungis

realm
þat weren more knowun to þe puple. Also þe worþy reume of

hindrances
fraunse, not-wiþ-stondinge alle lettingis, haþ translatid þe

bible & þe gospels wiþ oþere trewe sentensis of doctours out

25 of lateyn in-to freynsch, why shulden not engliȝsche men do

so? as lordis of englond han þe bible in freynsch, so it

against
were not aȝenus resoun þat þey hadden þe same sentense in

engliȝsch; for þus goddis lawe wolde be betere knowun & more

believed   *oneness*   *meaning*   *realms*
trowid for onehed of wit, & more acord be bi-twixe reumes.

30 & herfore freris han tauȝt in englond þe paternoster in

play   *York*
engliȝsch tunge, as men seyen in þe pley of ȝork, & in many

since   *Matthew's*
oþere cuntreys. siþen þe paternoster is part of matheus

gospel, as clerkis knowen, why may not al be turnyd to

since
engliȝsch trewely, as is þis part? specialy siþen alle

learned   *unlearned*   *must*   *in all ways*
35 cristenmen, lerid & lewid, þat shulen be sauyd, moten algatis

follow   *commons*
sue crist & knowe his lore & his lif. but þe comyns of

engliȝschmen knowen it best in þer modir tunge, & þus it were

one   *hinder*   *hinder*
al oon to lette siche knowing of þe gospel & to lette engliȝsch

follow   *I know   fault*
men to sue crist & come to heuene. Wel y woot defaute may be

                                          faults
in vntrewe translating, as myȝten haue be many defautis in   40

          Hebrew   Greek
turnyng fro ebreu in-to greu, & fro greu in-to lateyn, & from

                    live
o langage in-to anoþer. but lyue men good lif & studie many

                                        meaning
persones goddis lawe; & whanne chaungyng of wit is foundun,

                                        friars   work
amende þey it as resoun wole. sum men seyn þat freris trauelen

        supporters   *reasons*
& þer fautours in þis cause for þre chesouns, þat y wole not   45

          knows   whether   *true*
aferme, but god woot wher þey ben soþe. first þey wolden be

seen   *realm*
seun so nedeful to þe engliȝschmen of oure reume þat singulerly

        knowledge lay   meaning
in her wit   layȝ þe wit of goddis lawe, to telle þe puple goddis

lawe on what maner euere þey wolden. & þe secound cause herof

is seyd to stonde in þis sentense; freris wolden lede þe puple   50

in techinge hem goddis lawe & þus þei wolden teche sum, & sum

        curtail   *faults*
hide, & docke sum. For þanne defautis in þer lif shulden be

less truly

lesse knowun to þe puple, & goddis lawe shulde be vntreweliere

third

knowun boþe bi clerkis & bi comyns. þe þridde cause þat men

see   *orders (of friars)*

55   aspien stondiþ in þis as þey seyn; alle þes newe ordris

dreden hem þat þer synne shulde be knowun, & hou þei ben not

groundid in god to come in-to þe chirche, & þus þey wolden not

for drede þat goddis lawe were knowun in engliȝsch, but þey

myȝten putte heresye on men ȝif engliȝsch toolde not what

60   þey seyden. god moue lordis & bischops to stonde for

knowing of his lawe.

DAN MICHEL'S AYENBITE OF INWYT

Works of religious instruction were among the most widely circulated during the Middle Ages. One of those most widely known was the French *Somme des vices et des vertues* compiled by Friar Lorens in 1279 for King Philip le Hardi of France. It deals with the Ten Commandments, the Creed, the Ave Maria, the Lord's Prayer, the Seven Deadly Sins, the Seven Petitions of the Paternoster, and the Seven Gifts of the Holy Spirit. A version of this was one of the sources of Chaucer's "Parson's Tale," and Caxton translated it into English prose as *The Royal Book*. A less celebrated version is Dan Michel's *Ayenbite of Inwyt,* which literally means "again-biting of the inner wit," or remorse of conscience. Michel, who was a monk of St. Augustine's, Canterbury, completed the work in 1340, and his autograph copy survives as British Museum MS. Arundel 57. The work has great linguistic value because it is exactly dated, exactly localized, and accurately reflects the author's dialect.

Michel's writing tells us little about the word order or rhythm of the spoken language. His style is awkward and unidiomatic. In his verse statement of purpose, word order is twisted to fit the rhyme scheme (particularly ll. 5–6, 7–8). In the prose sections, syntax is distorted by imitation of the French original. Michel's phrase-by-phrase method of translation results in a rough rhythm (ll. 15–19, 21–22, 24–33).

What gives Michel's work linguistic value is his spelling, which reveals a great deal about the Kentish dialect of Canterbury. His use of "v" or "u" for "f" shows that "f" was voiced in his dialect: "uor" (l. 3), "uader" (l. 4), "uram" (l. 5), "uoul" (l. 6), "uolueld" (l. 11), "uorlet" (l. 17), "uri" (l. 19). Similarly, his use of "z" for "s" shows the voicing of "s": "zen" (l. 5), "yzed" (l. 7), "zaule" (l. 10), "zuo" (l. 20), "zone" (l. 25), "zit" (l. 29). Old English "y" appears as "e," as in "ken" (l. 4). The Old English diphthong "ea" appears as a long diphthong, written "ya," as in "dyad" (l. 10). Old English "æ" remains a front vowel, often spelled "e," as in "þet" (l. 1), "red" (l. 9).

Michel's dialect is almost entirely Southern in its grammatical features. The pronouns are "ich" (l. 1) for first person, "ham" (l. 5) and "hare" (l. 6) for third. The plural present indicative ends with "eþ" in "uorleteþ" (l. 18). The infinitive usually ends with "e," as in "berȝe" (l. 5), "deme" (l. 30). Past participles appear with the "y" prefix, and those of strong verbs usually omit the final "n": "ywent" (l. 1), "ywrite" (l. 2), "ymad" (l. 3), "ymende" (l. 11), "ybore" (l. 26). The present participle can end with the Southern "inde," as in "cominde" (l. 16), "eurelestinde" (l. 33), or with the Midland "ing," as in "beringe" (l. 14), "arizinge" (l. 33). An "en" plural appears in "halȝen" (l. 32); but "es" plurals are more common: "apostles" (l. 12), "heuenes" (l. 15), "yeldinges" (l. 18), "yelderes" (l. 18), "zennes" (l. 33).

Dan Michel's Ayenbite of Inwyt

I know how it come to pass
Nou ich wille þet ye ywyte hou hit is y-went:

written with
þet þis boc is y-write mid engliss of kent.

for unlearned
þis boc is y-mad uor lewede men /

father kin
Vor uader / and uor moder / and uor oþer ken /

them preserve from sin
ham uor to berʒe uram alle manyere zen /   5

their conscience remain foul spot
þet ine hare inwytte ne bleue no uoul wen.

who is like God (Hebrew Michael) said
"Huo ase god" is his name yzed /

give
þet þis boc made god him yeue þet bread /

counsel
of angles of heuene and þerto his red /

From *Dan Michel's Ayenbite of Inwyt or Remorse of Conscience,* ed. Richard Morris, EETS, OS 23 (London: The Early English Text Society, 1866), pp. 262–63. Reprinted by permission of The Council of the Early English Text Society.

10 *receive*   *soul*   *when*   *dead*
   and onderuonge his zaule huanne þet he is dyad. Amen.

   to be remembered   *completed (fulfilled)*
     Ymende. þet þis boc is uolueld ine þe eue of þe holy

   apostles Symon an Iudas, of ane broþer of þe cloystré of

Saint   *·Augustine*
sanynt austin of Canterberi, Ine þe yeare of oure lhordes

beringe. 1340.

   father   *hallowed*
15   Vader oure þet art ine heuenes, y-halȝed by þi name.

coming   *kingdom* *become*
cominde þi riche. y-worþe þi wil, ase ine heuene: and ine

          give *us*   *forgive*
erþe. bread oure echedayes: yef ous to day. and uorlet ous

   debts (yieldings)   *forgive*   *debtors*
oure yeldinges: ase and we uorleteþ oure yelderes. and

       temptation   *free*
ne ous led naȝt: in-to uondinge. ac vri ous uram

evil   *so*   *be* *it*
20 queade. zuo by hit.

     grace   *full*   *be* *with*   *blessed*
     Hayl Marie, of þonke uol. lhord by mid þe. y-blissed

among   *fruit*
þou ine wymmen. and y-blissed þet ouet of þine wombe.

so   *be* *it*
zuo by hit.

believe   *father*
Ich leue ine god, uader almiȝti. makere of heuene,

                              son   *single*
and of erþe. And ine iesu crist, his zone on-lepi, oure   25

          conceived   *born*
lhord. þet y-kend is, of þe holy gost. y-bore of Marie

          tormented   *to the cross*
Mayde. y-pyned onder pouns pilate. y-nayled a rode.

dead   *buried*   *went*   *third*
dyad. and be-bered. yede doun to helle. þane þridde day

        from   *dead*   *ascended*   *sits on the*   *side*
a-ros uram þe dyade. Steaȝ to heuenes. zit aþe riȝt half

                        thence   *judge*
of god þe uader al-miȝti. þannes to comene he is, to deme þe   30

living   *dead*   *believe*
quike, and þe dyade. Ich y-leue ine þe holy gost. holy

                      communion   *saints*   *forgiveness*
cherche generalliche. Mennesse of halȝen. Lesnesse of   32

sins   *flesh*   *everlasting*
zennes. of ulesse arizinge. and lyf eurelestinde.

so   *be* *it*
zuo by hyt.

THE ANCRENE RIWLE

During the twelfth and thirteenth centuries, when English was no longer the language of the court, it was still used for religious instruction. Copies of the homilies of Aelfric and Wulfstan were still circulated, and new works were also composed, some of them for nuns or women recluses who were not familiar with Latin. The most important of these works is *The Ancrene Riwle* (the rule of anchoresses), a devotional manual composed during the late twelfth or early thirteenth century for three noble sisters who had become recluses. The *Riwle* won an immediate audience and remained popular for three centuries: it was soon translated into French and Latin, was revised about 1230 for a larger community, was quoted by preachers and religious writers during the fourteenth century, and was a major source for the *Tretyse of Love,* printed by Wynkyn de Worde at the end of the fifteenth century.

One of the reasons for the popularity of the *Ancrene Riwle* was the author's vivid style, which resembles the plain style of Aelfric. The author of the *Riwle* frequently uses concrete descriptions, brief narratives, metaphors, and similes. In the following selection he develops the metaphor of Christ as a king wooing a lady, who represents the soul. The rhythm and syntax suggest the spoken language; a series of simple clauses are often joined by parataxis or coordination. Yet there is artful cadence and sentence variety, as with the introduction of rhetorical questions at lines 10 and 17, and correlative alliteration, as in lines 4–5, 7, 12, 14.

The style of the English version strongly influenced that of the Anglo-Norman translation, which does not have the trailing sentence structure typical of medieval French prose but follows the tighter structure and English word order of the original. In places where the English author used a French word, the translator adopted the same word: "destruite," "poure," "chastel," "beaubelez," "mestrie."

The original was written in a Southwestern dialect. Old English "æ" remains a front vowel, often written "e": "lefdi," "þet" (l. 1), "efter" (l. 5), "nes" (l. 17). West Saxon "ea" appears as "e" in "herd" (l. 8). The Old English diphthong "eo" becomes a rounded "o," spelled "eo": "heo" (l. 2), "eorðene" (l. 3), "heorted," "beon" (l. 9). Old English "y" remains a rounded front vowel, spelled "u", as in "murie" (l. 12). There is a rounding of "a" to "o" before a nasal, as in "lond," "one" (l. 2), "monie" (l. 5). Initial "f" is voiced:

118

"uoan" (l. 1), "uor" (l. 4), "ueole" (l. 6), "ueirest" (l. 11). The plural inflection for the noun is "es" in "beaubelez" (l. 6), "wordes" (l. 12), "wundres," "mestries" (l. 14), but "n" in "uoan" (l. 1), "sonden" (l. 5). The feminine nominative pronoun is "heo" (l. 2). In this selection the past participle appears without the "y" prefix: "biset" (l. 1), "destrued" (l. 2), "biturnd" (l. 3). The infinitive ends with "en" or "ien": "holden" (l. 7), "biholden" (l. 12), "arearen" (l. 13), "makien" (l. 16). There are no present tense forms because the story is narrated in the past.

The Ancrene Riwle

SOUTHWESTERN DIALECT (c. 1200)

lady   *with*   *foes*   *about*

A lefdi was. þet was mid hire uoan biset al abuten.

destroyed   *she*   *poor*

and hire lond al destrued. & heo al poure. wið innen one

earthen   *love*   *then*

eorðene castle. on mihti kinges luue. was þauh biturnd up on

immoderately very   *for*   *courtship*

hire. so vnimete swuðe. þet he uor wouhlecchunge. sende

messengers one after another   *together*   *many*

5   hire his sonden: on efter oþer. and ofte somed monie. &

jewels   *many*   *help*

sende hire beaubelez boðe ueole & feire. and sukurs of
boobbal

food   *great army*

liueneð. & help of his heie hird: to holden hire castel.

she   *received*   *thoughtless*   *hard*

heo underueng al. ase on unrecheleas þing. þet was so herd

From *The English Text of the Ancrene Riwle Edited from Cotton MS. Nero A xiv*, ed. M. Day and J. A. Herbert, EETS, OS, 225 (London: The Early English Text Society, 1952), p. 177. Reprinted by permission of the Council of the Early English Text Society.

hearted   *nearer*
i heorted. þet hire luue. ne muhte he neuer beon ðe neorre.

will   you   *showed*
hwat wult tu more. he com him sulf a last. and scheawede hire   10

          face   as was that   *fairest*
his feire neb. ase þe ðet was of alle men. ueirest forto

              very
biholden. and spec swuðe sweteliche. & so murie wordes.

they   might   the   *raise*   th
þet heo muhten ðe deade arearen urom deaðe to liue. and

      many   marvels   did *many   miracles*
wrouhte ueole wundres. and dude ueole meistries biuoren hire

sight   *showed*
eihsihðe. & scheawede hire his mihten. tolde hire of his   15

kingdom   *promised*   quccov
kinedome. and bead for to makien hire cwene. of al ðet he

possessed   *wasn't   astonishing   disdain*
ouhte. al þis ne help nout. nes þis wunderlich hoker:
          not

she   wasn't   worthy   for to   be   servant
vor heo nes neuer wurðe uorte beon his schelchine.

ANGLO-NORMAN (c. 1200)

a   lady   was of   her   enemies   besieged all   about   her land
| Une dame fut de ses enimis assise tout enuiron sa terre

From *The French Text of the Ancrene Riwle Edited from Cotton MS. Vitellius F vii*,
ed. J. A. Herbert, EETS OS, 219 (London: The Early English Text Society, 1944),
pp. 283–84. Reprinted by permission of The Council of the Early English Text Society.

all destroyed and she all poor within a castle of earth

20 t[ou]te destruite. et ele tout poure dedenz vn chastel de terre. /

the love nevertheless of a powerful king was toward her so immoderately

Lamour nepurquant dun poestif roi fust vers lui si tresademesure

given that he for courtship to her sent messengers one after the other

donee: quil pur dauneure lui enuea ses messages vn apres altre

often several together to her sent jewels beautiful and much

souent plusours ensemble lui enuea beaubelez beauz et plusours

help of food help of his people to hold her castle and

soucours de uitaille aide de ses genz pur tenir son chastel. Et

    vitailles

she received all as if it   nothing to her was and thus was hard of

25 ele recuest tout ausi come rien ne lui fust et issi fust dure de

heart so that to her love could not he be ever the nearer what want

queor. qe de samour ne poeit il estra ia le plus pres. qe volez

you more he came himself at last her showed his handsome face

vous plus. il vint meismes a la fin: lui moustra sa bele face

as he that was of all men the handsomest to look at

sicome cil qe fut de touz homes le plus beel a regarder.

spoke so very sweetly and words so joyful that they

Parla si tresdoucement et paroles si deliciouses qeles

could dead revive did many marvels and

30 porreient morz resusciter. oura mult des merueilles et

did great miracles before her eyes her showed his power

31 fist grant mestrie deuant ses oilz. Lui mostra son poer.

her told of his kingdom her offered to make queen of all

li cunta de son reigne. li offri de faire reine de tout

that   he   had   all   this   did   not   help   was not   this
ceo qil auoit. Tout cest rien ne valut. Ne fut ceo

astonishing   marvel   for   she   was not   once   worthy   to
escharnissable merueille qar ele ne fut vnqe digne de

be   his servant
estra sa baisse.   35

LYRICS

Since secular lyrics were mainly a popular, oral art form, relatively few have survived. More than half of those that have come down from before 1400 are preserved in British Museum, MS. Harley 2253, from which the following poems are taken. Most of the secular lyrics show the influence of the conventions of courtly love: in "Annot and Johon" and "Alysoun," we find the idea that love is to be greatly prized; an affirmation of the supreme value, beauty, and power of the lady; and a description of the suffering of the lover. A common characteristic of the lyrics is the association of nature with human emotion. References to spring, as in lines 1–4 of "Alysoun," became conventional as openings (witness the first lines of *The Canterbury Tales*). The lyrics exhibit a wide variety of form and meter appropriate to the modal motet music of the period.

The rhyme scheme of "Annot and Johon" is unusually complex. Each stanza consists of eight rhymed lines followed by a couplet. The lines are in the alliterative meter, most of them having four alliterative stresses, either falling on the same sound (ll. 1, 2), or divided between two sounds (ll. 3, 4). This complicated rhyme scheme sometimes results in a distortion of word order: the object precedes the verb and the verb the subject in l. 9; the object precedes the subject in l. 34, and it precedes the verb in l. 46.

The dialect of the poem is Southwestern. The author's allusions to Welsh folklore in the last stanza and his topographical references in lines 27 and 33 suggest an area near Wales. The pronouns are "he" (l. 5) for nominative feminine third person, "ich" (l. 10) and "y" (l. 22) for first person. The contraction "ichot" (l. 1) is typical of the South. The plural inflection for nouns is "es": "leres" (l. 12), "tonges" (l. 32), "folkes" (l. 46). The present indicative third person singular ends with "eþ": "lemeþ" (l. 3), "haueþ" (l. 8), "passeþ" (l. 13), "beteþ" (l. 21), "secheþ" (l. 34). The only plural verb form in the poem is "are" (l. 36). An "s" ending is used for second person singular in "þou . . . sys" (l. 18), but the author could have used "sys" as a rhyme word rather than as his customary form. The infinitive ends without an "n" in "leche" (l. 33), "fede" (l. 46). The past participle appears with a "y" prefix in "yholden" (l. 5), "ycud" (l. 7), "ytold" (l. 32), but without one in "dyht" (l. 6), "broht" (l. 19), "forsoht" (l. 20). Whether or not the prefix was used might have been determined by the rhythm of individual lines.

Various Southwestern pronounciations appear in the poem. Old English "y" remains a front vowel, spelled "u," in "cunde" (l. 15). The Old English diphthong "eo" becomes a rounded front vowel, spelled "eo," in "bleo" (l. 17). There is a rounding of "a" to "o" before a nasal in "nome" (l. 28), "mondrake" (l. 31), "mon" (l. 34). The spelling of "ant" (ll. 7, 18, 24) suggests an unvoicing of final "d."

The rhyme scheme and meter of "Alysoun" are simpler and more usual. The pattern of the stanza is ababcccd; that of the refrain (ll. 9–12), eeed. The last line of the refrain rhymes with the last line of each stanza. There is a fairly regular alternation of stressed and unstressed syllables. Most lines contain three or four stresses, the most common type of line in the lyrics. The meter is not alliterative, but alliteration is frequently used as an ornament (ll. 2, 5, 7, 9, 11–12). The rhyme scheme has caused some distortion of word order: the object precedes the subject in l. 9, and it precedes the verb in ll. 19, 27.

The dialect of this poem is also Southwestern. The pronouns are "he" (l. 7) for nominative feminine third person, "ich" (l. 5) for first person. Many contractions appear with "ich": "icham" (l. 8), "ichabbe" (l. 9), "ichot" (l. 10), "ichulle" (l. 19). The "es" plural inflection occurs with "wonges" (l. 23); "browe" and "eʒe" (l. 14) can be classified as "en" plurals, although the "n" has been dropped. The present indicative third person singular ends with "eþ" in "biginneþ" (l. 2). The same ending is used for the plural in "waxeþ" (l. 22). The infinitive can end in "e," as in "springe" (l. 2), "synge" (l. 4), "bringe" (l. 7), or with "en," as in "lyuen" (l. 19), "þolien" (l. 35), "mournen" (l. 36). The past participle appears with the "y" prefix in "yhent" (l. 9), "ymake" (l. 16), "ylent" (l. 25), "yʒyrned" (l. 34), but without it in "sent" (l. 10), "lent" (l. 11). The appearance of both "ylent" and "lent" suggests that the variation might have been called for by the rhythm.

Southwestern pronunciations appear in the use of "u" for Old English "y" in "lutel" (l. 3), "lud" (l. 4); in the use of a rounded vowel for Old English "eo" in "heu" (l. 13), "buen" (l. 18); and in the rounding of "a" to "o" before a nasal in "wonges," "won" (l. 23), "mon" (l. 26), "con" (l. 27), "swon" (l. 28).

Lyrics

ANNOT AND JOHON

I know   lady   bower
Ichot a burde in a bour ase beryl so bryht,

silver   comely
ase saphyr in seluer semly on syht,

jasper   shines
ase iaspe þe gentil þat lemeþ wiþ lyht,

garnet
ase gernet in golde & ruby wel ryht,

onyx   she   held
5   ase onycle he ys on yholden on hyht,

precious   she   dressed
ase diamaund þe dere in day when he is dyht.

she   known   emperor
he is coral ycud wiþ cayser ant knyht,

perfume
in the morning   maid
ase emeraude amorewen þis may haueþ myht.

pearl   maid beautiful
þe myht of þe margarite haueþ þis mai mere;

From *English Lyrics of the Thirteenth Century*, ed. Carlton Brown (Oxford: The Clarendon Press, 1932), pp. 136–39. By permission of The Clarendon Press, Oxford.

126

   garnet   *choose*   *countenance*
 ffor charbocle ich hire ches bi chyn & by chere.   10

  complexion   *branch*
Hire rode is ase rose þat red is on rys

     cheeks lovely
wiþ lilye-white leres lossum he is;

  primrose *she surpasses*   *periwinkle*   *value*
þe primerole he passeþ, þe peruenke of pris,

   horse parsley   *parsley* *anise*
wiþ alisaundre þareto ache & anys.

beautiful   *kind*
Coynte ase columbine, such hire cunde ys,   15

beautiful   *clothing* *fur*   *grey fur*
glad vnder gore in gro & in grys;

she   *complexion*   *linen*
he is blosme opon bleo brihtest vnder bis,

  celandine   *sage*
wiþ celydoyne ant sauge, ase þou þi-self sys.

          he
 þat syht vpon þat semly to blis he is broht,

  she *marigold*   *cure*   *sought*
 he is solsecle to sanne ys forsoht.   20

she *parrot*   *pine*   *amends*   *torment*
He is papeiai in pyn þat beteþ me my bale,

   turtle-dove *tower*
to trewe tortle in a tour y telle þe mi tale;

she   thrush   successful   dispute   hall
he is þrustle þryuen in þro þat singeþ in sale,

lark   hawk   woodpecker
þe wilde laueroc ant wolc & þe wodewale,

falcon   woods   most hidden
25   he is faucoun in friht, dernest in dale,

every   game   song
and wiþ eueruch a gome gladest in gale,

the Wye she   the Wirral
ffrom weye he is wisist in-to wyrhale.

name   nightingale
hire nome is in a note of þe nyhtegale

Annot   name   it   not
In annote is hire nome—nempneþ hit non!

whoever   rightly reads   whisper
30   whose ryht redeþ roune to Iohon.

mugwort she   moon
Muge he is ant mondrake þourh miht of þe mone,

remedy   throne
Trewe triacle ytold wiþ tonges in trone,

heal   the Lyn   the Lune
such licoris mai leche from lyne to lone,

sugar   seeks   cures   soon
such sucre mon secheþ þat saneþ men sone,

grants   prayer
35   bliþe yblessed of crist þat bayeþ me mi bone

      secret   *unworthy*   *secrets*
when derne dede is indayne, derne are done.

     gromwell   *grove*   *tip*
ase gromyl in greue grene is þe grone,

    cubeb   *cumin*   *known*   *wreath*
ase quibibe & comyn cud is in crone,

      known cumin   *cinnamon*   *coffer (chest)*
Cud comyn in court canel in cofre,

       ginger   *setwall*   *gillyflower*
wiþ gyngyure & sedewale & þe gylofre.   40

she   *covetous*   *power* *merciful*   *reward*
He is medierne of miht mercie of mede

ready   *Ragna*   *advise*
Rekene ase regnas resoun to rede,

      Tegeu-Eurvron tower   *Garwen*   *garment*
Trewe ase tegeu in   tour, ase wyrwein in wede,

bolder   *Bjorn*   *boar* *fought*
baldore þen byrne þat oft þe bor bede,

   Guilliadun   *she*   *doughty*
Ase wylcadoun he is wys, dohty of dede,   45

fairer   *Floripas*
ffeyrore þen floyres folkes to fede,

known   *Cradock*   *carved* *roast*
Cud as cradoc in court carf þe brede,

kinder   *Hilde-Gudrun*   *care for*
Hendore þen hilde þat haueþ me to hede,

she   *care for*   *kind one*

he haueþ me to hede þis hendy anon,

                    Jonas *she* *rejoices*   *John*

50   gentil ase ionas heo ioyeþ wiþ Ion.

ALYSOUN

        March   *April*

1   Bytuene mersh & aueril

        twigs   *bloom*

when spray biginneþ to springe,

        little

þe lutel foul haþ hire wyl

            outcry

on hyre lud to synge.

        live

5   Ich libbe in louelonginge

        most beautiful

for semlokest of alle þynge;
                    things

she

He may me blisse bringe,

I am   *power*

icham in hire baundoun.

            lucky   *fortune I have*   *received*

An hendy hap ichabbe yhent,

    I know

10   ichot from heuene it is me sent—

taken
from alle wymmen mi loue is lent,

& lyht on Alysoun.

hew   *hair*
On heu hire her is fayr ynoh,
        enough

hire browe broune, hire eȝe blake,

lovely   *countenance she*   *laughs*
Wiþ lossum chere   he on me loh;   15

wiþ middel smal & wel ymake.

unless she
Bote he me wolle to hire take
        desire

be   *mate*
forte buen hire owen make,

        I will
Longe to lyuen ichulle forsake

  fated
& feye fallen adoun.   20

        lucky   fortune
        An hendy hap, etc. (*repeat lines 9–12*)

        turn
Nihtes when y wende & wake—

therefore   *cheeks*
for-þi myn wonges waxeþ won—

lady
leuedi, al for þine sake,

bestowed
25 longinge is ylent me on.

wise
In world nis non so wyter mon

þat al hire bounte telle con;

neck
Hire swyre is whittore þen þe swon,

maid
& feyrest may in toune.

lucky
30   An hendi, etc. (*repeat lines 9–12*)

I am   *wooing*   *awake*
Icham for wowyng al forwake,

as   *weir*
wery so water in wore;

rob   *mate*
lest eny reue me my make

I have   *yearned*   *for long*
ychabbe y-ȝyrned ȝore.

suffer
35 Betere is þolien whyle sore

þen mournen euermore;

handsomest   *clothing*
geynest vnder gore,

listen　　　*song*
Herkne to my roun.

lucky
An hendi, etc. (*repeat lines 9–12*)

PIERS PLOWMAN

Piers Plowman is written in the alliterative meter that goes back to the Old English period. The alliterative style apparently survived in oral poetry and came to enjoy a new popularity in written verse during the fourteenth century. Most of the poems of the so-called "alliterative revival" are associated with the Northwest Midlands. But *Piers Plowman* is written in a dialect of the Southwest Midlands and was probably composed mainly in London. The life of the city infuses its spirit. Its theme is the popular tradition of social complaint, reflected in Chaucer's *Canterbury Tales,* where the figure of the ideal Plowman reappears. The name "Piers Plowman" was used as a rallying cry by John Ball in his letter to the peasants of Essex on the eve of the Peasants' Revolt of 1381. Some of the reasons for that revolt are revealed in the poem's attacks on political and social injustice.

Most of what is known about William Langland, the author, comes from autobiographical statements within the poem. He was born and educated in the West Midlands, became a clerk in minor orders, married, and lived with his wife in London, where he composed his satirical verse. The name Langland has been questioned, but the other statements about the author are supported by the subject matter and dialect of the poem. It exists in three versions: the A text (c. 1362–70); the B text (c. 1377), an expansion and revision of A; and the C text (c. 1390), a revision of B. More than fifty manuscripts of the poem have survived. The following selection is taken from Kane's edition of the A text, which is based on Trinity College, Cambridge, MS. R. 3. 14.

The prosody of *Piers Plowman* is looser in structure and richer in alliteration than that of Old English poetry. The line is divided into two half-lines, each containing two or more strong syllables. The strong syllables in the first half-line alliterate with each other and with at least one strong syllable in the second half-line. For example, all four strong syllables alliterate on "s" in the first line of the poem. The normal pattern is followed in line 2, with alliteration on "sh." In line 4, three strong syllables alliterate with each other in the first half-line and with one syllable in the second. The author sometimes employs a macaronic style, mixing Latin half-lines with English (l. 39).

The three versions of the poem were copied by many scribes in various dialects. But the dialect of the original was apparently West Midland with some Southern influence. The usual plural form for nouns is "es" or "is":

"werkis" (l. 3), "wondris" (l. 4), "hilles" (l. 5), "watris" (l. 9), dikes" (l. 16); an "en" plural occurs in "children" (l. 35), one of the few "en" forms preserved in Modern English. The normal genitive inflection is "s," as in "Luciferis" (l. 39). An unusual form appears in "heueneriche" (l. 27), where the neuter noun "riche" forms its genitive case with "e." Pronouns are "I" (l. 2) for first person; "hem" (l. 20), "here" (l. 34), "þei" (l. 31) for third person plural.

A mixture of Midland and Southern forms are found in the verbal inflections. The infinitive can end with "e," as in "here" (l. 4), "plese" (l. 30), or with "en," as in "cairen" (l. 29). Past participles appear with the Southern "y" or "i" prefix in "imakid" (l. 14), "ycrammid" (l. 41), but without it in "knowen" (l. 53), "fallen" (l. 62). Present participles end with "ing": "worching," "wandring" (l. 19), "settyng," "sowyng" (l. 21). The third person singular present indicative ends with "iþ": "askiþ" (l. 19), "semiþ" (l. 32), "prechiþ" (l. 38). The plural can end with "e," as in "putte" (l. 20), "coueite" (l. 29); with "en," as in "comen" (l. 24), "holden" (l. 28); with "eþ," as in "destroiȝeþ" (l. 22), or "iþ" as in "sewiþ" (l. 45).

Piers Plowman

In a somer sesoun whanne softe was the sonne

put   myself   rough clothing   shepherd
I shop me into a shroud as I a shep were;

dress   hermit
In abite as an Ermyte, vnholy of werkis,

Wente wyde in þis world wondris to here.

morning   Malverne
5   But on a may morwenyng on maluerne hilles

wonder   seemed
Me befel a ferly, of fairie me þouȝte:

tired out with wandering
I was wery [for]wandrit & wente me to reste

stream
Vndir a brood bank be a bourn[e] side,

And as I lay & lenide & lokide on þe watris

slumbered   sounded
10   I slomeride into a slepyng, it swiȝede so merye.

From *Piers Plowman: The A Version, Will's Visions of Piers Plowman and Do-Well*, ed. George Kane (London: The Athlone Press, 1960), pp. 175–80. Reprinted by permission of the Athlone Press of the University of London.

dream   *dream*

þanne gan I mete a merueillous sweuene,

knew

þat I was in a wildernesse, wiste I neuere where;

but   *on   high*

Ac as I beheld into þe Est an heiȝ to þe sonne

saw   tower   hill   excellently made

I saiȝ a tour on a toft triȝely Imakid;

A dep dale beneþe, a dungeoun þerinne   15

ditches

Wiþ depe dikes & derke & dredful of siȝt.

found

A fair feld ful of folk fand I þere betwene

poor

Of alle maner of men, þe mene & þe riche,

working   *requires*

Worching & wandringe as þe world askiþ.

played   seldom

Summe putte hem to plouȝ, pleiȝede ful selde,   20

planting   worked

In settyng & sowyng swonke ful harde;

[Wonne] þat þise wastours wiþ glotonye destroiȝeþ.

dressed

And summe putte hem to pride, aparailide hem þereaftir,

outward appearance
In cuntenaunce of cloþing comen disgisid.

25 In preyours & penaunce putten hem manye,

strictly
Al for loue of oure lord lyuede wel streite

of the kingdom of heaven bliss
In hope [for] to haue heueneriche blisse,

anchorites *hermits* *their*
As ancris & Ermytes þat holden hem in [here] cellis,

covet *go (careen)*
Coueite not in cuntre to cairen aboute

luxurious *livelihood* *body*
30 For no likerous liflode here likam to plese.

trade *prospered*
And somme chosen [hem] to chaffare, þei cheuide þe betere

thrive
As it semiþ to oure siȝt þat suche men þriuen.

can
And somme merþis to make as mynstralis conne,

singing *trust*
And gete gold wiþ here gle giltles, I trowe.

but *jesters* *chatterers*
35 Ac Iaperis & iangleris, Iudas children,

sought
Fonden hem fantasies & foolis hem make,

intelligence   *work*   *please*
And haue wyt at wille to wirche ʒif hem list.

Paul
þat poule prechiþ of hem I dar not proue it here:

who speaks   slander   *servant*
Qui loquitur turpiloquium [is] luciferis hyne.

                                    went
Bidderis & beggeris faste aboute ʒede   40

                          full to the brim
Til here bely & here bagge were bratful ycrammid;

quarrel
Flite þanne for here foode, fouʒten at þe ale.

                    knows
In glotonye, god wot, go þei to bedde,

                          lawless   vagabonds
And risen vp wiþ ribaudrie as robertis knaues;

    sloth   follow
Slep & sleuþe sewiþ hem euere.   45

                    arrange
Pilgrimes & palmeris pliʒten hem togidere

For to seke seint Iame & seintes at rome;

Wenten forþ in here wey wiþ many wise talis,

          permission lie
And hadde leue to leiʒe al here lif aftir.

hermits   *hooked*

50   Ermytes on an hep, wiþ hokide staues,

Wenten to walsyngham, & here wenchis aftir;

     louts   *work*

Grete lobies & longe þat loþ were to swynke

         copes

Cloþide hem in copis to be knowen from oþere;

        hermits

Shopen hem Ermytes here ese to haue.

      friars

55   I fond þere Freris, alle þe foure ordris,

                belly

Prechinge þe peple for profit of þe wombe;

interpreted   *them*   *pleased*

Gloside þe gospel as h[e]m good likide;

    greed   *copes*

For coueitise of copis construide it as þei wolde.

        masters

Manye of þise maistris may cloþe hem at lyking

     money

60   For here mony & here marchaundise meten togidere.

since   *merchant*   *confess*

Siþen charite haþ ben chapman & chief to shryue lordis

     wonders   *years*

Manye ferlis han fallen in a fewe ȝeris.

LAYAMON'S BRUT

In the opening lines of the *Brut*, Layamon states that he was a priest dwelling at Ernleʒe (King's Areley) on the Severn, and that he had decided "of Engle þa æðelæn tellen" (to tell of the noble deeds of the English). Since he speaks of Eleanor as having been Henry's queen, the poem was written after the death of Henry II (d. 1189) or Eleanor (d. 1204). It is a free, expanded paraphrase of Wace's *Roman de Brut* (written about 1155 in Anglo-Norman octosyllabic couplets), which is in turn a free rendition of Geoffrey of Monmouth's *Historia Regum Britanniae* (written about 1147 in Latin prose). Layamon's poem survives in two manuscripts, both in the British Museum: the earlier Cotton Caligula A IX, written in the first quarter of the thirteenth century (the basis for the following selection), and Cotton Otho C XIII, written about fifty years later.

The atmosphere of the *Brut* is that of Anglo-Saxon heroic epic rather than that of French romance. The tone is more somber and more fierce, as when Arthur speaks of cutting off Modred's head and cutting Queen Guenevere to pieces (ll. 29–30). Wace's characters are knights and courtiers, whereas Layamon's are Germanic warriors. Layamon adds many descriptions, such as the following account of Arthur's ominous dream, and uses much more dialogue; the dream is set within the context of a conversation, beginning with the question at line 10.

The prosody of the *Brut* derives from Anglo-Saxon versification but is much freer. In Old English poetry, one or both stressed syllables of the first half-line alliterated with the first stressed syllable of the second half-line (the "rhyme-giver"). The *Brut* alliterates on any stress or sometimes on none: for example, alliteration links the first and second half-lines in ll. 4, 7, 8, 9; it occurs only in the first half-line in ll. 3, 5; it is divided between two letters (m and h) in l. 14; and there is no alliteration in ll. 2, 12. Furthermore, the two half-lines are often linked by end rhyme, as in ll. 1, 2, 5, 10, 15, 16, 21.

The poem is in the West Midland dialect. Old English inflections are well preserved: the article retains an accusative ending in "þene ʒeonge cniht" (l. 5), a masculine dative with "m" reduced to "n" in "Arðure þan kinge" (l. 2), and a feminine dative in "þere eorðe" (l. 27). The dual nominative pronoun "wit" (already archaic in Old English) appears at l. 43. An uninflected genitive occurs in "suster" (l. 3), and plural "ene" genitives (a reduction of "ena") with the final "e" dropped in "wimmonen" (l. 22), "deoren" (l. 38).

There is a use of the "his" genitive with dropping of "h" in "Modred is hafd" (l. 29). Infinitives that had an "ian" ending in Old English preserve the "i," as in "sturien" (l. 7), "iwakien," "quakien" (l. 46), "biuien" (l. 47). The "i" prefix appears on the past participle in "iuaren" (l. 10), "iþoht" (l. 48). The "en" ending has been adopted as the plural form for "boden" (l. 4), "honden" (l. 23), "vðen" (l. 41), but "es" appears for "ærmes" (l. 8), "postes" (l. 21), "gripes," "fuʒeles" (l. 36).

There are many departures from the word order of Modern English. As in Old English, an object pronoun frequently precedes the verb (ll. 6, 13, 31, 43). In line 39, an object pronoun precedes the verb in the first half line but follows it in the second. Object pronouns also follow the verb in lines 10, 42, 44. The object occurs before the subject in lines 3, 17, 23, and before the verb in lines 21, 48, 50. The adverb "þa" initiates a verb + subject word order in lines 10, 18, 37, 45, 46, 47. The verb "gon" is used as a tense-carrying auxiliary in lines 7, 15, 34, 40, 46, and "com" in lines 18, 37, 44.

Several spellings reveal pronunciations typical of the West Midlands. The frequent use of "u" or "v" for "f" indicates the voicing of "f": "uæir" (l. 10), "iuaren" (l. 10), "þeruore" (l. 13), "uolke" (l. 18), "ueol" (l. 26). Old English "y" remains a front vowel, spelled "u": "sturien" (l. 7), "putte" (l. 31), "fur" (l. 47). Old English "eo" has become a front vowel, spelled "eo": "leofuest" (l. 22), "heo" (l. 23), "eorðe" (l. 27). Old English long "a" has not been rounded to "o": "aras" (l. 8), "agan," "wat" (l. 49). There is a frequent rounding of short "a" to "o" before a nasal: "mon" (l. 1), "gon" (l. 7), "lond" (l. 16), "honde" (l. 17).

Layamon's Brut

then   one time   brave

Þa com þer in are tiden an oht mon riden

and brohte tidinge Arðure þan kinge

sister's

from Moddrede his suster sune; Arðure he wes wilcume,

thought   messages very

for he wende þat he brohte boden swiðe gode.

the   young

Arður lai alle longe niht and space wið þene ȝeonge cniht,   5

wouldn't   tell   truth   went

swa nauer nulde he him sugge soð hu hit ferde.

in the morning   knights   did get up

Þa hit wes dæi a marȝen and duȝeðe gon sturien,

stretched

Arður þa up aras and strehte his ærmes;

as if   very   sick

he aras up and adun sat, swulc he weore swiðe seoc.

From *Selections from Layamon's Brut*, ed. G. L. Brook (Oxford: The Clarendon Press, 1963), pp. 109–10. By permission of The Clarendon Press, Oxford.

asked   *fair*   *lord*

10 Þa axede hine an uæir cniht, "Lauerd, hu hauest þu

fared
  iuaren toniht?"

        mind   *uneasy*

Arður þa andswarede—a mode him wes uneðe:

         bower

"Toniht a mine slepe, þer ich læi on bure,

  dreamed *dream*   *sorry*

me imætte a sweuen; þeruore ich ful sari æm.

  dreamed   *raised* *a* *hall (the roof)*

Me imette þat mon me hof uppen are halle;

   did *bestride* *as if*

15 þa halle ich gon bistriden, swulc ich wolde riden;

      possessed   *saw*

alle þe lond þa ich ah alle ich þer ouer sah,

  Gawain

and Walwain sat biuoren me; mi sweord he bar an honde.

      advanced   *countless* *army*

Þa com Moddred faren þere mid unimete uolke;

      battle-axe

he bar an his honde ane wiax stronge;

20 he bigon to hewene hardliche swiðe,

   cut down

and þa postes forheou alle þa heolden up þa halle.

saw   Guenevere   of women
Þer ich iseh Wenheuer eke, wimmonnen leofuest me;

great   pulled down
al þere muche halle rof mid hire honden heo todroh.

fall   fell
Þa halle gon to hælden and ich hæld to grunden,

broke
þat mi riht ærm tobrac; þa seide Modred, 'Haue þat.'   25

down   fell   fall
Adun ueol þa halle and Walwain gon to ualle

broken   both
and feol a þere eorðe; his ærmes brekeen beine.

grabbed   my
And ich igrap mi sweord leofe mid mire leoft honde

cut   off   head   rolled   field
and smæt of Modred is hafd þat hit wond a þene ueld

cut to pieces   precious
and þa quene ich al tosnaðde mid deore mine sweorede   30

then   her   dark   pit
and seoððen ich heo adun sette in ane swarte putte

army   powerful put   flight
and al mi uolc riche sette to fleme,

didn't know   they
þat nuste ich under Criste whar heo bicumen weoren.

but   did   stand   hill
Buten miseolf ich gon atstonden uppen ane wolden

       wander   *over*   *moor*
35 and ich þer wondrien agon wide ȝeond þan moren;

    saw griffins   *horrible*   *birds*
þer ich isah gripes and grisliche fuȝeles.

     golden   *lion traveled*
Þa com an guldene leo liðen ouer dune,

of animals most   *graceful*   *Lord*
deoren swiðe hende, þa ure Drihten make[de].

  lion   *ran*   *seized*
Þa leo me orn foren to and iueng me bi þan midle

      did   *go*   *sea went*
40 and forð hire gun ȝeongen and to þere sæ wende,

   saw   *waves in*
and ich isæh þæ vðen i þere sæ driuen

    lion in   *sea (flood) went*   *myself*
and þe leo i þan ulode iwende wið me seolue.

  we both   *waves*   *from her seized*
Þa wit i sæ comen, þa vðen me hire   binomen.

    fish passed   *carried*
Com þer an fisc liðe and fereden me to londe

              sorrow   *sick*
45 Þa wes ich al wet and weri of sorȝen and seoc;

  did   *wake*   *severely*   *shake*
þa gon ich iwakien, swiðe ich gon to quakien;

     tremble   *as if*   *in fire were burning*
þa gon ich to biuien, swulc ich al fur burne,

dream   *thought*
And swa ich habbe al niht of mine sweuene swiðe iþoht,

    know   *truly*   *gone*
for ich wat to iwisse agan is al mi blisse,

  always   *sorrow*   *must* *suffer*
for a to mine liue sorȝen ich mot driȝe.   50

alas   *don't have*
Wale þat ich nabbe here Wenhauer mine quene!"

SIR GAWAIN AND THE GREEN KNIGHT

Sir Gawain and The Green Knight is an alliterative Arthurian romance of the latter part of the fourteenth century relating two adventures of Gawain: his beheading match with the Green Knight, and his temptation by a lady in the castle of Sir Bertilak, who turns out to be the Green Knight. The outcome of the beheading match and the life of Gawain depend on his conduct at the castle, where his chastity and truthfulness are tested. The poem is found in British Museum, MS. Cotton Nero A x, together with three other alliterative poems, *Pearl, Patience,* and *Purity.* Because they are written in the same handwriting in the same Northwest Midlands dialect, have many stylistic parallels, and deal with similar moral themes, they are assumed to be by the same author. His description of North Wales and the forest of Wirral in *Gawain* (ll. 28–33) suggests that he was familiar with this area and expected his audience to be interested in it.

The poem is written in the alliterative style that enjoyed a revival during the fourteenth century. The long line is divided into two half-lines, each containing at least two stressed syllables and a variable number of unstressed syllables. The two half-lines are linked by alliteration, which usually falls on the two stresses of the first half-line and the first stress of the second. This pattern is followed in lines 2, 3, 5, 6, 8, 11, 12 ("h" alliterates with vowels). Three stressed syllables alliterate in the first half-line in lines 1, 4, 7, 10. The poem is composed in stanzas that contain between twelve and thirty-seven unrhymed alliterative long lines followed by five rhymed short lines: the first (called the "bob" by nineteenth-century prosodists) has one stressed syllable preceded by one or two unstressed; the remaining four (called the "wheel") have three stresses, separated by one or two unstressed syllables. In the wheel, the meter sometimes calls for pronunciation of final "e" (as in "made," l. 18).

The author of *Sir Gawain* employed a traditional poetic vocabulary with a large variety of synonyms. drawn from English, French, and Norse. In the following selection the synonyms for "man" include "segge" (OE, l. 4), "duk" (OF, l. 9), "knyȝt" (OE, l. 14), "sire" (OF, l. 16), "renk" (OE and ON, l. 22), "gome" (OE, l. 27), "freke" (OE, l. 34), "prynce" (OF, l. 45), "leude" (OE, l. 51), "lorde" (OE, l. 51), "burne" (OE, l. 68). The poet extended his vocabulary by using adjectives as nouns, as in "semly" (l. 3), "comly" (l. 5), "dere" (l. 9).

The *Gawain* poet took advantage of variant forms and pronunciations that existed in Middle English. But the basis of his language is a dialect of the Northwest Midlands. Northern features include the use of the Scandinavian preposition "til" for "to" (ll. 4, 28, 31); the use of "ande" for the present participle ending, as in "carande" (l. 5), "lowande" (l. 10); and the use of "es" for the third person present singular ending ("s" is often written as "ȝ" in this manuscript): "semeȝ" (l. 10), "rideȝ" (l. 22), "lengeȝ" (l. 24), "haldeȝ" (l. 29), "fareȝ" (l. 30). The plural occasionally ends in "es," as in "apendes" (l. 56), but the more common ending is the Midland "en," as in "maden" (l. 53). The past participle appears without a "y" prefix: "lost" (l. 6), "wroȝt" (l. 8), "dyȝt" (l. 9), "worþed" (l. 9), "lerned" (l. 51). The infinitive occurs without an ending or with "e": "fynde" (l. 7), "take" (l. 13), "karp" (l. 27). The usual plural inflection for nouns is "es": "spureȝ" (l. 1), "segges" (l. 4), ledeȝ" (l. 10), "knyȝteȝ" (l. 14); but an "en" plural occurs in "yȝen" (l. 15).

Several spellings reveal Western pronunciations: Old English "y" remains a front vowel, spelled "u," in "spured" (l. 44), "burþe" (l. 65); Old English "eo" appears as a front vowel, spelled "eu" in "leude" (1. 6) and "u" in "burneȝ" (l. 65); "a" is rounded to "o" before nasals in "londe" (l. 10), "mon" (l. 12), "gomneȝ" (l. 14), "mony" (l. 20), "bonk" (l. 31). Etymological "i" is sometimes spelled "e," as in "preue" (l. 45), "geuen" (l. 63); this indicates a lowering of "i," which became common in the fifteenth century.

Sir Gawain and the Green Knight

spurred
He sperred þe sted with þe spureʒ & sprong on his way

strongly   *sparks*
So stif þat þe ston-fyr stroke out þer-after;

saw   *fair (knight) sighed*
Al þat seʒ þat semly syked in hert,

truly   *together men*   *to*
& sayde soþly al same segges til oþer,

caring   *a shame*
5 Carande for þat comly, "bi Kryst, hit is scaþe

sir
þat þou, leude, schal be lost, þat art of lyf noble!

equal   *earth*   *easy*
To fynde hys fere vpon folde, in fayth, is not eþe;

more carefully   *sense*
Warloker to haf wroʒt had more wyt bene,

appointed yonder   *noble*   *become*
& haf dyʒt ʒonder dere a duk to haue worþed;

From *Sir Gawain and the Green Knight,* ed. Sir Israel Gollancz, EETS, OS, 210 (London: The Early English Text Society, 1940), pp. 25–26, 33. Reprinted by permission of The Council of the Early English Text Society.

brilliant   *men*

A lowande leder of ledeʒ in londe hym wel semeʒ,   10

destroyed

& so had better haf ben þen britned to noʒt,

beheaded   *elvish*   *excessive*

Hadet wyth an aluisch mon, for angardeʒ pryde.

Who knew euer any kyng such counsel to take,

trifling disputes   *Christmas*   *games*

As knyʒteʒ in cauel[aci]ounʒ on cryst-masse gomneʒ?"

was   *weltered*   *eyes*

Wel much watʒ þe warme water þat waltered of yʒen   15

fair   *went*   *dwellings*

When þat semly syre soʒt fro þo woneʒ

that

þad daye;

delay

He made non abode,

quickly

Bot wyʒtly went hys way,

wild

Mony wylsum way he rode,   20

þe bok as I herde say.

man   *realm*   *England*

Now rideʒ þis renk þurʒ þe ryalme of Logres,

side   *though*   *game*   *seemed*

Sir Gauan, on Godeʒ halue, þaʒ hym no gomen þoʒt;

    companionless   *stays*
Oft leudleȝ alone he lengeȝ on nyȝteȝ,

25   þer he fonde noȝt hym byfore þe fare þat he lyked,

              companion   *horse*   *woods*   *hills*
Hade he no fere bot his fole bi frytheȝ & douneȝ,

    man   *road*   *talk*
Ne no gome bot God bi gate wyth to karp,

    approached   *close*
Til þat he neȝed ful n[e]ghe in to þe Norþe Waleȝ;

         left *side*
Alle þe iles of Anglesay on lyft half he haldeȝ,

  goes
30   & fareȝ ouer þe fordeȝ by þe for-londeȝ,

                again shore
Ouer at þe Holy Hede, til he hade eft bonk

          dwelled   *few*
In þe wyldrenesse of Wyrale; wonde þer bot lyte

    either   *man*
þat auþer God oþer gome wyth goud hert louied.

    inquired   *went*   *men*
& ay he frayned, as he ferde, at frekeȝ þat he met,

       talk
35   If þay hade herde any karp of a knyȝt grene,

    region
In any grounde þer-aboute, of þe grene c[h]apel;

said no to him
& al nykked hym wyth nay, þat neuer in her lyue

saw   *man*   *was*   *hues*
þay seȝe neuer no segge þat watȝ of suche hweȝ

of grene.

roads
þe knyȝt tok gates straunge   40

dreary
In mony a bonk vnbene,

face   *did*   *turn*
His cher ful oft con chaunge,

þat chapel er he myȝt sene.

. . . .

was   *inquired*   *asked*   *tactful manner*
þenne watȝ spyed & spured, vpon spare wyse,

discreet questions
Bi preue poynteȝ of þat prynce, put to hymseluen,   45

acknowledged
þat he be-knew cortaysly of þe court þat he were,

noble   *courteous*   *alone*
þat aþel Arthure þe hende haldeȝ hym one,

noble
þat is þe ryche ryal kyng of þe Rounde Table;

was   *Gawain*   *dwelling*
& hit watȝ Wawen hym-self þat in þat won sytteȝ,

chance   *happened*
50   Comen to þat krystmasse, as case hym þen lymped.

man
When þe lorde hade lerned þat he þe leude hade,

laughed   *delightful*   *seemed*
Loude laʒed he þerat, so lef hit hym þoʒt,

castle
& alle þe men in þat mote maden much joye

promptly
To apere in his presense prestly þat tyme,

excellence   *refined*   *manners*
55   þat alle prys & prowes & pured þewes

belongs
Apendes to hys persoun, & praysed is euer;

earth   *honor*
By-fore alle men vpon molde his mensk is þe most.

man   *companion*
Vch segge ful softly sayde to his fere,

seemly   *displays of courteous manners*
"Now schal we semlych se sleʒteʒ of þeweʒ

faultless
60   & þe teccheles termes of talkyng noble;

success   *without asking*
Wich spede is in speche, vnspurd may we lerne,

received
Syn we haf fonged þat fyne fader of nurture;

has   given

God hatȝ geuen vs his grace godly forsoþe,

þat such a gest as Gawan graunteȝ vs to haue,

men   joyful   birth

When burneȝ blyþe of his burþe schal sitte   65

& synge.

understanding   manners   noble

In menyng of manereȝ mere

man

þis burne now schal vs bryng,

expect   who

I hope þat may hym here

love

Schal lerne of luf-talkyng."   70

RICHARD ROLLE'S

THE BEE AND THE STORK

During the latter part of the fourteenth century and the whole of the fifteenth, Richard Rolle was one of the most widely read authors in England. He was born about 1300 at Thornton Dale in Yorkshire and died at Hampole in 1349. As a young man he attended Oxford, but he left to take up the life of a hermit. He wrote many religious treatises in Latin and English. The English works were written during his later years for his women disciples.

The Bee and The Stork is found in the Lincoln Cathedral Thornton Manuscript (the basis for the following text), and in a copy at the Cosin Library in Durham. In this treatise Rolle uses the imagery of the Bestiaries to illustrate his doctrine of the pre-eminence of contemplative life. His prose looks toward modern usage in its idiomatic phrasing but harks back to the ornate styles of Aelfric and Wulfstan in its rhetorical flourishes. Alliteration (ll. 4, 13–14, 23, 29–30), parallel structure (ll. 21–24, 31–35), and rhythmic cadences (lines 3, 12–13, 46–49) give his style elevation. A series of rhyming present participles is one of his favorite stylistic devices (ll. 8–9).

Rolle wrote in the Northern dialect of Yorkshire. During the Middle English period the Northern dialects showed least change from Old English in phonology but most in morphology. Inflections are reduced almost as much as in Modern English. The only form for the definite article is "þe" (ll. 12, 15, 38, 39). The plural inflection for the noun is "es," "ys," or "is": "kyndis" (l. 1), "wyngez" (l. 6), "commandementes" (l. 14), "frendys" (l. 21), "saules" (l. 26), "thoghtes" (l. 27). The nominative feminine pronoun is "scho" (ll. 1, 2, etc.). Only "th" forms (often spelled "þ") appear for the plural pronoun: "þay" (l. 8), "thay" (l. 12), "thaym" (l. 2), "þaym" (l. 22), "thaire" (l. 13), "þaire" (l. 18). The third person present singular ending for the verb is "ys" or "es": "castys," "puttes" (l. 3), "flyes," "takes" (l. 4), "kepes" (l. 6), "turnes," "makes" (l. 25). The plural ends with "e," as in "take," "halde" (l. 11), or "es," as in "lufes" (l. 7), "afforces" (l. 19), "turnes" (l. 35), "rystes" (l. 36). The past participle appears without the "y" prefix: "blawen" (l. 12), "fedde" (l. 37), "chargede" (l. 49). The present participle ends with "and": "prayand," "thynkand," "redande" (l. 9). Rolle uses various adverbs, adjectives, pronouns, and prepositions typical of the North, including "mekill" (l. 22), "swylke" (l. 24), "wylke" (l. 29), "till" (ll. 24, 44), and "intill" (l. 28).

Many Northern pronunciations are revealed by the spelling. Old English long "a" remains as "a": "ane" (l. 1), "fra" (l. 10), "twa" (l. 14), "swa" (l. 18), "forgaa" (l. 29), "na" (l. 38), "gaa" (l. 41), "haly" (l. 47). Old English "o" is raised to "u" in "gud" (l. 14). The Old English fricative "sc" [ʃ], usually spelled "sh" in Middle English, has become "s" in "sulde" (l. 18).

Richard Rolle's
The Bee and the Stork

qualities   one   she

The bee has thre kyndis. Ane es, þat scho es never

idle   work

ydill, and scho es noghte with thaym þat will noghte wyrke,

bot castys thaym owte and puttes thaym awaye. Anothire es,

       feet

þat when scho flyes scho takes erthe in hyr fette, þat scho be

  easily   raised too high   air

5 noghte lyghtly overheghede in the ayere of wynde. The thyrde

es, þat scho kepes clene and brychte hire wyngez. Thus

righteous   either

ryghtwyse men þat lufes God are never in ydyllnes; for owthyre

  toil   praying   thinking   reading

þay ere in travayle, prayand, or thynkande, or redande, or

  good doing   reproving   showing

othere gude doande, or withtakand ydill men and schewand thaym

From *English Writings of Richard Rolle,* ed. Hope Emily Allen (Oxford: The Clarendon Press, 1931), pp. 54–56. By permission of The Clarendon Press, Oxford.

from   rest

worthy to be put fra þe ryste of heven, for þay will noghte   10

work

travayle. Here þay take erthe, þat es, þay halde þamselfe

blown

vile and erthely, that thay be noghte blawen with þe wynde of

vanyte and of pryde. Thay kepe thaire wynges clene, that es,

two   *good   conscience*

þe twa commandementes of charyte þay fulfill in gud concyens;

and thay hafe othyre vertus unblendyde with þe fylthe of syn   15

and unclene luste.

fighting

Arestotill sais þat þe bees are feghtande agaynes hym

should

þat will drawe þaire hony fra thaym. Swa sulde we do agaynes

endeavor   rob   poor

devells þat afforces tham to reve fra us þe hony of poure lyfe

and of grace. For many are þat never kane halde þe ordyre of   20

toward   kinsfolk   unrelated   either

lufe ynence þaire frendys, sybbe or fremmede; bot outhire þay

much   setting

lufe þaym over mekill, settand thaire thoghte unryghtwysely

on thaym, or þay luf thaym over lyttill, yf þay doo noghte all *such*

as þey wolde till þam. Swylke kane noghte fyghte for thaire

because   *wormwood*

25 hony, forthy þe develle turnes it to wormode, and makes þeire

often   *anguish*   *suffering*   *busyness*

saules oftesythes full bitter in angwys, and tene, and besynes

of vayne thoghtes, and oþer wrechidnes; for thay are so hevy

fly   *unto*

in erthely frenchype, þat þay may noghte flee intill þe lufe

which   *forgo*

of Jhesu Criste, in þe wylke þay moghte wele forgaa þe lufe

living

30 of all creaturs lyfande in erthe.

fowls

Wharefore accordandly Arystotill sais þat some fowheles

one

are of gude flyghyng, þat passes fra a lande to anothire;

some are of ill flyghynge, for hevynes of body, and for þaire

far

neste es noghte ferre fra þe erthe. Thus es it of thaym þat

35 turnes þam to Godes servys: some are of gude flyeghynge, for

rests

thay flye fra erthe to heven, and rystes thaym thare in

thoghte, and are fedde in delite of Goddes lufe, and has

thoghte of na lufe of þe worlde; some are, þat kan noghte

let

flyghe fra þis lande, bot in þe waye late theyre herte ryste,

    various   *as*

and delyttes þaym in sere lufes of men and women als þay come 40

 go   *one*

and gaa, nowe ane and nowe anothire, and in Jhesu Criste þay

   sweetness   *any*

kan fynde na swettnes; or if þay any tyme fele oghte, it es

swa lyttil and swa schorte, for othire thoghtes þat are in thaym,

    to   *stability*

þat it brynges thaym till na stabylnes; for þay are lyke till

          wings

a fowle þat es callede strucyo, or storke, þat has wenges, and 45

    weight   *so*

it may noghte flye for charge of body. Swa þay hafe

         holy

undirstandynge, and fastes and wakes and semes haly to mens

syghte; bot thay may noghte flye to lufe and contemplacyone of

  burdened

God, þay are so chargede wyth othyre affeccyons and othire vanytes.

CURSOR MUNDI

Cursor Mundi (over-runner of the world) is a comprehensive versification of biblical material, allegorical tales, and early Christian legend. The author's name is not known, but he identifies himself as a pastor at the end of the work. In the Prologue he gives his reasons for writing, provides a summary, and states that he used English rather than French so that the common people would understand him. He was evidently competing with the popular secular romances of the time, which he saw as not entirely beneficial. His style is informal. Moral points are often expressed in proverbs (as in lines 33–38).

The poem has survived in nine manuscripts in different dialects. British Museum, MS. Cotton Vespasian A III is the most complete version and probably best represents the Northern dialect of the original. It is written in a fourteenth-century hand by a scribe who faithfully followed an older copy. Bodleian Library, MS. Fairfax 14, copied in the first half of the fifteenth century, differs considerably in vocabulary and spelling from the Cotton manuscript. Comparing the two allows us to see the kind of changes that occurred as texts were copied by scribes over the centuries.

Many words in the Cotton manuscript were too archaic or unfamiliar to be retained by the later scribe. "Sere" is changed to "mony" at lines 2 and 12; however, "sere" remains at line 23. Unfamiliar words or spellings that were dropped or replaced include "yhernes" (l. 1), "bern" (l. 7), "were" (l. 14), "leth" (l. 31), "ai werrais" (l. 32), "scilwis" (l. 33), "alkyn" (l. 35). In the replacement of "strang" by "grete" (l. 5) and "knythes" by "kynges" (l. 11), we see one common word substituted for another. A stylistic change occurs at line 30, where "and pride" has been altered to "þe proude" to maintain parallel structure. Stylistic preferences also may account for use of the past tense of "lose" in the Fairfax manuscript at line 6, and the difference in word order at line 36.

In the Cotton manuscript, an "i" (spelled "j" if it follows an "i") is sometimes used to indicate a long vowel, a device common in northern texts: "strijf" (l. 5), "lijf" (l. 6), "leif" (l. 17); these words appear without the "i" or "j" in the Fairfax manuscript. In Cotton, words beginning with "wh" are sometimes spelled "qu" to indicate strong aspiration; these spellings are changed in Fairfax: "quam" is dropped entirely (l. 10), and "quat" is spelled "wat" (l. 34). Northern forms are replaced by Midland ones in the substitution of "frenche" for "frankys" (l. 24) and "drawes" for "draghus" (l. 28).

However, both manuscripts are written in a northern dialect. The plural inflection for the noun is "es", "ys," or "is": "rimes" (l. 1), "ferlys" or "ferles" (l. 11), "storis" (l. 21), "kynges" (l. 22). The third person plural pronoun usually appears with "th" forms, spelled "þ," but "h" forms occasionally occur: "þai" (l. 16), "þer" or "þaire" (l. 6), "þam" in Cotton but "ham" in Fairfax (l. 26). The third person present singular ending for the verb is "s": in the Cotton manuscript, we find "yhernes" (l. 1), "draghus" (l. 28), "werrais" (l. 32), "fettes" (l. 36), "coms" (l. 37), "beres" (l. 38); in Fairfax, "couettes" (l. 1), "drawes" (l. 28), "fecches" (l. 36), "beres" (l. 38). An "s" occurs as a plural verbal ending in "likes" (l. 26).

In both manuscripts, Old English long "a" usually appears as "a" but there is some variation between "a" and "o" forms: "bald" (l. 7) and "na" (l. 16) are found in the Cotton manuscript as opposed to "bold" and "noȝt" in the Fairfax; on the other hand, Fairfax has "nane" (l. 10) and "fra" (l. 36) as opposed to "non" and "fro" in Cotton. Both manuscripts have "a" spellings for "sanges" (l. 23), "wrang," "lath" (l. 29), "wrath" (l. 30). Old English "sc" becomes "s" in "Inglis" and "frankys" in Cotton, and in "Ingeles" in Fairfax (l. 24). A Western feature in the Fairfax manuscript is the occasional use of "o" for "a" before a nasal: "mony" (ll. 2, 6, 21), "mon" (l. 27).

Cursor Mundi

British Museum, Cotton Vespasian Ms. A III.	Bodleian Library, Fairfax Ms. 14.

    yearns
Man yhernes rimes for to here,

    covets
Men couettes rimes for to here

    romances   *many*
And romans red on maneres sere,

And romance rede of mony maner

Of Alisaundur þe conquerour;

of Alisander þe conquerour

Of Iuly Cesar þe emparour;

of Iuly cesar þe emperour

       strong
5 O grece and troy the strang strijf,

Of grece and troy þe grete strife

    lose
þere many thosand lesis þer lijf;

þer mony þousande lost þaire life

  man *bold*
O brut þat bern bald of hand,

of brute þat was bolde of hande

þe first conquerour of Ingland;

first conquerour of Ingelande.

     noble
O kyng arthour þat was so rike,

     noble
of kyng arþorow þat was rike

whom
10 Quam non in hys tim was like,

In his tyme was nane hym like

From *Cursor Mundi: A Northumbrian Poem of the Fourteenth Century*, ed. Richard Morris, EETS, OS, 57 (London: The Early English Text Society, 1874), pp. 8–10. Reprinted by permission of The Council of The Early English Text Society.

164

marvels   *befell*   *marvels that*   *befell*
O ferlys þat hys knythes fell,   of ferles at þer kynges felle

adventures many   *adventures*
þat aunters sere I here of tell,   of mony aunters I here of telle

Gawain   Kay   *firm*   *firm*
Als wawan, cai and oþer stabell,   of wawen cay and oþer stabil.

defend   *to*
For to were þe ronde tabell;   for til kepe þe rounde tabil.

Charlemagne   *Roland   fought*
How charles kyng and rauland faght,   how charles þe kyng and roland faȝt   15

desired   *peace*   *peace*
Wit sarazins wald þai na saght;   wit sarasynes walde þai noȝt saȝt

beloved Isolde
[Of] tristrem and hys leif ysote   of tristram and his lefe Isot

fool   *fool*
How he for here be-com a sote,   how he for hir bicome a sot

O Ioneck and of ysambrase,   of Ionek and of isombrase

O ydoine and of amadase   of ydoine and of amadase   20

strange
Storis als o ferekin thinges   storis als of mony þinges

O princes, prelates and o kynges;   of [prin]ces prelates and of kynges

songs   many   wonderful   *songs   many   wonderful*
Sanges sere of selcuth rime,   sa[nge]s sere of selcouþe rime

English French
Inglis, frankys, and latine,   Ingeles frenche and latine.

each one   ready   *each one   ready*
to rede and here Ilkon is prest,   to [re]de and here ilkan ys prest   25

pleases
þe thynges þat þam likes best.   þe þinges þat ham likes best.

þe wisman wil o wisdom here,   þe wyse mon wil of wisdome here

fool   *draws*
þe foul hym draghus to foly nere,   þe fole him drawes to foly nere.

loath
þe wrang to here o right is lath,   þe wrang to here of riȝt ys [lath]e

with obedience   *angry*   *obedience*
30   And pride wyt buxsumnes is wrath;   þe proude wit buxomnes Is wrath

lecher   *dislike*   *lecher*   *loath*
O chastite has lichur leth   of chastite ys licchour loþ

always makes war wrath   *warrior*   *wrath (angry)*
On charite ai   werrais   wreth;   wit charite ys werrour wroþ.

wise men
Bot be the fruit may scilwis se,   bot by þe frute men may see

what   *each*   *each*
O quat vertu is ilka tre   of wat [ver]tue ys ilka tree

all kinds   *each*
35   Of alkyn fruit þat man schal fynd,   of iche frute þat men may finde

fetches   *root its nature*   *root*   *its nature*
He fettes fro þe rote his kynd.   fra þe rote he fecches his kynde.

pear-tree
O gode pertre coms god peres,   of gode pertre gode peres

worse
Wers tre, vers fruit it beres;   of wers tre wers frute beres.

JOHN BARBOUR'S BRUCE

John Barbour, Archdeacon of Aberdeen, composed the *Bruce* in 1375. It is a poem dealing with events in Scottish history between 1304 and 1333, with emphasis on Scotland's struggles against England. It is not an exact history but a series of episodes telling stories about the perils and adventures of the heroes, chiefly Robert Bruce (who became king of Scotland), his brother Edward, and Sir James Douglas. Barbour called his work a romance. Although he embellished his stories to add to the artistic effect, he did not introduce any supernatural beings or incidents, and his basic method was realistic. His main theme was freedom, celebrated in an apostrophe in Book I (ll. 225–274). The poem, which heralds a long tradition of Scottish nationalistic verse, survives in two manuscripts: St. John's College, Cambridge, MS. G 23, copied in 1487 (the first part of which is missing), and one in the Advocates' Library, Edinburgh, copied in 1489 (the basis for the following selection).

Barbour was a skillful poet who narrated his stories in a lively, conversational style. His verse usually follows the syntax of the spoken language, although there is some inversion of word order (ll. 10, 33). The smooth movement is aided by the frequent use of enjambment (ll. 1–2, 9–10, 18–19, 21–22, 24–25). Alliteration was one of Barbour's favorite stylistic ornaments (ll. 3, 13, 15, 22, 23, 28, 34, 228, 229, 231). The apostrophe to freedom contains the rhetorical devices of repetition (ll. 225–227), contrast (lines 235–236), a simile (l. 240), and a philosophic maxim (ll. 241–242).

Barbour wrote in the Scots dialect of Aberdeen. Until about 1400, documents from the Humber to Aberdeen were written in a similar dialect. Thus Barbour's language resembles that of Richard Rolle and the *Cursor Mundi*. What is now called Lowland Scots is a rural, colloquial language derived from Old Northumbrian. Scots writers called this language "Inglis" until the end of the fifteenth century.

As in other Northern texts, the plural inflection for the noun is "is" or "ys": "storys" (l. 1), "thyngis" (l. 9), "dedys" (l. 18), "landis" (l. 32). The third person plural pronouns are "thai" (l. 2), "thaim" (l. 33), "thar" (l. 23). The third person present singular ending for the verb is "ys" or "is": "schawys" (l. 8), "giffis" (l. 227), "levys" (l. 228). The plural ends in "s" in "redys" (l. 17) and "representis" (l. 18). The present participle ends with "and": "likand" (l. 9), "plesand" (l. 10). In this text, the "ed" ending of the preterit and past participle of weak verbs is spelled "it" or "yt": "woydyt" (l. 26), "renownyt" (l. 32), "levyt" (l. 233), "wrechyt" (l. 235), "assayit" (l. 237). The short verbal forms "ma" (l. 33) and "mays" (l. 226) are characteristic of the North, as are the words "ger" (l. 16), "till" (l. 10), and "thartill" (l. 12).

In this manuscript the letters "v," "w," and "u" are completely interchangeable, as in "lywyt" (l. 19), "hawe" (l. 21), "chewalry" (l. 25). An "i" following a vowel often indicates length: "weill" (l. 21), "haiff" (l. 226). The guttural velar fricative is spelled "ch": "nocht" (l. 2), "rycht" (l. 8), "mycht" (l. 12), "wycht" (l. 22). Old English long "a" remains as "a": "schawys" (l. 8), "wald" (l. 11), "swa," "na" (l. 15), "haly" (l. 16), "wan" (l. 25), "knaw" (l. 234), "warld" (l. 240). Old English long "o" has become "u" in "gud" (l. 4) and "buk" (l. 33). Old English "sc" has become "s" in "suld" (ll. 3, 21, etc.).

John Barbour's Bruce

delightful
Storys to rede ar delitabill

Suppos that thai be nocht bot fabill;

should   *true*
Than suld storys that suthfast wer,

good
And thai war said on gud maner,

have   *pleasure*
Hawe doubill plesance in heryng.   5

pleasure   *speaking*
The fyrst plesance is the carpyng,

other   *truth*
And the tothir the suthfastnes,

shows   *right*
That schawys the thing rycht as it wes;

true   *pleasing*
And suth thyngis that ar likand

to
Tyll mannys heryng ar plesand.   10

From John Barbour, *The Bruce*, ed. Walter W. Skeat, EETS, ES, 11 (London: The Early English Text Society, 1870), pp. 1–2, 10. Reprinted by permission of The Council of the Early English Text Society.

gladly
Tharfor I wald fayne set my will,

if   intelligence   thereto
Giff my wyt mycht suffice thartill,

writing   true
To put in wryt A suthfast story,

last   always
That it lest ay furth in memory,

so   hinder
15 Swa that na lenth of tyme It let,

make   wholly
Na ger it haly be forʒet.

old
For aulde storys that men redys,

Representis to thaim the dedys

lived
Of stalwart folk that lywyt ar,

were
20 Rycht as thai than in presence war.

certainly   should   praise
And, certis, thai suld weill hawe prys

brave   prudent (wise)
That in thar tyme war wycht and wys,

hardship
And led thar lyff in gret trawaill,

conflict   of   battle
And oft in hard stour off bataill

won   praise   chivalry
Wan [richt] gret price off chewalry,   25

were freed (voided)   cowardice
And war woydyt off cowardy.

As wes king Robert off Scotland,

That hardy wes off hart and hand;

good   Sir   James
And gud Schyr Iames off douglas,

That in his tyme sa worthy was,   30

honor   excellence
That off hys price & hys bounte

far
In fer landis renownyt wes he.

make
Off thaim I thynk this buk to ma;

give   so
Now god gyff grace that I may swa

to
Tret It, and bryng It till endyng,   35

true
That I say nocht bot suthfast thing!

. . . .

225　A! fredome is A noble thing!

　　　　　makes　　　　　*have　pleasure*
　　Fredome mays man to haiff liking;

　　　　　　　　　　　　　gives
　　Fredome all solace to man giffis:

　　　lives
　　He levys at es that frely levys!

　　　　　　　　　no　　*ease*
　　A noble hart may haiff nane es,

230　Na ellys nocht that may him ples

　　　　　　fail　　　　*free will*
　　Gyff fredome failȝhe; for fre liking

　　desired　　*over*
　　Is ȝharnyt our all othir thing.

　　　　　　always　*lived*
　　Na he, that ay has levyt fre,

　　　　　　　　　　　condition
　　May nocht knaw weill the propyrte,

　　affliction　　　　　　*doom*
235　The angyr, na the wrechyt dome,

　　　　coupled　　　　　*thraldom*
　　That is cowplyt to foule thyrldome.

　　unless　　　*tried*
　　Bot giff he had assayit It,

　　　　by heart　　*should*　*know*
　　Than all perquer he suld It wyt;

should   *more*   *prize*
And suld think fredome mar to prys

world
Than all the gold in warld that Is.   240

contrary   *evermore*
Thus contrar thingis euir-mar,

other
Discoweryngis off the tothir ar.

QUESTIONS AND ASSIGNMENTS

1. Review the statements about the use of English made by Robert Mannyng in *The Story of Englande* (p. 75), Chaucer in the *Treatise on the Astrolabe* (p. 104), and Wyclif in *De Officio Pastorali* (p. 110). What do these remarks suggest about the status of English during the Middle English period?

2. Study the Middle English inflectional patterns in the Appendix, and compare them with the ones for Old English.

    a. Which endings survived from Old English?

    b. Which ones were lost because of the reduction of vowels in unstressed syllables?

    c. Which ones were lost due to analogy, that is, the assimilation of less common constructions or pronunciations to more familiar ones?

3. In Mark Twain's *A Connecticut Yankee in King Arthur's Court,* Hank Morgan, a pugnacious foreman in a gun factory, gets knocked on the head in a fight and wakes up in medieval England. Although he spoke the same language, he could have got into some good brawls by misinterpreting words that had changed meaning. The following sentences contain words that could have given Hank trouble:

> They are *lewd* students.
> She is a *buxom* woman.
> That is a *nice* thing to do.
> He is a *silly* man.

Look these words up in the *Oxford English Dictonary,* noting their meaning in Middle and Modern English. Go over the reading selections, and make a list of words that have undergone similar changes in meaning.

4. Examine the rhymes in the following lines, which appear in the selections you have read. Write the rhyme words in phonetic transcription, giving the probable Middle English and Modern English pronunciations of the words. What changes have occurred in the pronunciation of the vowels in the rhyme words?

    a. Robert Mannyng, *The Story of Englande*:
        lines   29–30   tale—Kendale
                56–57   selcouthe—mouthe

    b. Chaucer, The General Prologue to *The Canterbury Tales*:
        lines   5–6   breeth—heeth

lines	9–10	melodye—eye
	763–764	lye—compaignye
	773–774	noon (none)—stoon
	797–798	caas—solaas
	801–802	Canterbury—mury

c. Lyrics, *Annot and Johon*:
   lines 31–32   mone—trone (throne)
d. *Cursor Mundi*
   lines 24–25   rime—latine

5. Study the inflections and spellings in the *English Proclamation of Henry III* (1258) and the *Petition of the Folk of Mercerye* (1386). Then examine the Summary of Middle English Dialect Characteristics.

    a. Which Middle English dialect contains most of the features that appear in the English Proclamation?

    b. Which Middle English dialect contains most of the features that appear in the Petition?

    c. List some of the characteristics of the London dialect in the fourteenth century.

    d. Which of these characteristics have survived in Modern English?

    e. Cite some features of Modern English that have come from other dialects.

6. Examine the sample of literary dialect taken from the *Second Shepherds' Play*. What features does Mak use to distinguish the prestigious London dialect of the king's messenger from his own?

7. Look up the French words listed in the headnotes to the selections from Chaucer's General Prologue to *The Canterbury Tales* and *The Treatise on the Astrolabe* in the *Oxford English Dictionary*. What are the dates of the earliest citations for these words? What does this suggest about the introduction of French words into English?

8. Study the alliterative patterns and vocabulary in *Beowulf*, Laʒamon's *Brut*, *Sir Gawain and the Green Knight*, and *Piers Plowman*. What similarities and differences do you find in the alliteration and vocabulary of the Old English and Middle English selections?

9. Examine the inflections and spellings in Rolle's *The Bee and The Stork*, *Cursor Mundi*, and Barbour's *Bruce*. What similarities do you find between the northern dialects of Rolle and the *Cursor Mundi* and the Scots dialect of Barbour?

10. In Chaucer's "Wordes unto Adam, His Owne Scriveyn," the poet states:

    So ofte a-daye I mot [must] thy werk renewe
    It to correcte and eek to rubbe and scrape,
    And al is thorugh thy negligence and rape [haste].

Study the changes made by the scribe who copied the Fairfax manuscript of the *Cursor Mundi*. On the basis of these changes, do you think Chaucer's complaint about his scribe was probably justified? What kinds of changes would medieval scribes be likely to make in copying manuscripts?

11. Examine the inflections and spellings in the *Proclamation of Henry III,* Laʒamon's *Brut,* and the *Ancrene Riwle.* These works were written in different dialect areas, but they were all written in the thirteenth century. Do the features you find enable you to make any generalizations about the characteristics of early Middle English?

12. Go over the Middle English selections, and copy out some of the interrogative sentences. Compare them with the sentence patterns for questions in the Appendix.

    a. How do the sentence patterns differ from those of Modern English?
    b. Does the word order differ when an auxiliary verb appears?

13. Copy out some of the negative sentences in the Middle English selections. Compare them with the sentence patterns for negatives in the Appendix.

    a. How do the sentence patterns differ from those of Modern English?
    b. Which pattern seems to be more common, the one with "ne" or the one with "not"? Is there any difference in this respect between earlier and later works?
    c. Does the word order differ when an auxiliary verb appears?
    d. Do multiple negatives appear to be common?

14. Compare Barbour's dialect in *The Bruce* with Chaucer's representation of the northern dialect of the two students in *The Reeve's Tale,* and with Shakespeare's representation of the Scots dialect of Captain Jamy in *Henry V.* What similarities and differences do you find?

Late Middle English

WILLIAM CAXTON'S ENEYDOS

William Caxton, England's first printer, played an important role in helping to standardize his native language. He was born in Kent between 1415 and 1424. After having learned the trade of a mercer, he left England for the Low Countries, where he spent about thirty years as a member of the Merchant Adventurers. There he learned the art of printing and published his first two books in English. In 1476 he returned to England to set up his press at Westminster. He translated, edited, and printed about twenty-five volumes. He did not publish works in the native alliterative style but selected ones by authors who were influenced by French literature, such as Chaucer, Gower, Lydgate, and Malory. Most of his own translations were from the French.

The *Eneydos* (1490) is a translation of the *Livre des Eneydes*, printed at Lyon in 1483 by Guillaume Le Roy, or a manuscript of this work. In the Prologue, Caxton discusses some of the problems he faced as a translator. He tells an anecdote about a merchant who had trouble ordering eggs (the Scandinavian pronunciation), known to his hostess as "eyren" (the native English vocalization of the "g" after a front vowel), which illustrates the problem of dialect diversity in England. In discussing the change of language, he states that he could not translate Old English, which he compares to Dutch. He also discusses the difficulty of selecting a suitable vocabulary. Some people were in favor of sticking to a familiar, native vocabulary, whereas others believed in "augmenting" the language by borrowing foreign words. Caxton's critics called such words "over curious terms." In the sixteenth century, they were to be called "inkhorn terms." In associating archaic words with "uplondish" (rustic) men (l. 50), Caxton shows his awareness of folk conservatism. He states that he follows a middle-of-the-road course, but in practice he borrowed heavily from the French.

Caxton was influenced by the ornate French prose style of the late Middle Ages. It was characterized by long, asymmetric sentences drawn out by subordinate clauses; unfamiliar, Latinate words; and amplification by means of double or triple expressions. This is the style of Caxton's original prose as well as his translations. In the selection from the Prologue to *Eneydos*, trailing sentences appear at lines 1–7, 7–10, 10–15. The style becomes simpler (coordination replacing subordination) in the narration of the anecdote. Triple expressions are used at lines 1 and 47, and doublets at lines 3, 6, 8, 9, 11, 14–15, 17, 22–23, 24, 27,

43–44, 49, 52, 54. Among the French words in the Prologue are "dyuerse," "achieued," "paunflettis," "noble," "aduysed," "delybered," "doubted," "please," "gentylmen" (a loanblend), "curyous," "comyn," and "satisfye."

The French influence is even more pronounced in Caxton's translated prose. In the selection from Chapter XVI, trailing sentences appear at lines 57–61, 61–68, 68–72, 72–86. A French influence in phrasing is evident in lines 70–71, 88–89, and in the use of an adjective after a noun in lines 80, 81, 88, 89. Doublets, Caxton's favorite rhetorical ornament, appear in lines 57, 63, 66, 67, 75, 79, 80, 82, and 89. In a number of cases he has expanded single words in his source: "beten and cast" from "agitez" (l. 63), "borders and shores" from "orees" (l. 67), "pruneth or pycketh her" from "se sore" (l. 75), and "bystorye or wepen" from "bistorie" (l. 80). However, he reversed the process and used "susteyne" for "apvier et soustenir" at line 60. French words in this passage include "mountayne," "susteyne," "garnysshed," "sapyn," "issuen," "fontaines," "cesse," "border," "incontynent," "festye," "dysportes," "process," "pruneth," "edyfices," "deleectation," "royame," "magnifique," and "foundementes"; the *OED* cites the *Eneydos* for the first appearance of "bystorye" (l. 80).

Although Caxton freely borrowed words from his sources and was an innovator when it came to vocabulary, he was conservative in his spelling. He adopted the forms used in his manuscripts. Therefore, many of his spellings reflect pronunciations of the Middle English period, before the Great Vowel Shift and the simplification of consonant clusters. Since later printers followed his example, these archaic spellings tended to become standard. Caxton and other early printers often used "y" for "i"; "i" for "j" as well as "i"; and the same symbol for "u" and "v" ("v" was used initially but "u" in all other positions). A new practice was the use of "y" for "þ" or "th," as in "ye" (l. 58); this arose from the lack of "þ" in early continental type fonts and was reinforced by the way the character was formed in sixteenth century script.

Some of Caxton's spellings do reveal changes occurring in the spoken language. His variation between "e" and "i" in inflectional syllables shows that unstressed vowels were being reduced. For example, the plural inflection for the noun appears as "es," "is," or "ys": "werkes" (l. 1), "termes" (l. 11), "dayes" (l. 42), "egges" (l. 40), "eggys" (l. 34), "paunflettis" (l. 3), "bookys" (l. 3). The dental preterit is spelled "ed" or "id": "happened" (l. 3), "taryed" (l. 31), "vsid" (l. 20). The intrusive "h" on "harme" (l. 84) indicates improper aspiration or use of "h" as a silent letter. There is a lowering of "i" to "e" in "ded" (l. 19) and "wreton" (l. 21). Middle English "er" appears as "er" in "ferre" (l. 23), "derke" (l. 64), but as "ar" in "marchant" (ll. 29, 35). The vowel "a" is rounded to "o" before nasals in "vnderstonden" (l. 23), "forlond" (l. 31), "ony" (l. 42). All of these features appeared in the London dialect during the fifteenth century.

The conventions of punctuation used by Caxton differ from those of modern editors. As in later works, punctuation marks correspond to the major intonation patterns of speech and divide one portion of the text from another. But Caxton does not always use punctuation to separate clauses, series of words and phrases, or logical divisions. Furthermore, he employs the same symbol for more than one purpose: the slant bar (/) is used as a comma (lines 1, 6, 9) or period (lines 7, 10); the period (.) occasionally serves as a comma (lines 2, 3, 4). Names are often not capitalized (lines 7, 33, 69, 70, 71); on the other hand, capital letters are sometimes used arbitrarily (l. 47), and for decoration.

Inflections are preserved more fully in Caxton's prose than in Modern English. An "st" ending occurs for the second person singular present indicative in "hast" (l. 91). The third person singular ends in "eth": "varyeth" (l. 23), "waneth," "dyscreaseth" (l. 27), "feleth," "vnderstondeth" (l. 52). An "en" ending appears for the plural in "issuen" (l. 65). Past participles do not have an "i" prefix, but those of strong verbs usually retain the "en" ending: "wryton" (l. 19), "spoken" (l. 24), "forgoten" (l. 89), "understonden" (ll. 23, 56); at line 14 we find "understande," the reduced form of the original past participle, which was common until about 1575. The Modern form "understood" came into use in the latter part of the sixteenth century and was common by 1600.

PLATE III: WILLIAM CAXTON'S ENEYDOS

Early printed books were made to look as much like contemporary manuscripts as possible. Scribes employed a hierarchy of scripts, using different kinds of handwriting for different classes of books, and printers followed the same practice. Caxton used an angular Gothic print for Latin texts but a cursive one for works in English, modeled on the *lettre bâtarde* or Bastard script popular at the Court of Burgundy. It was a cursive bookhand in a set calligraphic style that was used for copying many finely illuminated manuscripts in the vernacular. Caxton's type number 2, the first font used in England, was modeled on *lettre bâtarde*. His type number 6, a recasting of number 2, was used for vernacular works printed between 1489 and 1491, including the *Eneydos*.

As in medieval manuscripts, *u* and *v* appear interchangeably, *v* initially and *u* in other positions. The letter *y* is used for thorn in the abbreviation "yt" ("that," l. 29). Caxton's earliest fonts of type from the Continent did not include thorn, and he used *y* as a substitute. Other abbreviations include "&" (l. 7), and a line over a vowel to indicate omission of a following *n* or *m*, as in "fraūce" (France, l. 5), "whā" (when, l. 26).

Some words that are now written as one were then written as two, such as "a longe" (l. 14), "by cause" (l. 15). On the other hand, the definite article is often joined to the following word when it begins with a vowel, as in "thystorye" ("the history," l. 12). End-line divisions were not standardized as in modern printing: for example, "ha-uyng" (ll. 1–2), "whi-che" (ll. 5–6), "gre-te" (ll. 8–9), "wy-fe" (ll. 10–11), "hone-st" (ll. 15–16).

The virgule or slant bar (/) is used to indicate a comma or period, and the period sometimes serves as a comma. Note the signature number (A 1) at the bottom of the page. Four pages were printed on each side of a sheet and the sheet then folded to make a gathering of four leaves (eight pages). The letters were placed at the foot of the first page to show the order in which the gatherings were to be bound.

After dyuerse werkes made/ translated and achieued/ ha
uyng noo werke in hande. I sittyng in my studye where as
laye many dyuerse paunflettis and bookys. happened that
to my hande cam a lytyl booke in frenshe .whiche late was
translated oute of latyn by some noble clerke of fraūce whi
che booke is named Eneydos/ made in latyn by that noble
poete & grete clerke Vyrgyle/ whiche booke I sawe ouer and
rede therin. How after the generall destruccyon of the gre
te Troye, Eneas departed beryinge his olde fader anchises
vpon his sholdres/his lityl son yolus on his honde.his wy
fe wyth moche other people folowynge/and how he shypped
and departed wyth alle thystorye of his aduentures that he
had er he cam to the achieuement of his conquest of ytalye
as all a longe shall be shewed in this present booke.In whi:
che booke I had grete playsyr.by cause of the fayr and hone
st termes & wordes in frenshe/Whyche I neuer sawe to fo
re lyke.ne none so playsaunt ne so wel ordred .whiche boo:
ke as me semed sholde be moche requysyte to noble men to see
as wel for the eloquence as the historyes/How wel that
many hondred yerys passed was the sayd booke of eneydos
wyth other werkes made and lerned dayly in scolis specyal:
ly in ytalye & other places/whiche historye the sayd Vyrgyle
made in metre/And whan I had aduysed me in this sayd bo
ke .I delybered and concluded to translate it in to englysshe
And forthwyth toke a penne & ynke and wrote a leef or
tweyne /Whyche I ouersawe agayn to correcte it/And whā
I sawe the fayr & straunge termes therin/I doubted that it
sholde not please some gentylmen whiche late blamed me
sayeng ȳ in my translacyons I had ouer curyous termes
whiche coude not be vnderstande of comyn peple /and desired
me to vse olde and homely termes in my translacyons. and

A   i

PLATE III: From Caxton's Prologue to the *Eneydos* (Copy in the British Museum,
Sig. A 1). Reproduced by Permission of the Trustees of the British Museum.
After dyuerse werkes made/ translated and achieued/ ha

William Caxton's Eneydos

PROLOGUE

After dyuerse werkes made/ translated and achieued/

hauyng noo werke in hande. I sittyng in my studye where as

pamphlets

laye many dyuerse paunflettis and bookys. happened that to my

hande cam a lytyl booke in frenshe. whiche late was translated

5   oute of latyn by some noble clerke of fraunce whiche booke is

named Eneydos/ made in latyn by that noble poete & grete

    clerke

vyrgyle/ . . . And whan I had aduysed me in this sayd boke.

deliberated

I delybered and concluded to translate it in to englysshe And

page   two

forthwyth toke a penne & ynke and wrote a leef or tweyne/

10   whyche I ouersawe agayn to corecte it/ And whan I sawe the

From William Caxton, *Eneydos*, Westminster, c. 1490, sigs. A1-A2, E3^v-E4. Transcribed by Diane Bornstein.

words *feared*
fayr & straunge termes therin/ I doubted that it sholde not

that
please some gentylmen whiche late blamed me sayeng yt in my

erudite
translacyons I had ouer curyous termes whiche coude not be

vnderstande of comyn peple/ and desired me to vse olde and

familiar
homely termes in my translacyons. and fayn wolde I satysfye   15

euery man/ and so to doo toke an olde boke and redde therin/

rough *unrefined (broad)*
and certaynly the englysshe was so rude and brood that I coude

not wele vnderstande it. And also my lorde abbot of westmynster

have shown *documents*
ded do shewe to me late certayn euydences wryton in olde

translate
englysshe for to reduce it in to our englysshe now vsid/ And   20

certaynly it was wreton in suche wyse that it was more lyke to

translate
dutche than englysshe I coude not reduce ne brynge it to be

vnderstonden/ And certaynly our langage now vsed varyeth ferre

from that. whiche was vsed and spoken whan I was borne/ For we

25   englysshe men ben borne vnder the domynacyon of the mone.

whiche is neuer stedfaste/ but euer wauerynge/ wexynge one

decreases

season/ and waneth & dyscreaseth another season/ And that

comyn

englysshe that is spoken in one shyre varyeth from a nother.

In so moche that in my dayes happened that certayn marchauntes

Thames

30   were in a ship in tamyse for to haue sayled ouer the see

at the

into zelande/ and for lacke of wynde, thei taryed atte forlond.

and wente to lande for to refreshe them/And one of theym

asked   food

named sheffelde a mercer cam in to an hows and axed for mete.

and specyally he axyd after eggys. And the goode wyf answerde.

35   that she coude speke no frenshe. And the marchant was angry.

for he also coude speke no frenshe. but wolde haue hadde egges/

and she vnderstode hym not/ And thenne at laste a nother sayd

eggs

that he wolde haue eyren/ then the good wyf sayd that she

vnderstod hym wel/ Loo what sholde a man in thyse dayes now

wryte. egges or eyren/ certaynly it is harde to playse euery   40

man/ by cause of dyuersite & chau*n*ge of langage. For in these

dayes euery man that is in ony reputacyon in his cou*n*tre.

communication

wyll vtter his co*m*mynycacyon and maters in suche maners &

termes/ that fewe men shall vnderstonde theym/ And som honest

and grete clerkes haue ben wyth me and desired me to wryte   45

erudite

the moste curyous termes that I coude fynde/ And thus bytwene

unrefined   *erudite*

playn rude/ & curyous I stande abasshed. but in my Iudgemente/

easier

the comyn termes that be dayli vsed ben lyghter to be

vnderstonde than the olde and au*n*cyent englysshe/ And for as

rough   *rustic*

moche as this present booke is not for a rude vplondyssh man   50

to laboure therin/ ne rede it/ but onely for a clerke & a noble

deeds

gentylman that feleth and vnderstondeth in faytes of armes

in loue & in noble chyualrye/ Therfor in a mcanc bytwene bothe

I haue reduced & translated this sayd booke in to our

unrefined   erudite

55 englysshe not ouer rude ne curyous but in suche termes as

shall be vnderstanden by goddys grace accordynge to my copye.

CHAPTER XVI

A. 'as   giant

This Athlas was a geant strong and myghty a boue alle

the

other/ & bycause that ye heuens were not stedfast of one

syde & sometyme dyde bowe atte other part the goddes dide

60 tourne hym in to a hyghe mountayne for to susteyne the

hairs

heuens And vpon his hed in stede of herys he is all

fir   holly

garnysshed of sapyn trees and of hooly trees that be

greatly

contynully beten & cast of the wyndes and sore couered with

clowdes fulle derke/ his sholdres are couered with snowe atte

65 alle season of the yere. & out of his grete chyne issuen

grete flodes & fontaines rening doune without cesse alonge

his terrible berde of whiche the borders and shores in

hairs   ice   at once

stede of heres ben garnyshed with thycke yse/ And incontynent

Mercury   *greet*
the sayd mercuryus drewe thyderwarde for to festye the sayd

that
athlas yt was his vncles brother vnto his moder named   70

Laya
laye/ & sette hymself vpon his sholdres where he was a whyle

to reste hym/ And after toke his flyghte as a byrde streyght

                        Libya   *then   high*
towarde the see of lybye fleyng lowe & syn hie restynge

himself vpon the roches alonge the shores of the see. takynge

        diversions
hys dysportes as a byrde that pruneth or pycketh her/ so that   75

        course
he cam by processe of tyme from a boue the sholdres of his

said vncle/ vnto the sandy shores of the see of Lybye/ &

                        Carthage   *Aneas*
from thens he entred wythin cartage. where he fonde eneas that

buylded towres & other grete edyfices. all ocupyed for to make

                        dagger   *of green stone*
vp the cytee of cartage/ and had a bystorye or wepen crysolite/   80

as it were a lityl swerde crosseles that hafted was wyth

iasper wel enryched & garnysshed wyth fyne golde hangynge at

a silken lase by his side/ and hadde a sleue vpon his

left   *arm*   *crimson cloth*
lifte harme of fyne cremoysin alle drawen ouer wyth golde

   thread   *gaily*   *noble*   *Dido*
85   wyer right wauntanly wouen/ whiche the ryche dydo had made

wyth her owne handes & had gyue it to hym to the whiche

eneas the sayd mercuryus adressed him & said in this manere/

                                               delight
Man effemynate wythout honour rauysshed in to deleectacion

                              realm   *abandoned*
femynyne that hast lefte & forgoten thi royame & habandouned

                   to attend   *the*   *thou*
90   thyn owne thynges for tentende to ye strange. why wylt yu

                                  thou
edyfie this citee thus moche magnyfique. wherof yu hast

      foundations   *that*
taken the foundementes in this place yt is not thyne/ That

                  that
same god regnynge in the clere heuyn yt of his godhed

                the earth
doeth moeue bothe the heuens & therth/ hath commaunded me to

                                the air
95   come hastely towarde the thrugh the hie regyons of thayer

to brynge vnto the his commaundementes.

SIR THOMAS MALORY'S
BOOK OF KING ARTHUR

Sir Thomas Malory, a knight with a strong interest in chivalry and warfare, completed his version of the Arthurian epic in 1469. It was based on various French prose romances of the thirteenth century as well as two English poems, the alliterative *Morte Arthure* and the stanzaic *Le Morte Arthur*. Caxton's edition of 1485 was the only known version of Malory's work until 1934, when a manuscript closer to the original was discovered at the Fellows' Library of Winchester College. This was the basis for Vinaver's edition, from which the following selection is taken.

Although Malory adopted most of his material from his sources, he treated it very freely. He telescoped or combined scenes and characters, unravelled interwoven motifs, substituted dialogue for narrative, divided narrative units into smaller sections, omitted material that did not interest him, and made his own additions. In the following selection, he interweaves material from the French prose *Mort Artu* and the English stanzaic *Le Morte Arthur* and adds his own comments in lines 60–74.

His style was not at all influenced by that of the French prose romances. He employed a simple, colloquial style that followed the rhythm and syntax of spoken English. Clauses are linked by parataxis or coordination with "and" as the most common conjunction. The vocabulary is predominantly Anglo-Saxon with few French borrowings. Malory effectively portrays the moods and personalities of his characters in dialogue, as in lines 29–43. Questions, longer sentences, parallel structure, and repetition are used to suggest the dignity of the Bishop of Canterbury. This contrasts with the short phrases and imperative exclamations of Mordred. Mordred uses the familiar "the" (l. 37) and "thou" forms (ll. 36, 42, 43), whereas the Bishop uses the polite "ye" (l. 29) and "you" forms (ll. 32, 35, 38) of the second person pronoun. Parallel structure and repetition are skillfully employed in Malory's address to Englishmen (ll. 66–74).

Syntactic forms are close to those of Modern English. Constructions that differ include the word order of adverb + verb + subject in lines 27, 56, 60, 63 (which harks back to the *Anglo-Saxon Chronicle*); the use of a dative pronoun with verbs of emotion or obligation (ll. 38, 39); and the use of "thou" or "you" after an imperative verb (ll. 36, 38). Among the spellings of vowels that may be noted are the frequent use of "i" or "y" in unaccented syllables, as in "lettirs" (l. 2), "lordys" (l. 5), "togydir" (l. 5), "unclys," "fadirs" (l. 10), "modirs brothir" (l. 31), "candyll" (l. 35), "gyffyn" (l. 65), "upholdyn" (l. 69); the appearance of "ar" in "harte" (l. 13), "warste" (l. 36), "warke" (l. 41), "warre" (l. 50); the lowering of "i" to "e" in "ded" (l. 44); and the rounding of "a" to "o" before nasals in "Inglonde" (l. 1), "hondis" (l. 26), "ony" (l. 43), "londe" (l. 60), "londis" (l. 65).

Sir Thomas Malory's
Book of King Arthur

ordered made

As sir Mordred was rular of all Inglonde, he lete make

lettirs as thoughe that they had com frome beyonde the see, and

the lettirs specifyed that kynge Arthur was slayne in batayle

with sir Launcelot. Wherefore sir Mordred made a parlemente,

and called the lordys togydir, and there he made them to chose   5

hym kynge. And so was he crowned at Caunturbyry, and hylde a

feast

feste there fiftene dayes.

And aftirwarde he drew hym unto Wynchester, and there

he toke quene Gwenyver, and seyde playnly that he wolde wedde

her (which was hys unclys wyff and hys fadirs wyff). And so   10

appointed

he made redy for the feste, and a day prefyxte that they

From *The Works of Sir Thomas Malory*, ed. E. Vinaver (Oxford: The Clarendon Press, 1967), III, 1227–29. By permission of The Clarendon Press, Oxford.

shulde be wedded; wherefore quene Gwenyver was passyng hevy. _very_ _sad_

But she durst nat discover her harte, but spake fayre, and _reveal_

aggreed to sir Mordredys wylle.

15   And anone she desyred of sir Mordred to go to London to

byghe all maner thynges that longed to the brydale. And bycause _buy_ _were required for_

of her fayre speche sir Mordred trusted her and gaff her leve; _permission_

and so whan she cam to London she toke the Towre of London,

and

suddeynly in all haste possyble she stuffed hit with all maner _it_

20   of vytayle, and well garnysshed hit with men, and so kepte hit. _food_ _supplied_

And whan sir Mordred wyst thys he was passynge wrothe _knew_ _very_ _angry_

oute of mesure. And shorte tale to make, he layde a myghty

syge aboute the Towre and made many assautis, and threw

engynnes _war engines_

unto them, and shotte grete gunnes. But all myght nat prevayle, for quene Gwenyver wolde never, for fayre speache nother for   25

foule, never to truste unto sir Mordred to com in hys hondis

agayne.

Than cam the Bysshop of Caunturbyry, whych was a noble

clerke and an holy man, and thus he seyde unto sir Mordred:

"Sir, what woll ye do? Woll ye firste displease God and

then
sytthyn shame youreselff and all knyghthode? For ys nat kynge   30

Arthur youre uncle, and no farther but youre modirs brothir,

and uppon her he hymselffe begate you, uppon hys owne syster?

Therefore how may ye wed youre owne fadirs wyff? And

therefor,

sir," seyde the Bysshop, "leve thys opynyon, other ellis I shall

curse you with booke, belle and candyll."   35

"Do thou thy warste," seyde sir Mordred, "and I defyghe

the!"

know
"Sir," seyde the Bysshop, "wyte you well I shall nat feare

spread rumors
me to do that me ought to do. And also ye noyse that my lorde

40 Arthur ys slayne, and that ys nat so, and therefore ye woll

work

make a foule warke in thys londe!"

"Peas, thou false pryste!" seyde sir Mordred, "for and

anger

thou chauffe me ony more, I shall stryke of thy hede!"

So the Bysshop departed, and ded the cursynge in the

proud   *manner*

45 moste orguluste wyse that myght be done. And than sir Mordred

sought the Bysshop of Caunturbyry for to have slayne hym.

Than the Bysshop fledde, and tooke parte of hys good with hym,

Glastonbury

and wente nyghe unto Glassyngbyry. And there he was a preste-

hermit

ermyte in a chapel, and lyved in poverte and in holy prayers;

50 for well he undirstood that myschevous warre was at honde.

Than sir Mordred soughte uppon quene Gwenyver by lettirs

messengers

and sondis, and by fayre meanys and foule meanys, to have her

to com oute of the Towre of London; but all thys avayled

nought,

secretly

for she answered hym shortely, opynly and pryvayly, that she *rather*

had levir sle herselff than to be maryed with hym.   55

Than cam there worde unto sir Mordred that kynge Arthure

raised

had areysed the syge frome sir Launcelot and was commynge

army

homwarde wyth a grete oste to be avenged uppon sir Mordred,

wherefore sir Mordred made wryttes unto all the baronny of thys

londe. And muche people drew unto hym; for than was the

comyn   60

voyce amonge them that with kynge Arthur was never othir lyff

but warre and stryff, and with sir Mordrede was grete joy and

defamed

blysse. Thus was kynge Arthur depraved, and evyll seyde off;

and many there were that kynge Arthur had brought up of

nought,

and gyffyn them londis, that myght nat than say hym a good

worde.   65

Lo ye all Englysshemen, se ye nat what a myschyff here

greatest

was? For he that was the moste kynge and nobelyst knyght of

the worlde, and moste loved the felyshyp of noble knyghtes,

and by hym they all were upholdyn, and yet myght nat thes

70 Englyshemen holde them contente with hym. Lo thus was the

olde custom and usayges of thys londe, and men say that we

of thys londe have nat yet loste that custom. Alas! thys

fault
ys a greate defaughte of us Englysshemen, for there may no

thynge us please no terme.

WILLIAM GREGORY'S CHRONICLE

During the fifteenth century, historical works again began to appear in English prose. They included comprehensive compilations, such as John Capgrave's *Chronicle of England*, and *The Brut*, as well as briefer narratives dealing with contemporary events set down by people who witnessed them. Among the latter, one of the most interesting is the *Chronicle* of William Gregory, a member of the Skinners Company and Mayor of London in 1451. His most valuable contribution is his account of Cade's rebellion in 1450, from which the following selection is taken.

Gregory wrote in an unstudied, colloquial style that probably reflected the speech of the middle classes of London. His language is particularly idiomatic at lines 8–9 and 50–51. The *OED* cites Gregory's *Chronicle* for the first appearance of "riff raff" (l. 51). In lines 57–59, he makes his point by quoting a proverb. The casualness of speech is suggested by the rambling sentence structure. Coordination with "and" is the usual method of linking clauses. The word order is consistently subject + verb + object. The constructions that differ most markedly from Modern English are the possessives. Rather than the group genitive of Modern English (for example, the king of England's name), we find the Middle English form, "the kyngys name of Engelonde" (l. 24) and "our soverayne lordys the kyng" (l. 39). At lines 28 and 55, the possessive is formed by addition of the separate particle "ys." This form, common in the fifteenth and sixteenth centuries, was often identified with and written as "his," which suggests that "his" was pronounced without an "h."

Many spellings point to contemporary pronunciations. The use of "y" in "fylde" (ll. 6, 25) suggests that the vowel already had its Modern [i] sound. Middle English "er" appears as "ar" in "warre" (l. 7), "marchaunte" (l. 55), but as "er" in "herte" (l. 46), "Clerkyn welle" (l. 28). The vowel "a" is rounded to "o" before nasals in "londe" (ll. 7, 29), "Engelonde" (ll. 24, 25). We find "e" lowered to "a" in "massyngerys" (l. 11), and "i" lowered to "e" in "thedyr" (l. 23). The vowel in unstressed syllables is usually "i" or "y," as in "aftyr," "comyns" (l. 1), "othyr," "schyrys" (l. 2), "compellyd," "gentellys" (l. 3). A reduction of the vowel and a loss of the final consonant occurs in "Syn John" (l. 28). An "s" is dropped in "Leyceter" (l. 14) and an "r" in "fowarde" (l. 34). On the other hand, an intrusive "n" occurs in "noke" (l. 9). The letter "w" appears for "v" in "wery" (l. 59), and "th" for "t" in "whythe" (l. 46). The "w" in "with" (l. 1) is often replaced by "wh" (ll. 3, 4, 21, etc.), which suggests that both spellings were pronounced the same way.

William Gregory's Chronicle

arose

Ande aftyr that the comyns of Kent a rosse with certayne

chose   *them*

othyr schyrys, and they chesse hem a captayne, the whyche

nobility   *arise*   *with*

captayne compellyd alle the gentellys to a-rysse whythe hem.

Ande at the ende of the Parlyment they come whythe a grete

army

5   myght and a stronge oste unto the Blacke hethe, be syde

Grene wyche, the nomber of xlvjM; and there they made a fylde,

ditched

dykyd and stakyde welle a-bowt, as hyt ben in the londe of warre,

save only they kepte ordyr among them, for als goode was Jacke

oak   *pigs' feet*

Robyn as John at the Noke, for alle were as hyghe as pygysfete,

10   unto the tyme that they shulde comyn and speke with suche

From *The Historical Collections of a Citizen of London in the Fifteenth Century*, ed. J. Gairdner (London: Camden Society, 1876), pp. 190–92.

officials
statys and massyngerys as were sende unto hem; thenne they put

their
alle hyr pouer unto the man that namyd hym captayne of alle

army
hyr oste. And there they a-bode certayne days too the comyng of

Leicester
the kynge fro the Parlymentte at Leyceter. Ande thenne the kyng

send unto the captayne dyvers lordys bothe spyrytualle and   15

know
temporalle, to wytte and to have knowleche of that grette

misadvised
assembelynge and gaderyng of that grete a[n]d mysavysyd

feleschyppe. The captayne of hem sendyng worde agayne unto

welfare
the kynge, that hyt was for the wele of hym our soverayne

destroy
lorde, and of alle the realme, and for to dystrye the traytours   20

beyng a-boute hym, whythe othyr dyvers poyntys that they wolde

see that hyt were in schorte tyme a-mendyde. Uppon whyche

thither
answere that the kyng, thedyr sent by hys lordys, dyd make a

crye in the kyngys name of Engelonde that alle the kyngys lege

leave

25   men of Engelonde shulde a-voyde the fylde. And a-pon the

gone

nyght aftyr they were alle voydyd and a-goo.

pieces

The morne aftyr, the kynge rode armyd at alle pecys

saint

from Syn John ys be-syde Clerkyn welle thoroughe London; and

whythe hym the moste party of temporalle lordys of thys londe

array

30   of Engelond in there a beste raye. Aftyr that they were every

lorde whythe hys retenowe, to the nombyr of xM personys, redy

as they alle shulde have gon to batayle in to any londe of

heraldic devices

Crystyn-dome, whythe bendys a-bove hyr harnys that every lorde

schulde be knowe from othyr. And yn the fowarde, as they

wolde have folowyde the captayne, was slayn Syr Umfray

35   Stafforde

and Wylliam Stafford, squyer, one the mannylste man of alle

more   *low rank*

thys realme of Engelonde, whythe many moo othyr of mene

Sevenoaks   *rebelling*

personys at Sevenocke, in Kentt, in hyr oute ragyng fro hyr

army
oste of our soverayne lordys the kyng, Harry the vj. And the

kyng loggyd that nyght at Grenewyche, and sone aftyr every 40

lorde whythe hys retynewe rood home in to hyr contraye.

July
  Ande aftyr that, uppon the fyrste day of Juylle, the

same captayne come agayne, as the Kenttysche men sayde, but

hyt was a-nothyr that namyd hymselfe the captayne, and he come

to the Black Hethe. And uppon the morowe he come whythe a 45

  army   *white*
grette hoste yn to Sowtheworke, and at the Whythe Herte he

toke his loggynge. And a-pon the morowe, that was the Fryday,

before *evening*   *draw*
a gayn evyn, they smote a sondyr the ropys of the draught

bridge   *very*
brygge and faught sore a manly, and many a man was mortheryde

       know
and kylde in that conflycte, I wot not what [to] name hyt for 50

the multytude of ryffe raffe. And thenne they enteryde in to

the cytte of London as men that hadde ben halfe be-syde hyr

     fury
wytte; and in that furynes they wente, as they sayde, for the

        welfare

comyn wele of the realme of Ingelonde, evyn strayght unto a

55   marchaunte ys place i-namyd Phylyppe Malpas of London. Yf

                                                                             consign

hyt were trewe as they surmysyd aftyr ther doyng, I remytte

      ink   *paper*   *God*   *knows and I*   *not*

me to ynke and pauper—*Deus scit et ego non.* But welle I

 know   *ill*   *ill*

wote that every ylle begynnynge moste comynly hathe an ylle

                                            very

endyng, and every goode begynnyng hathe the wery goode

     endyng.

THE PASTON LETTERS

Informal private letters often tell us a great deal about developments in the spoken language. This is particularly true in the Late Middle and Early Modern English periods, when spelling had not yet become standardized, and there were a great many writers unshackled by a scribal tradition. *The Paston Letters* were written to or by members of the Paston family, who belonged to the landed gentry of Norfolk and took their name from the village of Paston. The manor of Oxnead (mentioned in line 36) was the principal family residence. The letters, which were sometimes written by the Pastons and sometimes by secretaries whom they employed, date from 1422 to 1509.

The following letter was sent by Margery Paston to her husband John on December 18, 1477. It opens with a formal greeting (ll. 1–3), for the conventions of the age demanded that women address their husbands with humility. But Margery soon adopts an intimate tone, urging John to buy her cloth for a new gown (ll. 10–13), and humorously complaining about the discomfort caused by her pregnancy (ll. 18–22, 40–42). The rhythm of conversation is suggested by the loose, rambling, coordinate sentence structure. Margery adopts the polite "you" form of the second person pronoun: "ye" is used for the nominative case (ll. 4, 10, 11), and "yow" for the dative and accusative (ll. 3, 4, 5, 8, 10); the particle "ys" appears separately with "your" to form the possessive at line 43. The third person singular present indicative ends in "th": "hath" (l. 23), "makyth" (l. 41). The pronoun "it" is often attached to the preceding word (ll. 8, 11, 13, 17, 18).

The spelling points to many features of pronunciation. The vowel "e" often appears for "i": "worscheful" (ll. 1, 2), "wete" (l. 5), "sek" (l. 23), "hedyr" (l. 25), "leve" (l. 30), "dede" (l. 34), "Trenyte" (l. 34), "hese" (l. 35), "wretyn" (l. 36), "reyng" (l. 38), "emage" (l. 38). On the other hand, "y" (an alternate spelling for "i") appears for "e" in "wylfare" (l. 3). Middle English "er" remains in "hertyly" (l. 3) but becomes "ar" in "harde" (l. 29). The appearance of "w" for "wh" in "wanne" (ll. 7, 41) indicates lack of aspiration. The intrusive "h" on "ham" (ll. 13, 21) indicates improper aspiration or use of "h" as a silent letter. Consonants are dropped in "worscheful" (ll. 1, 2), "lyer" (l. 12), "seyetyka" (l. 23), "rememraunse" (ll. 39, 40). An intrusive "w" occurs in "dyskevwyrd" (ll. 26, 30), and "w" replaces "v" in "wechesaf" (ll. 10, 19). The "d" is spelled "t" in "reverent" (ll. 1, 2), and the "t," "th" in "ryth" (ll. 1, 2, 36), "nyth" (l. 41). Metathesis occurs in "towlmonyth" (l. 29) and "Thrusday" (l. 36). "Elisabet" (l. 22) is spelled according to its old pronunciation, which is reflected in the nickname "Betty."

A Letter of Margery Paston

To myryth reverent and worscheful husbond, Jon Paston:
right   *reverend*   *worshipful*

right
Ryth reverent and worscheful husbond, I recomaunde

me to yow, desyryng hertyly to here of yowr wylfare,

thankyng yow for the tokyn that ye sent me be Edmunde Perys,

know
preyng yow to wete that my modyr sent to my fadyr to London   5

grey woolen cloth
for a goune cloth of mustyrddevyllers to make of a goune

when
for me; and he tolde my modyr and me wanne he was comme

home,

charged   *buy it*
that he cargeyt yow to beyit, aftyr that he were come oute

of London.

vouchsafe
I pre yow, yf it be not bowt, that ye wyl wechesaf to   10

From *The Paston Letters*, ed. J. Gairdner (London: Constable & Co. Ltd., 1900), III, 214–15. Reprinted by permission of Constable & Co. Ltd.

byit, and sendyt home as sone as ye may, for I have no goune

lyard (spotted with grey)

to weyre this wyntyr but my blake and my grene a lyer,

cumbersome   *am*

and that is so comerus that I ham wery to weryt.

belt   *promised*

As for the gyrdyl that my fadyr be hestyt me, I

went

15   spake to hym ther of a lytyl before he zede to London last,

fault   *you*

and he seyde to me that the faute was in yow, that ze wolde

have it made

not thynk ther uppe on to do makyt; but I sopose that ys not

excuse

so; he seydyt but for a skwsacion. I pre yow, yf ye dor

vouchsafe   *before*

takyt uppe on yow, that ye wyl weche safe to do makyt a yens

20   ye come home, for I hadde never more nede ther of than I

well-formed

have now, for I ham waxse so fetys that I may not be gyrte

belt

in no barre of no gyrdyl that I have but of one. Elisabet

sick   *sciatica*

Peverel hath leye sek xv. or xvj. wekys of the seyetyka,

should

but sche sent my modyr word be Kate, that sche xuld come

should   *wheeled*

hedyr wanne God sent tyme, thoow sche xuld be crod in a   25

wheel-barrow.

barwe.

revealed (discovered)

Jon of Damm was here, and my modyr dyskevwyrd me to

hym, and he seyed, be hys trouth that he was not gladder of

heard   *twelve-month*

no thyng that he harde thys towlmonyth, than he was ther of.

live

I may no lenger leve be my crafte, I am dysscevwyrd   30

of alle men that se me.

should

Of alle odyr thyngys that ye deseyreyd that I xuld

sende yow word of, I have sent yow word of in a letter that I

dede wryte on Ouwyr Ladyis Day laste was. The Holy Trenyte

have yow in Hese kepyng.   35

Wretyn at Oxnede, in ryth gret hast, on the Thrusday

next be fore Seynt Tomas Day.

ring   *image*

I pre yow that ye wyl were the reyng with the emage

of Seynt Margrete, that I sent yow for a rememraunse, tyl

such

40   ye come home; ye have lefte me sweche a rememraunse, that

night

makyth me to thynke uppe on yow bothe day and nyth wanne I

sleep

wold sclepe.

Your ys, M. P.

THE CELY LETTERS

The Cely family were merchants of the Staple who did business in London and owned land in Essex (including a house called Bryttys Place, mentioned at line 28). Their surviving letters, which often deal with commercial transactions, date from 1475 to 1488. The spelling in these documents is very phonetic. It resembles that of the *Paston Letters*, but there is greater variation in vowel and consonant forms. The *Cely Letters* probably illustrate the dialect of the merchant class in fifteenth-century London.

The following letter was written by Richard Cely to his son George in 1479. The tone is businesslike, direct, almost peremptory. Short declarative statements are joined by coordination or parataxis. There is a shift to the imperative mood as Cely instructs his son about the purchase of a cart (ll. 18–22). He uses the "ye" (l. 10) and "you" (l. 1) forms of the second person pronoun. Ellipsis occurs, with elimination of "he," at line 9. Cely tends to omit the "n" on the past participle of strong verbs, as in "wryt" (ll. 3, 36), "understande" (l. 4).

Cely's writing tells us a great deal about his pronunciation. The vowel "e" appears for "i" in "weche" (l. 3), "schepys" (l. 26), "sekenese" (l. 33); "i" (spelled "y") appears for "e" in "wyll" (ll. 2, 3) and "rydy" (l. 19). Middle English "er" remains "er" in "pertys" (l. 28) but becomes "ar" in "clarke" (l. 7), "warke" (l. 19), "Parcar" (l. 21). The vowels are diphthongized in "hyar" (l. 17) and "traywe" (l. 22). The "h" is usually dropped on "his" (ll. 7, 8, 11, 32, 34). An intrusive initial "h" appears in "hassche" and "hexsyd" (l. 18), which indicates improper aspiration or treatment of "h" as a silent letter. Loss of aspiration is indicated by the "w" spelling in "weche" (l. 3), "were" (ll. 10, 27), and "wan" (l. 34). The consonant "t" is voiced to "d" in "Dorney" (l. 10), "abods" (l. 14), and (whatever the phonetic value) spelled "th" in "weythe" (l. 14) and "carthe" (ll. 16, 17, 18). The process is reversed, with "th" spelled "t," in "wyt" (ll. 11, 15). Intrusive consonants appear in "wolde" (l. 17) and "baras" (l. 29). On the other hand, consonants are dropped in "Randofe" (l. 31) and "helle" (l. 35).

A Letter of Richard Cely

letter

To George Cely at Caleys be thys lecter delyverd.

well   *letter*

I grete yow wyll and I have resayved a lecter from you

which   *well*

wryt at Caleys the xxxj [day] of May the weche lecter I have wyll

bookcase (*binder*)

understande and also the same day I have resayved a boykys

5 therin v lecters of payment acordyng to youre wrytyng and I

have schewede the lecters [unto] John Domynyco Bartholomeo

Lombarde

his clerk

to ys clarke and he saythe the lecter schall be payd at the

his

day and I have schewyd to John Spynyell Lombard ys lecter

and hathe promysyd payment at the day but as for Phyllypys

Tournai   *where*

10 Sellar of Dorney ye meste wryte to me were I schall speke

From *The Cely Papers*, ed. Henry E. Malden (London: Longmans Green & Co. Ltd., 1900), pp. 18–19. Reprinted by permission of Longmans Green & Co. Ltd.

with
wyt hym at ys comyng to London the xiiij day of Jun. I

schewyd the Lombardys lecters at London. I wrote to you a

cellars
lecter I send to yow be John Rose and ij salt salers of

weight   *ounces*   *abouts*
sylver of the weythe of x unse or xj or there abods bothe

jewel
wyt a jw ryng, and I spake to John Rose for to speke to you   15

cart
for to bye for me a carthe at Caleys for j horse a schorte

without metal rims (unshod)   *here*   *old*
carthe bare unschude the wyllys for I have hyar of my wolde

ash   *axised (axled)*
Caleys carthe. Se the carthe body be good hassche and hexsyd

ready   *work*
rydy for goe to warke for I have gret nede ther to. I

clouts (patches) cord   *nails*
sopose it wyll coste a vj or vij clotys   lynys pynys and   20

all. Praye John Parcar for helpe you or Thomas Granger

believe   *know*
for I traywe ye can but lytyll skyll of syche ware. I wrote

to you in the lecter send be John Rose as for all syche

money as ye have resayved for me and schall resayve in this

market   *much*
25   marte, I wyll ye make home to me as meche as ye can for I

ships
here saye ther schall goe schepys of war to the see

wherefore   *us*
were for God send wsse pese. Ye schall here myche more in

parts   *Bryttys Place*
thys pertys nor I can at Brytys. I wyll ye bye for me v

Arras   *market*
or vj c of good baras canvase at the marte for I am avysyde

wool
30   for to by more woll. I have marvele that ye send me no

wrytyng be Randofe of syche maters as he com to London for

his   *place*
I fere me ys comyng ys for grete maters for the plase and

world (state of things) follow   *sickness*
here ys but strange warlede for to sue non. The sekenese

struck   *severely*   *when*
rayned sore at London. God send wan ys wyll ys. At

health
35   the wrytyng of thys lecter we were all in good helle I

thanke God. Wryte at London the xiiij day of Jun in

grete haste.

per Rychard Cely.

QUESTIONS AND ASSIGNMENTS

1. Between the Middle English and Modern English periods, the long vowels underwent a systematic shift in their place of articulation, called the Great Vowel Shift. The Middle English high vowels were diphthongized and the others were raised, resulting in the following changes in pronunciation:

Vowel Change	Sample Word	Middle English	Modern English
[i] > [aɪ]	mice	[mis]	[maɪs]
[u] > [au]	house	[hus]	[haus]
[e] > [i]	geese	[ges]	[gis]
[o] > [u]	moon	[mon]	[mun]
[ɔ] > [o]	stone	[stɔn]	[ston]
[a] > [e]	fame	[famə]	[fem]

An important source of evidence for earlier pronunciations is that of rhyme words, such as the ones you studied in Question 4 on Middle English. Which Great Vowel Shift changes are illustrated by those rhymes?

Make a list of words containing the Modern English Great Vowel Shift sounds. Give phonetic transcriptions for their present and Middle English pronunciations. Which phonetic forms tend to be closest to the standard spellings?

2. Go over the selections for the Late Middle English period, and copy out the non-standard spellings that suggest Modern English pronunciations of vowels (i.e., *fylde*, Gregory's *Chronicle*, l. 6).

   a. In which selections do you find most of these spellings?
   b. Do your findings suggest any correlation between stylistic level and closeness to the spoken language?

3. In the Prologue to the *Eneydos*, Caxton tells about the difficulty a merchant had when he tried to order eggs, which his hostess knew as "eyren." Have you ever had trouble understanding a pronunciation or word used by a person from another dialect area? For example, have you ever been confused by someone's use of the pronunciation [pɪn] for "pen," or [kɑt] for "caught"?

An Englishman would be likely to use the following words, but they might puzzle an American. If you are not familiar with them, look them up in a dictionary, and give the American English equivalents: boot (of a car),

215

costermonger, cotton wool, bonnet (of a car), pram, public school, plimsolls, lorry.

Americans from certain regions might puzzle other Americans by using the following words. If you do not know them, look them up: pale fence, nicker, whicker, shivaree, fire dogs, smearcase, chitlins, snap beans.

4. The conventions of punctuation used by Caxton and other early printers differed considerably from those of modern editors. Capital letters were often not used for proper nouns; on the other hand, they were sometimes used arbitrarily or for decoration. The slant bar (/) served as a comma or period, and the period was sometimes used as a comma. There was a tendency to use punctuation to indicate brief pauses in reading, even when these did not coincide with divisions between clauses. The selection from *Eneydos* reveals the punctuation used by Caxton in his original edition. Re-punctuate it according to modern conventions.

5. Compare the speech of Mercury in Caxton's *Eneydos* (p. 190) with the exchange between Mordred and the Bishop of Canterbury in Malory's *Book of King Arthur* (p. 195).

     a. What are some characteristic features of the language in each passage (sentence structure, vocabulary, inflections)?
     b. Do you think that any Englishman ever spoke like Mercury?
     c. Do you think that Englishmen may have spoken like Mordred and the Bishop?

6. Go over the Late Middle English selections, and copy out some of the interrogative and negative sentences. How do these sentence patterns differ from those you found in earlier Middle English?

7. Make a list of sentences or clauses that contain the relative pronouns "who," "which," and "that." What restrictions, if any, seem to govern their use? Are they the same restrictions that apply in Modern English?

8. Make a list of genitive (possessive) constructions that appear in the Late Middle English selections, including both inflected forms and phrases.

     a. Do you find any constructions that differ from those of Modern English?
     b. Do you find any examples of the group genitive (ex.: the Queen of England's crown)?

Early Modern English

THE DIARY OF HENRY MACHYN

Henry Machyn was a merchant-tailor in London who worked primarily as an undertaker or furnisher of funerals. In 1550, when he was over fifty years old, he began a diary, which he continued until 1563. The initial entries are mainly records of deaths and funerals, but as the work progresses we find reports of city pageants as well as the gossip and news of the day. The following selection was written in June 1557. Since Machyn had little education, his diary is a valuable record of sixteenth-century, middle-class London English. His form of English, written when Roger Ascham and Sir Thomas Wilson were using "standard English," can be considered an early example of "class" dialect. Although most of its individual features occur in the informal writings of the upper class, they do not appear in such profusion.

Machyn's style has the casual, colloquial quality of unstudied speech. He employs a loose, trailing sentence structure, often joining a series of clauses or participial phrases with "and." Ellipsis occurs with omission of the relative pronoun before "was" (l. 2), and the verb before "favorable" (ll. 6–7).

Machyn's writing contains a large number of words in which "i" is lowered to "e": in this selection we find "menysters" (l. 4), "consperacy" (l. 5), "cete" (l. 14), "ennes" (l. 15), "sterope" (l. 28); "i" appears instead of "e" in "inter-teyned" (l. 9). Other vowel changes include monophthongization of the vowel in "he" and "sant" (l. 12); shortening of the vowel (indicated by a double consonant) in "latt" (l. 2), "grett" (l. 20), "shutt" (l. 26); lowering of "er" to "ar" in "harroldes" (l. 7), "stremars" (l. 13), "clarkes" (ll. 15, 18), "hartt" (l. 21).

Machyn often omits or misplaces his "h's." The pronoun "his" consistently appears without the "h" (ll. 3, 5, 10, 26, 27, 28, 29, 30). At line 27, it is omitted on "hit." On the other hand, an intrusive "h" occurs in "blohyng" (l. 7), "folowhyng" (l. 22).

Consonant spellings also reveal a great deal about Machyn's pronunciation. Loss of aspiration is indicated by the "w" in "wyche" (l. 10); the appearance of "wh" instead of "w" in "whettes" (ll. 14, 18) and "whent" (l. 16) suggests that both spellings were pronounced the same way. An intrusive "w" replaces the "h" in "howswold" (l. 21). We find "th" instead of "d" in "althermen" (l. 8); the process is reversed, with "d" replacing "th," in "furdered" (l. 3), "odur" (l. 9). Consonants are dropped in "Hamtun" (l. 20), "Norfoke" (l. 24). Archaic pronunciations are indicated for "rayme" (l. 10) and "mo" (l. 10).

The Diary of Henry Machyn

The vij day of Juin was a proclamassyon in London by

the quen['s] grace, of the latt duke of Northumberland was

his
supported and furdered by Henry the Frenche kyng and ys

ministers
menysters, and by the heddes of Dudley, Asheton, and by the

his
5 consperacy of Wyatt and ys trayturs band; and the sayd

plot   *give (yield)*
kynges mynysters dyd secretly practysse and gyff, and they

heralds
favorabulle; with trumpeters blohyng and a x harroldes of

aldermen
armes, and with my lord mayre and the althermen; and by the

lat Stafford and with odur rebelles whom he had interteyned

realm   *more*
10 in ys rayme, and dyver odur mo, the wyche be ther yett

on-taken. . . .

From *The Diary of Henry Machyn, Citizen and Merchant–Taylor of London, from A.D. 1550 to A.D. 1563*, ed. John G. Nichols (London: Camden Society, 1848), pp. 138–39.

The viij day of Juinj cam a goodly prossessyon unto

St. Paul's   *high altar*   *saint*
Powlles, and dyd oblassyon at the he auter, sant Clementes

     outside   *Temple-bar (gateway)*
parryche with-out Tempylle-bare, with iiijxx baners and stremars,

    waits (musicians)   *city*
and the whettes of the cete playing; and a iijxx copes,

               inns
and prestes and clarkes, and dyver of the ennes of the cowrt   15

whent next the prestes; and then cam the parryche with

whytt rodes in ther handes, and so bake agayne with the

waits
whettes playing, and prestes and clarkes syngyng, home-warde.

The x day of Junij the Kyng and the Quen toke ther

jorney toward Hamtun courte for to hunt and to kyll a grett   20

              household   *remained*
hartt, with serten of the consell; and so the howswold tared

at the Whytthalle, tylle the Saterday folowhyng they cam

a-gayne to Whytthalle.

The xvj day of June my yong duke of Norfoke rod

              small pistol
abrod, and at Stamford-hylle my lord havyng a dage hangyng   25

shoot   it

on ys sadylle bow, and by mysse-fortune dyd shutt yt, and

hit one   rode

yt on of ys men that ryd a-for, and so by mysse-forten

one

ys horse dyd flyng, and so he hangyd by on of ys sterope[s],

and so thatt the horse knokyd ys brayns owt with flyngyng

30   owt with ys leges.

LETTERS OF QUEEN ELIZABETH

The letters of Queen Elizabeth range from informal notes to impersonal administrative documents: they include letters written by the Queen herself; letters dictated to ministers or secretaries by the Queen, who sometimes added postscripts in her own hand; letters written by ministers under instructions from the Queen; and letters sent to officers of the state that were entirely the work of the Queen's ministers. All of these documents tell us something about Elizabeth as a ruler, but those belonging to the first category reveal most about her language.

Both of the following letters, written by Elizabeth herself, concern plots that centered around Mary, Queen of Scots. After the Scottish lords had revolted in 1567, Mary fled to England, where she remained as a captive until her death in 1586. She was a focus for the plotting of discontented Catholic noblemen, chief of whom was the Duke of Norfolk. After having been implicated in a conspiracy involving Mary, he was imprisoned in 1569, and again in 1572, when he was condemned to death for high treason. Nevertheless, the Queen was reluctant to order his execution and delayed it by sending Lord Burghley the following letter on April 11. But the reprieve was temporary; Norfolk was beheaded on June 2.

Since Burghley was the Queen's most trusted minister, she addressed him in an informal style. She used the "the" form of the second person pronoun (l. 10). The opening sentence is particularly colloquial (ll. 1–3). In form and meaning the letter is straightforward and direct.

The second letter was sent to King James VI of Scotland on February 14, 1586. Although he was Elizabeth's cousin, she addressed him in a formal, circumspect manner. She used the polite "you" form of the second person pronoun (ll. 1, 5, 6, etc.). The formal tone is set by the opening periodic sentence (ll. 1–3) and carried on by the frequent use of parallel structure (ll. 8–9, 10–11, 11–12, 12–14, 20). Of course, Elizabeth was writing about a touchy matter, the death of James' mother, Mary, Queen of Scots. In 1586 a number of Catholics conspired to murder Elizabeth and set Mary on the throne. The plot was discovered, the conspirators executed, and Mary tried and found guilty. Elizabeth signed the warrant for Mary's execution but was unwilling to have it dispatched. Burghley and other members of the Council sent it on their own responsibility, and Mary was executed on February 8.

Elizabeth has been condemned for hypocrisy in this matter, but the letter seems to express genuine feelings of regret.

Both of the letters tell us something about the Queen's pronunciation. In the first, the spelling of "Levetenant" (l. 3) reflects the traditional and usual British pronunciation; the American pronunciation is based on the standardized spelling. An "s" inflection appears on the verb in the impersonal verb "thinkes" (l. 1) and in "nides" (l. 11) with the second person singular. The "i" in "nides" points to the Modern English pronunciation. An identification or confusion of "er" and "ar" sounds is indicated by the "ar" spellings in "hindar" (l. 2), "ordar" (l. 4), "defar" (l. 4), "furdar" (l. 5); at line 6 we find "further." The "n" is detached from "myn" and attached to the following vowel in "my none" (l. 12). Although the spelling is more careful in the second letter, there are some departures from usual forms: a shortened form appears for the past participle of "abide" in "bid" (l. 9); an initial "y" is added to "yerksom" (l. 6); initial "w" is dropped in "owld" (l. 8). The archaic pronunciation is indicated for "moe" (l. 7). The third person singular present indicative ends with "s" in "overwhelms" (l. 2) and "fits" (l. 13) but with "th" in "hath" (ll. 3, 4).

PLATE IV: QUEEN ELIZABETH'S LETTER
TO LORD BURGHLEY

During the sixteenth century, it was still not uncommon for an educated person to write more than one hand (this was a continuation of the medieval scribal tradition). A particularly fashionable one was the humanistic or Italian hand, an imitation of Caroline miniscule that became popular in Italy and served as the basis for modern Italic print. Roger Ascham taught this script to Elizabeth. When she became queen, however, she usually wrote in the straggly hand exhibited in the letter to Lord Burghley. She apparently had little time for careful penmanship. Nevertheless, her elaborate signature suggests her interest in the art.

The letters *e*, *h*, and *s* differ most from their later forms. Also note the angular *y*, which resembles thorn. As in contemporary books and earlier manuscripts, a line over a vowel indicates omission of a following *m* or *n*, as in "cōmitted" (l. 13).

My lord me thinkes that I am more beholdinge to the hindar
part of my hed than wil dare trust the forwards side
of the same and therfor sent to the Levetenant
and the S: as you knowe best the order to
defar this execution till the here funday
and that this may be done I doute nothing
witout carrocihe of any furer warrant
for that her rasche determination upon
a very unfit day was countermanded by
your considerat admonition the cause that
moved me to this ar not now to be expressed
lest an irrevocable dede be in mene while
comitted. If the wyl nide a warrant
let this suffice all writen with my none
hand. Your most loving soverain

Elizabeth R

PLATE IV: Queen Elizabeth's Letter to Lord Burghley (Bodleian Library, MS. Ashmole
1729, Folio 13 r). Reproduced by permission of the Bodleian Library.
My Lord me thinkes that I am more beholdinge to the hindar

Letters of Queen Elizabeth

Queen Elizabeth to Lord Burghley: April 11, 1572.

seems
My Lord, me thinkes that I am more beholdinge to the

back
hindar part of my hed than wel dare trust the forwards side

sergeant
of the same, and therfore sent to the Levetenant and the S.,

as you knowe best, the ordar to defar this execution till

they   *further*
the here furdar. And that this may be done I doubte   5

attention
nothing, without curiositie of my further warrant, for that

ther rasche determination upon a very unfit day was

countermaunded by your considerat admonition. The causes

that move me to this ar not now to be expressed, lest an

thee
irrevocable dede be in mene while committed. If the wyl   10

From *Original Letters Illustrative of English History*, ed. Sir Henry Ellis (London: Harding, Triphook & Lepard, 1824), II, 262–63.

need
nides a warrant, let this suffice, all written with

mine own
my none hand.

> Your most lovinge Soveraine
> Elizabeth R.

Queen Elizabeth to King James the Sixth: February 14, 1586.

My deare Brother, I would you knewe (though not felt)

the extreme dolor that overwhelms my mind, for that miserable

accident which (far contrary to my meaninge) hath befalen.

I have now sent this kinsman of mine whom ere now yt hath

5   pleased yow to favor, to instruct yow trewly of that which

irksome
ys to yerksom for my penne to tell yow. I beseche yow that

more
as God and many moe knowe, how innocent I am in this case:

would
so you will believe me that yf I had bid ought I owld

abided
have bid by yt. I am not so bace minded that feare of any

10   livinge creature or prince should make me afrayde to do

From *Original Letters Illustrative of English History*, ed. Sir Henry Ellis (London, 1824), III, 22–23.

that were just, or don to denye the same. I am not of so

base a linage, nor cary so vile a minde. But, as not to

disguise fits not a Kinge, so will I never dissemble my

to be shown
actions, but cawse them shewe even as I ment them. Thus

assuringe yourself of me, that as I knowe this was deserved, 15

yet yf I had ment yt I would never laye yt on others shoulders;

no more will I not damnifie my selfe, that thought yt not.

The circumstance yt may please yow to have of this

bearer. And for your part, thincke yow have not in the World

a more lovinge kinswoman, nor a more deare frend then my 20

self; nor any that will watch more carefully to preserve yow

and your estate. And who shall otherwise perswade yow, judge

them more partiall to others then yow. And thus in hast I

leave to troble yow: besechinge God to send yow a longe Reign.

The 14th of Feb. 1586. 25

Your most assured lovinge sister and cosin
Elizab. R.

HUGH LATIMER'S
SERMON ON THE PLOUGHERS

A majority of the books published in sixteenth-century England were concerned with religion. Reformers and defenders of the establishment debated the questions of the day in pamphlets, philosophic treatises, and sermons. One of the greatest Protestant preachers was Hugh Latimer, the son of a yeoman farmer in Leicestershire. He attended Cambridge, became Professor of Greek at the University, preached before Henry VIII in the 1530s, and was consecrated Bishop of Worcester in 1535. Unable to accept the Six Articles proclaimed by Henry VIII, Latimer resigned his See in 1539 and was imprisoned. He was released and allowed to preach during Edward's reign but was again in trouble when Mary came to the throne. In 1555 he was burnt at the stake at Oxford together with Bishop Ridley.

The kind of preaching that led to Latimer's fiery death is exemplified by the *Sermon on the Ploughers*, first preached outside St. Paul's on January 18, 1548, and printed three times within the year. He attacked the establishment and the rich citizens of London in a racy, colloquial style (see particularly ll. 7–10, 74–77, 85–88), using all the tricks of rhetoric to arouse his audience. He used the sentence structure and rhythm of colloquial English and was not influenced by Latin syntactic patterns. Even his Latin quotations from the Bible are translated very idiomatically (ll. 13–16). His metaphors and similes are taken largely from agriculture and domestic occupations. In lines 5–33, he defends his use of metaphor against attacks by literal-minded critics and in lines 40–59 develops the traditional comparison of the preacher to the plowman (found in *Piers Plowman* and elsewhere). Rhetorical questions (ll. 23–24, 31–32, 60–61, 64–66), repetition (ll. 55–59, 67–69), and abrupt changes of pace hold the attention of the audience. The address grows more rhetorical in the apostrophe to London (ll. 67–74), returns to colloquial in the anecdote about the sensitive citizens of London (ll. 74–78), and rises again in the comparison of burgesses to butterflies (ll. 78–85).

Latimer's syntactic forms differ in only minor ways from later Modern English. He uses the nominative "ye" (ll. 2, 5) for the second person plural pronoun (driven out by "you") as well as the nominative "thou" (l. 68) and objective "the" (l. 69) for the singular. The relative pronoun "whatsoever" appears for a person at line 36, but "whosoever" at lines 37, 38. The second person singular present indicative ends in "est" or "st," as in "heareste" (l. 68), "haste" (l. 70), and the third person singular in "th": "hath" (ll. 7, 18, 19, etc.), "doth" (l. 19), "sayth" (l. 30), "setteth" (l. 48), "tilleth," "breaketh" (l. 49).

Since publishers did less standardizing than they do today, the spelling in early printed books tends to be closer to that of the author and may tell us something about his pronunciation. In the following selection, we find "e" for "i" in "geue" (l. 26), and "i" for "e" in "oprission" (l. 66). Middle English "er" appears as "ar" in "swaruinge" (l. 56). A long vowel or diphthong is suggested by the "ou" spelling in "doungeth" (l. 52), "pourgeth" (l. 53). The "u" in "rightuous" (l. 59) may be based on an analogy with "virtuous." Intrusive vowels appear in "fayethfull (l. 38), "fayeth" (l. 56), "dueties" (l. 72), and "hatered" (l. 80).

Hugh Latimer's
Sermon on the Ploughers

For preachynge of the Gospel is one of Goddes plough

workes, and the preacher is one of Goddes plough men. Ye may

simile
not be offended wyth my similitude: in that I compare

preachynge to the laboure and worke of ploughinge, and the

5   preacher to a ploughman. Ye maye not be offended wyth thys

slandered
my similitude, for I haue ben sclaundred of some personnes

for such thynges. It hath ben sayde of me, Oh Latimer, nay

as for hym I wil neuer beleue hym whyle I lyue, nor neuer

compared
truste hym, for he lykened our blessed Ladye to a saffrone

10   bagge, where in deede I neuer vsed that similitude. But it

was as I haue sayde vnto you before nowe, accordinge to that

From *Sermon on the Ploughers*, ed. Edward Arber (London: Alex Murray & Son, 1868), pp. 18–19, 22–23.

whiche Peter sawe before in the spirite of prophesy and sayde

that there shoulde come afterwarde men: *Per quos via*

veritatis maledictis afficeretur, there should come felowes

by whom the waye of truth should be yll spoken of and   15

sclaundred. But in case I had vsed this similitude, it had

not bene to be reproued, but myght haue bene without reproche.

For I might haue sayde thus, as the saffrone bagge that hath

bene full of saffron or hath had saffron in it, doth euer

after sauoure and smel of the swete saffron that it   20

conteyned: so oure blessed Ladye which conteyned and bare

Christe in her wombe, dyd euer after resemble the maners and

vertues of that precious babe which she bare. And what had

oure blessed Ladie bene the worse for thys? or what

dishonour was thys to oure blessed Ladie. But as preachers   25

                                          that

must be ware and circumspect yat they geue not any iust

occasion to be sclaundered and yll spoken of by the

hearers, so must not the auditours be offended without cause.

For heauen is in the gospel likened to a musterde seede.

30   It is compared also to a piece of leauen, and Christ sayth

that at the last day, he wyl come lyke a thiefe. and what

dishonoure is thys to God? or what derogation is thys to

heauen. Ye maye not then, I say, be offended with my similitude,

for because I lyken preachyng to a ploughmans laboure and a

35   prelate to a ploughman. But now you wyll aske me whom I cal a

that

prelate. A prelate is that man, what soeuer he be, yat hath a

flocke to be taughte of hym, who soeuer hath any spirituall

charge in the fayethfull congregation, and who so euer he be

spiritual charge
that hath cure of soule.

compared

40   And wel may the preacher and the ploughman be lykened

together. Fyrste for their labour of all ceasons of the yere.

For there is no tyme of the yere, in whiche the ploughman

hath not some speciall worke to do, as in my countrey in

Lecestre Shire, the ploughe man hath a tyme to set furth and

45   to assaie hys plough, and other tymes for other necessari

workes to be done. And then they also maye be likenede

together, for the diuersitie of workes and varietie of offices

that
yat they haue to do. For as the ploughman first setteth

furth hys plough and then tilleth hys lande and breaketh it

in furroughes, and sometime ridgeth it vp agayne. And at   50

an other tyme harroweth it, and clotteth it, and somtyme

dungs
doungeth it, and hedgeth it, diggeth it, and weedeth it,

purges
pourgeth and maketh it cleane. So the prelate, the preacher

hath mani diuers offices to do. He hath fyrst a busie worke,

to bringe his parishioners to a ryght fayth, as Paule calleth   55

swerving
it. And not to a swaruinge fayeth, but to a fayeth that

embraceth Christe, and trusteth to hys merites, a liuely

fayth, a iustifyng fayth, a fayth that maketh a man

rightuous wythout respecte of workes. . . .

Nowe what shall we saye of these ryche citizens of   60

London? What shall I saye of them? shal I cal them proude

men of London, malicious men of London, mercylesse men of

London. No, no, I may not saie so, they wil be offended wyth

me than. Yet must I speake. For is there not reygning in

65   London, as much pride, as much coueteousnes, as much crueltie,

as much opprission, as much supersticion, as was in Nebo?

Yes, I thynke and muche more to. Therfore I saye, repente

O London. Repent, repente. Thou heareste thy faultes tolde

the, amend them, amend them. I thinke if Nebo had had the

that

70   preachynge yat thou haste: they wold haue conuerted. And you

rulers and officers be wise and circumspect, loke to your

charge and see you do your dueties and rather be glad to amend

your yll liuyng then to be angrye when you are warned or tolde

fuss

of your faulte. What a do was there made in London at a

75   certein man because he sayd, and in dede at that time on a

iust cause. Burgesses quod he, nay butterflies. Lorde what

that

a do there was for yat worde. And yet would God they were no

worse then butterflies. Butterflies do but theyre nature,

the butterflye is not couetouse, is not gredye of other mens

goodes, is not ful of enuy and hatered, is not malicious,   80

is not cruel, is not mercilesse. The butterflye gloriethe

not in hyr owne dedes, nor preferreth the tradicions of men

before Gods worde; it committeth not idolatry nor worshyppeth

false goddes. But London can not abyde to be rebuked

suche is the nature of man. If they be prycked, they wyll   85

gall (wound)
kycke. If they be rubbed on the gale: they wil wynce.

although
But yet they wyll not amende theyr faultes, they wyl not

ill
be yl spoken of.

RICHARD HOOKER'S OF THE LAWS
OF ECCLESIASTICAL POLITY

Richard Hooker was born of poor parents at Heavetree near Exeter and attended Oxford University, where he became a teacher of Hebrew. When he was appointed master or chief preacher at the Temple in 1585, he got into a controversy with Walter Travers, the assistant preacher, who was the chief Puritan authority on church government. Travers was dismissed by Archbishop Whitgift, but Hooker continued to ponder the questions he had raised. The result was his philosophic treatise, *Of the Laws of Ecclesiastical Polity*. The first five books were published between 1593 and 1597, and the last three posthumously (Books VI and VIII in 1648, and Book VII in 1662). The following selection is taken from Book I, which contains Hooker's general treatise on the law.

The church had often been attacked with street-corner invective in colloquial language. Hooker defended it in the ornate formal style that had been developed by humanists under the influence of Cicero and Quintilian. This style imitated the periodic sentence structure of Ciceronian Latin prose in its extensive use of subordination, lengthy periods, and suspended meaning. Periodic sentences occur at lines 1–11, 33–36, 40–44, and most dramatically, at lines 49-68; here we have a two-hundred word sentence consisting of six "if" clauses followed by a rhetorical question. Within the "if" clause beginning at line 61, a series of examples are set forth in parallel structure (ll. 61–65). Hooker also recognized the effectiveness of parataxis, which he used together with parallel openings at lines 19–22. Polysyllabic, Latinate phrases give his prose a slow, dignified movement: "signify the infinite greatness" (ll. 23–24), "established by solemn injunction" (l. 33), "importeth the establishment" (l. 36), "manifestation by execution" (ll. 38–39), "intermit her course" (ll. 49–50), "irregular volubility" (ll. 56–57). The *OED* cites Hooker as the first writer to use "volubility" to mean "revolving." Sir John Cheke and his circle condemned such neologisms as "inkhorn terms," but many Latinate words introduced by Renaissance humanists have become a permanent part of the language.

As in other early printed books, "u" and "v" are used interchangeably ("v" initially and "u" in all other positions); "i" stands for "i" and "j"; and "ie" is often used for "y." This selection illustrates the way Elizabethan writers freely

238

used capital letters for emphasis. The spelling is quite regular and does not reveal much about Hooker's pronunciation. But we can observe some differences between the syntax and morphology of his prose and that of later Modern English. The relative pronoun "which" is used for a person at line 58. A predicate adjective occurs before the subject and verb at line 9, and an adjective follows the noun at lines 30, 39. The verb "did" is used as an auxiliary in declarative sentences at lines 29, 30, 44. The usual ending for the third person singular present indicative of the verb is "th," as in "hath" (l. 16), "attributeth" (l. 18), "seemeth" (l. 25), "importeth" (l. 35), "commeth" (l. 40); but an "s" ending appears in "takes" (l. 41).

Richard Hooker's *Of the Laws*
of Ecclesiastical Polity

although

Wherefore to come to the law of nature, albeit thereby

we sometimes meane that manner of working which God hath

set for each created thing to keepe: yet for as much as

those things are termed most properly naturall Agents which

unconsciously

5   keepe the Law of their kind vnwittingly, as the Heauens and

Elements of the World, which can doe no otherwise then they

doe; and for as much as wee giue vnto intellectual natures the

name of voluntary Agents, that so wee may distinguish them

from the other; expedient it will be, that wee seuer the Law

10   of Nature obserued by the one, from that which the other is

tyed vnto. Touching the former, their strict keeping of

From *Of the Laws of Ecclesiastical Politie* (London, 1617), pp. 6–7. Transcribed by Diane Bornstein.

tenor (course)

one Tenure, Statute, and Law is spoken of by all, but hath

in it more then men haue as yet attained to know, or perhaps

work

euer shall attaine, seeing the trauell of wading herein is

giuen of God to the sonnes of Men, that perceiuing how much   15

the least thing in the World hath in it more then the wisest

are able to reach vnto, they may by this meanes learne

humilitie. Moses, in describing the worke of Creation,

attributeth speech vnto God, God said, Let there be light:

let there be a firmament: let the Waters vnder the Heauen   20

be gathered together into one place: Let the Earth bring

forth: Let there be Lights in the Firmament of Heauen.

Was this onely the intent of Moses, to signifie the infinite

greatnesse of Gods power, by the easinesse of his accomplishing

work

such effects without trauell, paine, or labour? Surely it   25

seemeth that Moses had herein, besides this, a further

purpose, namely, first, to teach that God did not worke as a necessary but a voluntary Agent, intending beforehand and

decreeing with himselfe that which did outwardly proceed from

30   him: Secondly, to shew that God did then institute a

law naturall to be obserued by creatures, and therfore according

to the manner of Lawes, the Institution thereof is described,

as being established by solemne iniunction. His commanding

those things to be which are, and to be in such sort as they

                                        tenor
35   are, to keepe that tenure and course which they doe,

importeth the establishment of Natures Law. This Worlds

first Creation, and the preseruation since of things created,

what is it but only so far forth a manifestation by

execution, what the Eternall Law of God is concerning

40   things naturall? And as it commeth to passe in a kingdome

rightly ordered, that after a Law is once published, it

                                ranks of society
presently takes effect far and wide, all States framing

themselues thereunto; euen so let vs thinke it fareth in

the naturall course of the World: since the time that God

did first proclaime the Edicts of his Law vpon it, Heauen   45

and earth haue harkned vnto his voyce, and their labour

hath bin to doe his will: He made a Law for the Raine,

He gaue his Decree vnto the Sea, that the Waters should not

discontinue

passe his commandement. Now, if nature should intermit her

course, and leaue altogether, though it were but for a while,   50

the obseruation of her own Lawes; if those principall and

Mother Elements of the World, whereof all things in this

lower World are made, should lose the qualities which now

they haue; if the frame of that Heauenly Arch erected ouer

our heads should loosen and dissolue it self; if Celestial   55

accustomed

Spheres should forget their wonted Motions, and by irregular

revolving

volubilitie turne themselues any way as it might happen;

if the Prince of the Lights of Heauen, which now as a

Gyant doth run his vnwearied course, should as it were

through a languishing faintnesse, begin to stand and to rest   60

himselfe, if the Moone should wander from her beaten way,

the times and seasons of the yeere blend themselues by

disordered and confused mixture, the Winds breathe out their

last gaspe, the Clouds yeeld no Raine, the Earth be defeated

65 of Heauenly Influence, the Fruits of the Earth pine away

as Children at the withered brests of their Mother, no

longer able to yeeld them reliefe; what would become of

Man himselfe, whom these things now doe all serue? See

wee not plainly that obedience of Creatures vnto the

70 Law of Nature is the stay of the whole World?

THE KING JAMES BIBLE

The religious disputes of the sixteenth and seventeenth centuries led to a large number of biblical translations. Protestant reformers translated the Bible from newly available Greek and Hebrew manuscripts, published their books wherever they could manage to do so, and smuggled them into England. William Tyndale translated the New Testament from the Greek (copies appeared in England by 1526) and portions of the Old Testament, including the Pentateuch, from the Hebrew. Basing his work on that of Tyndale, Miles Coverdale produced a complete English Bible in 1535. In 1539 he published an officially sponsored revision known as the Great Bible. Between 1557 and 1560, English Protestant scholars in exile produced the Geneva Bible, which became the most popular version for private reading. After the accession of Elizabeth, Archbishop Parker commissioned another revision, which resulted in the Bishops' Bible of 1568. In response to Genevan and Anglican competition, a group of English Catholic refugees translated the Latin Vulgate and published the New Testament at Rheims in 1582 and the Old Testament at Douai between 1609 and 1610. The King James Bible was initiated by King James I in 1604 as a revision of the Bishops' Bible. It was compiled by more than fifty clergymen and scholars representing both the Anglican and Puritan wings of the church and published in 1611.

Each group of translators used the work of their predecessors. Since Tyndale's translation thus served as a basis for the King James Bible, we may consider the factors that influenced him. In his Preface to the "Obedience of a Christen Man," he tells us that he had read the *English Chronicle* when he was a child. The style of the chronicle, with its coordinate or paratactic sentence structure and simple vocabulary, is the one he used in narrative sections of the Bible, and later translators followed his example. The parable of the prodigal son is written in such a style (ll. 1–43). The sentence structure is coordinate, the vocabulary mainly Anglo-Saxon. Another influence that went back to the Old English period was the homiletic tradition. English prose was never abandoned as a vehicle for sermons and devotional treatises. Therefore, a continuous tradition links the homilies of Aelfric and Wulfstan, the *Ancrene Riwle*, the treatises of Rolle and other mystics, and the biblical translations. These translations also reflect the style of the Greek original. The parallelism in the Greek reinforced Tyndale's use of parallel structure, as in the passage from Corinthians (ll. 44–69). The King James translators improved the rhythm of Tyndale's version and substituted "charity" (used in the Rheims Bible) for "love." They were aiming at language that would be effective in oral delivery. The classical training of the translators, the consummate rhetoric of the original Greek and Hebrew texts, the pastoral imagery, the excellence of the base provided by Tyndale, the heritage of English prose—all these things combined to produce the magnificent style of the King James Bible.

This style has come to be identified by many readers as biblical prose. Its spelling, punctuation, and vocabulary retain vestiges of Elizabethan English. In addition, in this section we find the "th" ending for the third person singular present indicative, as in "falleth" (l. 3), "hath" (l. 31), "profiteth" (l. 51), "suffereth" (l. 52), "enuieth" (l. 53); the "st" ending for the second person singular, as in "gauest" (l. 37), "hast" (l. 39); the second person singular pronouns, "thee" (l. 15), "thy" (l. 16), "thou" (l. 36); the relative pronoun "which" for a person (l. 38); "spake" as the past tense of "speak" (l. 63); "did" (l. 11) or "do" (l. 35) as auxiliaries in declarative sentences, and a reversal of subject and verb in lines 33–34, 35, 36.

The King James Bible

LUKE 15.11–32

And hee said, A certaine man had two sonnes: And the

yonger of them said to his father, Father, giue me the portion

of goods that falleth to me. And he diuided vnto them his

liuing. And not many dayes after, the yonger sonne gathered

altogether, and tooke his iourney into a farre countrey, and   5

there wasted his substance with riotous liuing. And when he

had spent all, there arose a mighty famine in that land, and

he beganne to be in want. And he went and ioyned himselfe to

a citizen of that countrey, and he sent him into his fields

to feed swine. And he would faine haue filled his belly with   10

the huskes that the swine did eate: & no man gaue vnto him.

And when he came to himselfe, he said, How many hired seruants

From *The Holy Bible, Conteyning the Old Testament, and the New, Newly Translated out of the Originall Tongues* (London, 1611). Transcribed by Diane Bornstein.

of my fathers haue bread inough and to spare, and I perish

with hunger: I will arise and goe to my father, and will say

15   vnto him, Father, I haue sinned against heauen and before thee.

And am no more worthy to be called thy sonne: make me as one

of thy hired seruants. And he arose and came to his father.

But when he was yet a great way off, his father saw him, and

had compassion, and ranne, and fell on his necke, and kissed

20   him. And the sonne said vnto him, Father, I haue sinned

against heauen, and in thy sight, and am no more worthy to be

called thy sonne. But the father saide to his seruants,

Bring foorth the best robe, and put it on him, and put a

ring on his hand, and shooes on his feete. And bring hither

25   the fatted calfe, and kill it, and let vs eate and be merrie.

For this my sonne was dead, and is aliue againe; hee was

lost, & is found. And they began to be merie. Now his

elder sonne was in the field, and as he came and drew nigh

to the house, he heard musicke & dauncing, And he called one

30   of the seruants, and asked what these things meant. And he

said vnto him, Thy brother is come, and thy father hath killed

the fatted calfe, because he hath receiued him safe and sound.

And he was angry, and would not goe in: therefore came his

father out, and intreated him. And he answering said to his

father, Loe, these many yeeres doe I serue thee, neither   35

transgressed I at any time thy commandement, and yet thou

neuer gauest mee a kid, that I might make merry with my

friends: But as soone as this thy sonne was come, which

hath deuoured thy liuing with harlots, thou hast killed for

him the fatted calfe. And he said vnto him, Sonne, thou art   40

euer with me, and all that I haue is thine. It was meete

that we should make merry, and be glad: for this thy brother

was dead, and is aliue againe: and was lost, and is found.

1 CORINTHIANS 13.1–13

Though I speake with the tongues of men & of Angels,

and haue not charity, I am become as sounding brasse or a   45

tinkling cymbal. And though I haue the gift of prophesie,

and vnderstand all mysteries and all knowledge: and though

I haue all faith, so that I could remooue mountaines, and haue

no charitie, I am nothing. And though I bestowe all my goods

50   to feede the poore, and though I giue my body to bee burned,

and haue not charitie, it profiteth me nothing. Charitie

suffereth long, and is kinde: charitie enuieth not:

charitie vaunteth not it selfe, is not puffed vp, Doeth not

behaue it selfe vnseemly, seeketh not her owne, is not easily

55   prouoked, thinketh no euill, Reioyceth not in iniquitie, but

reioyceth in the trueth: Beareth all things, beleeueth all

things, hopeth all things, endureth all things. Charitie

neuer faileth: but whether there be prophesies, they shall

faile; whether there bee tongues, they shall cease; whether

60   there bee knowledge, it shall vanish away. For we know in

part, and we prophesie in part. But when that which is

perfect is come, then that which is in part, shalbe done

away. When I was a childe, I spake as a childe, I vnderstood

as a childe, I thought as a childe: but when I became a man,

65   I put away childish things. For now we see through a glasse,

darkely: but then face to face: now I know in part, but

then shall I know euen as also I am knowen. And now abideth

faith, hope, charitie, these three, but the greatest of

these is charitie.

RICHARD HAKLUYT'S DIVERS VOYAGES
TOUCHING THE DISCOVERIE OF AMERICA

Richard Hakluyt was a preacher educated at Christ Church, Oxford, but the gospel he preached in his writing was colonization of foreign lands for the glory of England and the "advauncement of the kingdome of Christ." He tried to encourage colonization by compiling and publishing various travel narratives and works on geography including *Divers Voyages Touching the Discoverie of America* (1582), *De Orbe Novo* (1587, in Latin), *A Notable History Containing Four Voyages Made by Certain French Captains into Florida* (1587, a translation from the French), and *The Principal Navigations, Voyages and Discoveries of the English Nation* (1589, and an enlarged edition, 1598–1600). His first work, the *Divers Voyages*, was designed to inform his countrymen of what was known about North America and to serve as a manual for potential colonists. The following selections have been taken from the opening and closing sections: the first tells of Sebastian Cabot's voyage, financed by Henry VII in 1498, and of the three Indians he brought home; the second, written by Hakluyt's cousin (Richard Hakluyt the elder, a lawyer of the Middle Temple), provides instructions on how to establish a new colony.

Both selections are written in a simple, expository style. Hakluyt tends to favor relative clauses (ll. 1, 6, 15, 21, 23, 25); "which" is used for a person at lines 1 and 23, and "what" at line 25. The use of the ablative absolute at lines 7–8, 9–10, and the inversions of word order at lines 4, 11–12, may be due to the influence of Latin syntactic patterns. Richard Hakluyt the elder relies more on coordination (ll. 32–38, 39, 41). The spelling of "Bristowe" (ll. 5, 11, 14 — from "brycg stow," bridge place) reflects the earlier pronunciation.

The third person singular present indicative ends with "s" in "becomes" (l. 37), but "eth" in "standeth" (l. 50), "behoueth" (l. 51). Hakluyt uses a plural and an "er" spelling in "merchandizes" (l. 12), but his cousin writes "marchandize" (ll. 31, 39). His cousin also uses "th" for "t" in "inhabithantes" (l. 36) and an "i" for "e" in "interprice" (l. 37). These details point to the unsettled state of written English at the end of the sixteenth century. It was this uncodified language that the earliest colonists brought to America.

Richard Hakluyt's Divers Voyages
Touching the Discoverie of America

This yeere the King, (by meanes of a Venetian whiche

made himselfe very expert and cunning in knoweledge of the

circuite of the worlde and Ilandes of the same, as by a

map
Carde and other demonstrations reasonable hee shewed) caused

     supply   *Bristol*
to man and victuall a shippe at Bristowe, to searche for an   5

Ilande, whiche hee saide hee knewe well, was riche and

replenished with riche commodities. Which Ship thus manned

and victualed at the kinges cost, diuers merchants of London

ventured in her small stockes, being in her as chiefe

Patrone the saide Venetian. And in the companie of the   10

saide shippe sayled also out of Bristowe three or foure

From *Diuers Voyages Touching the Discouerie of America* (London, 1582), sigs. A-3, K-1, 2. Reprinted by Permission of University Microfilms, Ann Arbor, Michigan, 1966.

loaded

small ships fraught with freight and grosse merchandizes,

thread lace

as course cloth, Caps, Laces, points and other trifles,

and so departed from Bristowe in the beginning of May:

mayor's

15   of whome in this Maiors time returned no tidings.

This yeere also were brought vnto the king three men

taken in the new founde Iland, that before I spake of in

mayor

William Purchas time being Maior. These were clothed in

beastes skinnes, and ate rawe fleshe, and spake such speech

20   that no man coulde vnderstand them, and in their demeanour

like to bruite beastes, whom the king kept a time after.

Of the which vpon two yeeres past after I saw two apparelled

after the maner of Englishe men in Westminster pallace, which

at that time I coulde not discerne from Englishe men, till

25   I was learned what they were. But as for speech I heard

none of them vtter one worde. . . .

Notes framed by a Gentleman heretofore to bee giuen to one

that prepared for a discouerie, and went not

settle

The people there to plant and to continue are eyther to

trade

liue without trafficke, or by trafficke and by trade of   30

marchandize. If they shall liue without sea trafficke, at

the first they become naked by want of linen and wollen, and

very miserable by infinite wantes that will otherwise ensue,

and so will they be forced of them selues to depart, or els

Spanish   French

easely they will bee consumed by the Sp. by the Fr. or by   35

the naturall inhabithantes of the countrey, and so the

hindrance

interprice becomes reprochfull to our nation, and a lett

to many other good purposes that may be taken in hande.

unless

And by trade of marchandize they can not liue, excepte

the sea or the lande there may yeelde commoditie for   40

commoditie. And therefore you ought to haue most speciall

settle

regarde of that point, and so to plant, that the naturall

colony

commoditics of thc place and seate, may drawe to you accesse

of Nauigation for the same, or that by your owne Nauigation

45   you may carie the same out, and fetche home the supplye of

colony

the wantes of the seate.

Such nauigation so to bee employed, shall besides the

supply of wantes, bee able to encounter with forreyne force.

trade

And for that in the ample vente of suche thinges as are

England

50   brought to you out of engl. by sea, standeth a matter of

great consequence, it behoueth that all humanitie and

curtesie and much forbearing of reuenge to the inland people

be vsed, so shall you haue firme amitie with your neyghbours,

so shall you haue their inland commodities to maintayne

trade

55   trafficke, & so shall you waxe rich and strong in force.

Diuers & seuerall commodities of the inland are not in

great plentie to be brought to your handes, without the

                   navigable   *lake*

ayde of some portable or Nauigable ryuer, or ample lacke,

and therefore to haue the helpe of suche a one is most

60   requisite: And so is it of effecte for the dispersing

of your owne commodities in exchange into the inlandes.

QUESTIONS AND ASSIGNMENTS

1. The writings of Richard Cely and Henry Machyn reveal many deviations in grammar and spelling from the formal, "standard" English of their time. Do the same kinds of deviations occur in the dialects of Modern English?

2. In her letters to Lord Burghley and King James, Queen Elizabeth follows the principle of functional variety, using a different style to address each man.

    a. What are the distinguishing features of each style?

    b. Are there any specific words that function as code labels, that is, expressions that help to identify the stylistic level?

3. Hugh Latimer's *Sermon on the Ploughers* exhibits a considerable range in style, from colloquial to rhetorical. Point out some of the differences in the language in the various sections. Do similar characteristics distinguish colloquial and rhetorical styles in later Modern English?

4. Look up the following words from Hooker's *Of the Laws of Ecclesiastical Polity* in the *Oxford English Dictionary*: expedient, import, injunction, institute, intermit, volubility.

    a. What are the dates of the first few citations?

    b. What do your findings suggest about the introduction of Latin words into English during the sixteenth century?

5. During the sixteenth century the upper class London dialect, which was becoming the Received Standard, was in the process of changing the inflection of the third person singular of the verb from "th" to "s."

    a. Make a list of the third person singular verb forms that appear in the Early Modern selections.

    b. Does the same writer follow a different practice for different words?

    c. Do any words consistently appear with "th" or "s"?

    d. What do your findings suggest about the manner in which a linguistic change occurs?

6. Early printers used various abbreviations and typographical devices that are unfamiliar to a modern reader. One that often causes confusion is the use of "y" for "th" or "þ," which arose from the lack of "þ" in early Continental type fonts. This practice resulted in forms such as: ye = "the" or "thee," yat or yt = "that." A line over a vowel indicates omission of a following "n" or "m," as in "sō" (some), "thē" (then, them) (this device was very common in manuscripts). Final "e's" were occasionally employed to "justify" lines of type,

that is, to even out right-hand margins. The letter "y" was often used for "i," and "i" for "j" as well as "i." The same symbol was used for "u" and "v," "v" initially and "u" in all other positions. These last two practices also followed those of medieval scribes.

Go over the selections by Latimer, Hooker, and Hakluyt, which are transcribed just as they are found in the early printed editions, and list some examples of these printing practices.

7. The language of the King James Bible has often been praised as a model of English prose. Some of its features are characteristic of the work itself (such as the use of parallel structure). Others are general features of Early Modern English (such as the inflections of verbs). Make a list of items that belong in each category.

8. The selection by the Hakluyts has a simple vocabulary, but many of the words have lost the meanings that their context in *Diuers Voyages* demands.

    a.   Make a list of such words. You might wish to look them up in the *Oxford English Dictionary* in order to find other examples of the lost meanings.

    b.   Have the words become more specialized or more generalized in later Modern English?

9. Make a list of sentences and clauses that contain relative pronouns. Are the restrictions that govern their use the same as in later Modern English?

10. Make a list of negative and interrogative sentences in the Early Modern selections. Are the sentence patterns closer to those of Middle English or later Modern English?

11. Make a list of sentences that contain the verb "do" in the Early Modern selections, placing them under the following categories:

    a.   main verb (ex.: He *did* the job.)

    b.   substitute verb (ex.: I read the book and so *did* Bill.)

    c.   causative verb (ex.: She *did* him to die.)

    d.   mark of emphasis (ex.: They *do* want to come.)

    e.   tense carrier (ex.: He *did* leave = He left.)

Do you find any examples of "do" as a tense carrier in negative and interrogative sentences? (ex.: *Did* he leave? He *did* not leave.)

12. Compare Henry Machyn's language (p. 220) to that of Mistress Quickly, hostess of the Boar's Head Tavern, in Shakespeare's *Henry V* (p. 320). What are some of the similarities and differences?

Colonial American English

JOHN SMITH'S GENERALL HISTORIE OF VIRGINIA,

NEW ENGLAND, AND THE SUMMER ISLES

John Smith, the son of a tenant farmer and land owner in Lincolnshire, was educated at the grammar schools of Louth and Alford and apprenticed to a merchant of Lynn. Finding this life boring, he ran away from home at fifteen, went to sea, served as a soldier in France and the Low Countries, and sailed to Virginia in 1607 with the first expedition sent out by the Royal Virginia Company of London. He wrote several works to encourage colonization including *A True Relation of Such Occurences and Accidents of Note as Hath Hapned in Virginia* (1608); *A Map of Virginia* (1612); and *The Generall Historie of Virginia, New England, and the Summer Isles* (1624), the first publication to claim to be a history of English territory in the New World.

The following selection from the *Generall Historie* tells of the customs of Powhatan's tribe. Smith's description was influenced by the utopic works of the Renaissance, such as Sir Thomas More's *Utopia*; he praises the Indians for being ruled better than many so-called civilized men and portrays their government in terms of English institutions. However, he is unable to use such an analogy in dealing with their domestic life (ll. 46–60), and does not try to do so in discussing executions (ll. 83–97). At line 31, he calls Powhatan's bodyguard a "corps du guard," using an elegant French term first introduced into English at the end of the sixteenth century. He states that the Indians do not have a written language but provides English spellings and translations for some of their words. On this list we find the familiar terms "mockasins" (l. 114) and "tomahacks" (l. 122), which first appear in Smith's *Map of Virginia*.

Like many of the early colonists of Virginia and New England, Smith came from an eastern county, spoke a variety of English close to the London dialect, and had received some training in written English. His writing contains the usual vocabulary and forms found in the London dialect of the late sixteenth and early seventeenth centuries. The plural inflection for the noun is normally "s," as in "magistrates" (l. 2), "places" (l. 4), "kings," "governours" (l. 6); an "n" occurs in "brethren" (l. 56). The third person singular present indicative usually ends in "eth," as in "ruleth" (l. 6), "taketh" (l. 7), "hath" (ll. 9, 15, etc.), "seemeth" (l. 25), "doth" (l. 28); however, an "s" appears in "beats" (l. 89). Both "be" (l. 1) and "are" (l. 105) occur for the third person plural of "to be." Syntactic features that differ from those of later Modern English include use of the relative pronoun "which" for a person (l. 71), "do" as an auxiliary in declarative sentences (ll. 28, 33, 78, 93, 94, 106), formation of a question without an auxiliary (l. 108), and occasional reversal of subject and verb in a subordinate clause (ll. 1–2).

John Smith's Generall Historie
of Virginia, New England,
and the Summer Isles

Although the Country people be very barbarous, yet haue

they amongst them such government, as that their Magistrates

for good commanding, and their people for due subiection, and

obeying, excell many places that would be counted very civill.

The forme of their Common-wealth is a Monarchicall

    government,   5

one as Emperour ruleth ouer many Kings or Governours. Their

chiefe ruler is called Powhatan, and taketh his name of his

principall place of dwelling called Powhatan. But his proper

name is Wahunsonacock. Some Countries he hath which haue

    beene

From *The Generall Historie of Virginia, New England, and the Summer Isles* (London, 1624), pp. 37–38, 40. Reprinted by permission of University Microfilms, Ann Arbor, Michigan, 1966.

10 his ancestors, and came vnto him by inheritance, as the

Country called Powhatan, Arrohateck, Appamatuck, Pamaunkee,

Youghtanund, and Mattapanient. All the rest of his

Territories expressed in the Mappe, they report haue beene

his severall Conquests. In all his ancient inheritances, he

15 hath houses built after their manner like arbours, some 30.

some 40. yards long, and at every house provision for his

entertainement according to the time. At Werowcomoco on the

Northside of the river Pamaunkee, was his residence, when I

was delivered him prisoner, some 14 myles from Iames Towne,

20 where for the most part, he was resident, but at last he

tooke so little pleasure in our neare neighbourhood, that he

retired himselfe to Orapakes, in the desert betwixt

Chickahamanta and Youghtanund. He is of personage a tall

sour
well proportioned man, with a sower looke, his head somwhat

25 gray, his beard so thinne, that it seemeth none at all, his

age neare sixtie & of a very able and hardy body to endure

any labour. About his person ordinarily attendeth a guard

of 40 or 50 of the tallest men his Country doth afford.

Every night vpon the foure quarters of his house are foure

           bow   shot

Sentinels, each from other a flight shoot, and at every halfe   30

         body   of soldiers

houre one from the Corps du guard doth hollow, shaking his

lips with his finger betweene them; vnto whom every Sentinell

doth answer round from his stand: if any faile, they

presently send forth an officer that beateth him extremely.

A myle from Orapakes in a thicket of wood, he hath a   35

house in which he keepeth his kinde of Treasure, as skinnes,

copper, pearle, and beads, which he storeth vp against the

time of his death and buriall. Here also is his store of red

paint for oyntment, bowes and arrowes, Targets and clubs.

             visited

This house is fiftie or sixtie yards in length, frequented   40

onely by Priests. At the foure corners of this house stand

foure Images as Sentinels, one of a Dragon, another a Beare,

the third like a Leopard, and the fourth like a giantlike

man, all made evill favouredly, according to their best

45　workemanship.

He hath as many women as he will, whereof when he

lieth on his bed, one sitteth at his head, and another at his

feet, but when he sitteth, one sitteth on his right hand

and another on his left. As he is weary of his women, he

50　bestoweth them on those that best deserue them at his hands.

When he dineth or suppeth, one of his women before and after

meat, bringeth him water in a wooden platter to wash his hands.

Another waiteth with a bunch of feathers to wipe them in

stead of a Towell, and the feathers when he hath wiped are

55　dryed againe. His kingdomes descend not to his sonnes nor

children, but first to his brethren, whereof he hath 3.

namely, Opitchapan, Opechancanough, and Catataugh, and after

their decease to his sisters. First to the eldest sister,

then to the rest, and after them to the heires male or

60　female of the eldest sister, but never to the heires of the males.

He nor any of his people vnderstand any letters, whereby

to write or reade, onely the lawes whereby he ruleth is custome.

pleases

Yet when he listeth his will is a law and must be obeyed: not

onely as a King, but as halfe a God they esteeme him. His

inferiour Kings whom they call Werowances, are tyed to rule by   65

customes, and haue power of life and death at their command in

that nature. But this word Werowance, which we call and

interpret

construe for a King, is a common word, whereby they call all

commanders: for they haue but few words in their language,

and but few occasions to vse any officers more then one   70

commander, which commonly they call Werowance, or

     Caucorouse,

which is Captaine. They all know their severall lands, and

habitations, and limits, to fish, foule, or hunt in, but they

hold all of their great Werowance Powhatan, vnto whom they

pay tribute of skinnes, beads, copper, pearle, deere, turkies,   75

wild beasts, and corne. What he commandeth they dare not

disobey in the least thing. It is strange to see with what

great feare and adoration, all these people doe obey this

Powhatan. For at his feet they present whatsoever he

80   commandeth, and at the least frowne of his brow, their greatest

spirits will tremble with feare: and no marvell, for he is

very terrible & tyrannous in punishing such as offend him. /

For example, he caused certaine malefactors to be bound hand

and foot, then having of many fires gathered great store of

85   burning coales, they rake these coales round in the forme of a

cockpit, and in the midst they cast the offenders to broyle

to death. Sometimes he causeth the heads of them that offend

him, to be laid vpon the altar or sacrificing stone, and one

with clubbes beats out their braines. When he would punish

90   any notorious enemy or malefactor, he causeth him to be tyed to

a tree, and with Mussell shels or reeds, the executioner

cutteth off his ioynts one after another, ever casting what

off
they cut of into the fire; then doth he proceed with shels and

strip
reeds to case the skinne from his head and face; then doe they

rip his belly and so burne him with the tree and all. Thus   95

themselues reported they executed George Cassen. Their ordinary

correction is to beate them with cudgels. We haue seene a man

kneeling on his knees, and at Powhatans command, two men haue

beate him on the bare skin, till he hath fallen senselesse in a

swoon
sound, and yet never cry nor complained. And he made a woman   100

for playing the whore, sit vpon a great stone, on her bare

breech twenty-foure houres, onely with corne and water, every

three dayes, till nine dayes were past, yet he loued her

exceedingly: notwithstanding there are common whores by

    profession.   105

Because many doe desire to know the manner of their Language,

I haue inserted these few words.

Ka ka torawines yowo.   What call you this.

Nemarough,   a man.

Crenepo,   a woman.   110

Marowanchesso,   a boy.

Yehawkans,　　Houses.

Matchcores,　　Skins or garments.

Mockasins,　　Shooes.

115 Tussan,　　Beds.

Pokatawer,　　Fire.

Attawp,　　A bow.

Attonce,　　Arrowes.

Monacookes,　　Swords.

120 Aumouhhowgh,　　A Target.

Pawcussacks,　　Gunnes.

Tomahacks,　　Axes.

Tockahacks,　　Pickaxes.

Pamesacks,　　Kniues.

125 Accowprets,　　Sheares.

Pawpecones,　　Pipes.

Mattassin,　　Copper.

Vssawassin,　　Iron, Brasse, Silver, or any white mettall.

WILLIAM BRADFORD'S
HISTORY OF PLIMOTH PLANTATION

William Bradford, the son of a farmer and a shopkeeper's daughter in Yorkshire, was a devoted student of the Bible from his early youth. He joined a Puritan group that met at the house of William Brewster, stayed with it when it withdrew from the Anglican Church, migrated to Holland with a group of Separatists in 1608, and sailed to America aboard the Mayflower in 1620. His *History of Plimoth Plantation* traces the fortunes of the colony from 1620 to 1647. The following extract describes the Pilgrims' hazardous landing at Plymouth.

Bradford states that he writes "in a plaine stile, with singuler regard unto the simple trueth in all things." His work is characterized by a sincere, religious tone and a simple, straightforward style. His loosely constructed sentences follow the rhythm and syntax of the spoken language, sometimes shifting direction, as in his mingling of indirect and direct discourse at lines 16–21. The relative pronoun "which" refers to a person in line 16. The third person singular present indicative sometimes ends in "th," as in "doth" (l. 33). Both "bid" (l. 18) and "bad" (lines 5, 16) appear for the past tense of "bid"; this verb had a variety of forms from the Old English period on since two originally distinct verbs, "beodan" and "biddan," were conflated.

Bradford's spelling is fairly phonetic. The "oa" in "broake" (lines 3, 8) and the "ou" in "floud" (l. 11), "could" (l. 27) suggest a diphthongal pronunciation. An "ar" spelling occurs in "darke" (l. 22), where it became standard, and in "harts" (1. 46). An "e" appears for "i" in "devided" (l. 25). A double consonant is often used to indicate a preceding short vowel: "cupple" (l. 4), "gett" (l. 7), "wett" (l. 28), "fitt" (l. 40), "shipp" (l. 45). "Desemr" (l. 47) is an abbreviation rather than a phonetic spelling.

PLATE V: WILLIAM BRADFORD'S
HISTORY OF PLIMOTH PLANTATION

Bradford's handwriting, like his style, is clear and plain. He wrote in the secretary hand, the native English script used for business, record keeping, and other everyday purposes. The letters that differ most from later forms are the *e*, as in "fros*e*," and the *h* in "*h*ard" (line 1). Abbreviations include "&" (line 1), "ye" for "the" (l. 3), "desemr" (l. 15), and a line over a vowel to indicate omission of *n* or *m*, as in "sunshinīg" (l. 4), "cōmand" (l. 36). Bradford's punctuation is close to modern usage. He underlines for emphasis and employs periods, semicolons, and commas to indicate syntactic divisions.

north-west, & it frose hard. But though this had been a day, & night
of much troub...nger vnto them; yet god gaue them a morning of
comforte & refreshing (as vsually he doth to his children) for ye next
day was a faire sunshininge day, and they found them selues to be
on an ysland secure from ye yndeans; wher they might drie their
stufe, fixe their peeces, & rest them selues; and gaue god thanks for
his mercies, in their manifould deliuerances. And this being the last
day of ye weeke, they prepared ther to keepe ye Sabath; on munday they
sounded ye harbor, and founde it fit for shiping, and marched into
ye land, & found diuerse cornfeilds, & little runing brooks, a place as
they supposed) fit for situation, at least it was ye best they could find,
and ye season, & their presente necessitie made them glad to accepte of
it. so they returned to their shipe againe with this news to ye rest of
their people, which did much comforte their harts.
On ye 15. of desem: they wayed anchor to goe to ye place they had disco-
uered, & came within 2. leagues of it, but were faine to bear vp a-
gaine, but ye 16. day ye winde came faire, and they arriued safe in
this harbor. And after wards tooke better veiw of ye place, and re-
solued wher to pitch their dwelling; and ye 25. day begane ~~firs~~
to erecte ye first house, for comone vse to receiue them, and
their goods.

<hr>

The ~~f~~ chap ~~ ~~ The 2. booke

<hr>

The rest of this history (if god giue me life, & opportunitie) I
shall (for breuitis sake) handle by way of annalls; noteing onl
the heads of principall things, and passages as they fell in or-
dor of time. And may seeme to be profitabe to know, or to
make vse of. And this may be as ye 2. booke.

<hr>

The remainder of An^o: 1620, & ~~An 1621~~

<hr>

I shall a litle returne bake and begine with a combination made by them before they came ashore; being ye first foundation of their gouermente in this
place. Occasioned partly by ye discontented & mutinous
speeches that some of the strangers amongst them,
had let fall from them in ye ship; That when they came
ashore they would vse their owne libertie; for
none had power to comand them, the patente they
had being for Virginia, and not for newengland,
which belonged to an other gouerment, with which ye virginia company had nothing to doe. And partly that shuch an
acte

PLATE V: From William Bradford's *History of Plimoth Plantation* (Massachusetts State Library).
north-west, & it frose hard. But though this had been a day & night

273

William Bradford's
History of Plimoth Plantation

After some houres sailing, it begane to snow & raine,

       the   *the*   *the*   *the*

& aboute ye midle of ye afternoone, ye wind increased, & ye

sea became very rough, and they broake their rudder, & it was

as much as 2. men could doe to steere her with a cupple of

                   told

5   oares. But their pillott bad them be of good cheere, for he

    the   *the*

saw ye harbor; but ye storme increasing, & night drawing on,

they bore what saile they could to gett in, while they could

see. But herwith they broake their mast in 3. peeces, & their

saill fell over bord, in a very grown sea, so as they had like

10   to have been cast away; yet by Gods mercie they recovered

                     the tide   *the*

them selves, & having ye floud with them, struck into ye

From *History of Plimoth Plantation* (Boston: Wright & Potter Printing Co., 1899), pp. 105–7.

the
harbore. But when it came too, ye pillott was deceived in

the   *the*
ye place, and said, ye Lord be mercifull unto them, for his

that   *master*
eys never saw yt place before; & he & the mr. mate would

the
have rune her ashore, in a cove full of breakers, before ye   15

strong
winde. But a lusty seaman which steered, bad those which

rowed, if they were men, about with her, or ells they were all

cast away; the which they did with speed. So he bid them be

vigorously
of good cheere & row lustly, for ther was a faire sound

before them, & he doubted not but they should find one place   20

or other wher they might ride in saftie. And though it was

hard   *the*
very darke, and rained sore, yet in ye end they gott under

the   *that*
ye lee of a smalle iland, and remained ther all yt night in

saftie. But they knew not this to be an iland till morning,

the
but were devided in their minds; some would keepe ye boate   25

the

for fear they might be amongst ye Indians; others were so

cold

weake and could, they could not endure, but got a shore,

& with much adoe got fire, (all things being so wett,) and

the *the*

ye rest were glad to come to them; for after midnight ye wind

30　　shifted to the north-west, & it frose hard. But though this

had been a day & night of much trouble & danger unto them,

yet God gave them a morning of comforte & refreshing (as

the

usually he doth to his children), for ye next day was a faire

sunshining day, and they found them sellvs to be on an iland

the

35　　secure from ye Indeans, wher they might drie their stufe,

guns

fixe their peeces, & rest them selves, and gave God thanks

for his mercies, in their manifould deliverances. And this

the

being the last day of ye weeke, they prepared ther to keepe

the *the*

ye Sabath. On Munday they sounded ye harbor, and founde it

the
fitt for shipping; and marched into ye land, & found   40

diverse cornfeilds, & litle runing brooks, a place (as they

        settlement   *the*
·supposed) fitt for situation; at least it was ye best they

     the
could find, and ye season, & their presente necessitie,

made them glad to accepte of it. So they returned to their

        the
shipp againe with this news to ye rest of their people,   45

which did much comforte their harts.

   the   *the*
   On ye 15. of Desemr they wayed anchor to goe to ye

place they had discovered, & came within 2. leagues of it,

    obliged   *the*   *the*
but were faine to bear up againe; but ye 16. day ye winde

came faire, and they arrived safe in this harbor. And after   50

        the
wards tooke better view of ye place, and resolved wher to

       the   *the*
pitch their dwelling; and ye 25. day begane to erecte ye

first house for com*m*one use to receive them and their goods.

PLYMOUTH RECORDS

Local records of New England town meetings are a valuable source of information about Colonial American pronunciation. At more prestigious institutions, such as the General Court at Boston or the House of Burgesses in Virginia, records were kept by trained clerks who used the standard written forms of the language. But the clerks of small towns often had little formal training and spelled words as they sounded to their ears.

The following selections from the Plymouth Records contain a number of spellings that provide insights concerning pronunciation. The spelling "Leiftenant" (l. 3) reflects the traditional British pronunciation, which was common in America in the seventeenth and eighteenth centuries; the later American pronunciation was modeled on the standardized spelling. An identification of "er" and "ar" sounds is revealed in "cellar" (l. 1), "perticular" (l. 14), "persell" (l. 16). An "e" appears for "i" in "minnesters" (l. 2), "publeck" (l. 17), "bredg" (l. 23). Both of these features appeared in British English as early as the fifteenth century. An "i" appears for "e" in "privilidg" (l. 32), "ingagement" (l. 11). Pronunciation of [ɛ] as [ɪ] before "n," prevalent in various regions of the South from where it has traveled to the urban areas of the North, was a common feature of Colonial English. The spelling "apinted" (l. 37) indicates that the diphthong [ɔɪ] was pronounced [aɪ]; this was considered good usage until the end of the eighteenth century, when avoiding it became a mark of careful speech. The spelling "rooade" (l. 38) suggests a diphthongal long "o," which was a characteristic New England pronunciation.

At the beginning of the eighteenth century the syntax and morphology of English were still not entirely standardized. A collective noun occurs with a plural verb at line 1 but with a singular verb at line 7. The third person singular present indicative ends with "s" in "requires" (l. 7), "needs" (l. 35), but with "th" in "runeth" (l. 30), "goeth" (l. 34).

Plymouth Records

Meeting of 1667:

The Towne have agreed that a leantoo and a Cellar shalbe

made and erected to the minnesters house; to bee about halfe

the length of the house; It being left unto Leiftenant Morton

and Serjeant harlow to agree with workmen to doe it; as they

shall Judge most Convenient;   5

It is ordered by the Towne that notice be given to those

that are the owners of the mill That the Towne Requires them

either by a fflood gate or otherwise to take Course that the

herrings
herrings or Alwives may have free libertie to goe up to spawn

att the season therof according to a former agreement and   10

Ingagement; and in case they shall Refuse or neglect soe to

doe that then the Towne will take Course that it shalbe done.

From *Records of the Town of Plymouth* (Boston: W. B. Clarke & Co., 1889), I, 98,
290–91.

Meeting of 1701:

    said

At sd Meting Nathaniel Warren was Chosen to gather the

Money that is due from perticular persons Relating to the

    their

15   scooling there Children the last year.

    said   *parcel*

At sd meeting The town voted to sell A persell of

Meadow Neere unto Will. Elless for to defraying publeck

Charge & gave power to the select men to sell it for the

    aforesaid

Ends aforsd.

20   Voted that the first Monday in october Next to be a

Town Meeting.

    said

At sd Meeting The Town granted Liberty to Richard seers

        bridge

to Make A swing bredg over the town pond Creek.

    said

At sd Meeting Totman had liberty to bring his family

25   into the town.

    said

At sd Meting George Morton Ephraim Morton Nathaniel

Morton Josiah ffinney Benjamin Warren Ebenazur holmes &

Thomas ffaunce Requested of the Town that in Case they Can

great
Make a stream from the grate south pond soe Caled into the

Eel
brook that Runeth through finneys Medows into the Eale River   30

herrings   *said*
in order to the leting up alwives into sd pond that the town

would grant them the privilidg of two or three pole breadth

said   *said*
on Each side of sd strem; of land down along sd strem soe

said
far as the town Comons goeth; which sd Request was granted

to them & to stop the pond when it needs.   35

said
      At sd Meting the select men or any two of them are

appointed
Apinted to lay out A highway from the sandy hill to Lakenham

& from sandwedg Rooade A Mile & a half over dubble brooks

towards Agawam.

THE WINTHROP LETTERS

John Winthrop was born in 1588 in Suffolk, England. He was lord of Groton Manor in that county, a member of the Puritan party, and a lawyer. In 1618 he married Margaret Tyndal, his third wife, the daughter of Sir John Tyndal of Essex. Throughout their marriage, Winthrop was busily occupied in trying to form the Massachusetts Bay Company and to establish a colony in America. In 1630, as Governor of the Massachusetts Bay Colony, he sailed to New England along with about seven hundred Puritan gentlemen, yeomen, and indentured servants. His wife joined him in 1631. In the following letter, Governor Winthrop tells his wife what to pack for her trip to America. Margaret's letter was written in 1637, when her husband was attending the annual General Court of Elections at Newtown (Cambridge).

In both of these letters we find an interesting usage of the second person pronouns. This point of grammar became a political issue in the seventeenth century. The Quakers interpreted the use of "thou" and "you" for familiar and polite address as a denial of the equality of all men and argued for employing the two forms solely on the basis of number. This is the practice followed by John Winthrop. He uses the second person singular forms to address his wife: "thee" (ll. 1, 53, 55), "thou" (ll. 22, 24, 44), "thy" (l. 69); "you" at line 39 probably refers to her as well as her traveling companions; "you" (ll. 56, 57) and "yor" (l. 58) are used to address his children. Margaret Winthrop is less consistent. She refers to her husband as "thee" at line 84 but as "you" at line 72 and uses "your" (ll. 84, 86) for the possessive.

Along with the second person singular pronouns the verb forms "shalt" (l. 22) and "seest" (l. 24) occur in John Winthrop's letter. He generally uses an "s" ending for the third person singular present indicative: "upholds" (l. 10), "makes" (l. 14), "beginnes" (l. 16), "bends" (l. 18), "stirres" (l. 19); but "th" appears in "hath" (ll. 7, 27, 48). The singular for "to be" is "be" at lines 12, 46, but "is" at line 17; the plural is normally "are" (ll. 10, 18, 20, 48), but "be" occurs at line 33, where it could be interpreted as a subjunctive. In Margaret Winthrop's letter the third person singular ends with "s" in "makes" (l. 73), "meanes" (l. 74), but with "th" in "knoweth" (l. 82); only "is" occurs as the singular of "to be" (ll. 81, 82).

John Winthrop's spelling is quite regular. The forms "or" (ll. 7, 10, etc.), "wth" (l. 16), "wch" (l. 18) are abbreviations. The spelling "shewed" (l. 20) indicates the pronunciation that was common until the eighteenth century. An "e" appears for "i" in "hether" (ll. 23, 24), and an "i" for "e" in "togither" (l. 42).

Margaret Winthrop's spelling is more phonetic and reveals the hand of a less practiced writer. An "e" is used for the vowel in unaccented syllables in "honered" (l. 70), "opertunytye" (l. 72), but an "i" in "hir" (l. 70). An "e" appears for "i" in "sperits" (l. 73), "spiret" (l. 79). An "ar" spelling occurs in "hart" (l. 79). In "rituusnesse" (l. 78) we find an obtrusive vowel. A final consonant is dropped in "husban" (l. 70), and a medial syllable in "wondringe" (l. 74).

The Winthrop Letters

Governor Winthrop to His Wife: July 23, 1630.

My Deare Wife, I wrote to thee by my brother Arthur,

but I durst write no more; then I need not care though it

miscarried, for I found him the olde man still; yet I would

have kept him to ease my brother, but that his owne desire to

5   returne, & the scarcitye of provisions heer, yielded the

stronger reason to let him goe. Now (my good wife) let us

join   *our*
ioyne in praysinge or mercifull God, that (howsoever he hath

afflicted us, both generally & particularly mine owne family

in his stroke upon my sonne Henry) yet myselfe & the rest of

our
10 or children & familye are safe & in health, & that he upholds

our   *our*
or hearts that we fainte not in all or troubles, but can yet

From *Some Old Puritan Love Letters*, ed. Joseph A. Twichell (New York: Dodd, Mead & Co., 1894), pp. 163–67, 180–81.

waite for a good issue. And howsoever our fare be but

coarse in respect of what we formerly had, (pease, puddings

our
& fish, beinge or ordinary diet, yet he makes it sweet &

wholesome to us, that I may truely say I desire no better: 15

with
Besides in this, that he beginnes wth us thus in affliction,

it is the greater argument to us of his love, & of the goodnesse

which   *Satan*
of the worke wch we are about; for Sathan bends his forces

against us, & stirres up his instruments to all kinde of mischief,

so that I thinke heere are some persons who never shewed so

much   20

wickednesse in England as they have doone heer. Therefore be

not

discouraged (my deare Wife) by anythinge thou shalt heare from

our   *hither*
hence, for I see no cause to repente of or coming hether, &

our
thou seest (by or experience) that God can bringe safe hether

even the tenderest women & the youngest children (as he did

25   many

in diverse shippes, though the voyage were more teadious than

formerly hath been knowne in this season.) Be sure to be warme

clothed, & to have store of fresh provisions, meale, eggs putt

up in salt or grounde mault, butter, ote meale, pease, & fruits,

30   & a large stronge chest or 2: well locked, to keepe these

provisions in; & be sure they be bestowed in the shippe where

which
they may be readyly come by, (wch the boatswaine will see to &

the quartermasters, if they be rewarded beforehande,) but for

these thinges my sonne will take care, Be sure to have ready at

35   sea 2: or 3: skilletts of severall syzes, a large fryinge

panne, a small stewinge panne, & a case to boyle a pudding in;

white wine
store of linnen for use at sea, & sacke to bestowe among the

saylers: some drinkinge vessells, & peuter & other vessells:

medicine
& for phisick you shall need no other but a pound of Doctor

medicinal paste
40   Wright's Electuarium lenitivum, & his direction to use it, a

scurvy-grass (herb)

gallon of scirvy grasse to drinke a litle 5: or 6: morninges

with

togither, wth some saltpeter dissolved in it, & a little

grated or sliced nutmege.

Thou must be sure to bringe no more companye than so

many as shall have full provisio*n* for a yeare & halfe, for   45

though the earth heere be very fertile yet there must be

tyme & meanes to rayse it; if we have corne enough we may live

which

plentifully. Yet all these are but the meanes wch God hath

our

ordayned to doe us good by: or eyes must be towards him, who

withhold

as he can wthhould blessings from the strongest meanes, so he   50

can give sufficient vertue to the weakest. I am so streightened

with

wth much businesse, as can no waye satisfie myselfe in wrightinge

to thee. The Lorde will in due tyme lett us see the faces of

our

each other againe to or great comforte: Now the Lord in mercye

blesse, guide & supporte thee: I kisse & embrace thee my deare   55 wife. I kisse & blesse you all my deare children, Forth, Mary,

Deane, Sam, & the other: the Lorde keepe you all & worke his

true feare in yor hearts. The blessing of the Lorde be upon all

salutation

my servants, whom salute from me, Jo: Samford, Amy etc.,

60   Goldston, Pease, Chote etc.: my good freinds at Castlins & all

my good neighbors, goodman Cole & his good wife, & all the

rest:

with

Remember to come well furnished wth linnen, woollen,

some more beddinge, brasse, peuter, leather bottells, drikinge

hornes etc.: let my sonne provide 12: axes of severall sorts of

the Braintree Smithe, or some other prime workman, whatever

65   they

(tools for boring holes)

coste, & some Augers great & smale, & many other necessaryes

which

wch I cant now thinke of, as candles, sope, & store of beife suett,

etc.: once againe farewell my deare wife.

Thy faithfull husband, Jo: Winthrop.

Margaret Winthrop to Her Husband: 1637.

To hir Honered husban these be delivered. 70

    Deare in my thoughts, I blush to thinke howe much I have

neclected the opertunytye of presenting my love to you. Sad

spirits *which*

thoughts posses my sperits, and I cannot repulce them wch makes

me unfit for any thinge wondringe what the Lord meanes by all

these troubles amonge us — shure I am that all shall worke to 75

the best, to them that love God, or rather are loved of hime,

obscurity

I know he will bring light out of obcuritye, and make his

righteousness *noon*

rituusnesse shine forth, as clere as the noune daye, yet I

intractable

finde in my selfe an aferce spiret, and a tremblinge hart not

so wilinge to submit, to the will of God, as i desyre. Thear 80

which *which*

is a time to plant and a time to pul up that wch is planted, wch

I could desyre mite not be yet, but the Lord knoweth what is

best and his wilbe done, but i will rite no more, hopeinge to

see thee to morrow my best affections being commended to your

selfe, the rest of our frends at Nuetone, I commit thee to God. 85

          Your lovinge wife, Margaret W.

JONATHAN EDWARDS' SINNERS IN
THE HANDS OF AN ANGRY GOD

Jonathan Edwards was born in 1703 at Windsor, Connecticut, the son and grandson of preachers. He received his M.A. from Yale in 1723, preached at a Presbyterian church in New York, returned to Yale as a tutor, and in 1727 became a minister at his grandfather's church at Northampton, Massachusetts, where he remained for twenty-three years. Edwards was highly regarded as an author in America and Europe. As a supporter of the doctrines of Calvin, he played a major role in the religious controversies that took place in eighteenth-century New England. Between 1736 and 1746 he led the party that favored the movement known as the Great Awakening, a wave of religious enthusiasm stirred up by revivalist preachers who tried to induce emotional upheavals and conversions in their hearers. It began in Northampton and spread over the whole eastern coast from Maine to Georgia. Edwards' *Sinners in the Hands of an Angry God,* preached at Enfield in 1741, belongs to this movement. Reverend Eleazar Wheelock reported that, "there was such a breathing of distress, and weeping, that the preacher was obliged to speak to the people and desire silence, that he might be heard." The sermon was published in Boston in 1741 and went through at least four editions and six reprintings before the nineteenth century.

Edwards' most important stylistic model was the King James Bible. He often uses biblical imagery, as in his figures of the lake of burning brimstone (l. 4), fire (l. 6), clouds (l. 42), storms (ll. 43–45), and chaff (l. 48). He employs parallel structure (ll. 4, 5-8), word pairs (ll. 21–22, 23, 25), and repetition (ll. 30–34) to emphasize his points.

Edwards' careful writing shows the influence of eighteenth-century prescriptive grammar. When he was about sixteen years old, he set down a number of rules for writing on the cover of his *Notes on Natural Science.* One was to follow the recommendations of *The Ladies Library,* a work by Mary Wray (granddaughter of Jeremy Taylor) that contained the precepts adopted by most eighteenth-century grammarians. Edwards' spelling conforms to the standard written forms of the language. Most of his inflections are those of later Modern English. The third person singular present indicative usually ends in "s":

"holds" (l. 9), "makes" (l. 19), "groans" (l. 29), "does" (l. 30), "stays" (l. 46); but a "th" appears in "hath" (l. 41). The verbs "hath" and "doth" maintained a "th" inflection until the latter part of the eighteenth century.

Jonathan Edwards' Sinners in the Hands of an Angry God

The use of this awful subject may be for awakening

unconverted persons in this congregation. This that you have

heard is the case of every one of you that are out of Christ.

That world of misery, that lake of burning brimstone, is

5   extended abroad under you. There is the dreadful pit of the

glowing flames of the wrath of God; there is hell's wide gaping

mouth open; and you have nothing to stand upon, nor any thing

to take hold of; there is nothing between you and hell but the

air; it is only the power and mere pleasure of God that holds

10   you up.

You probably are not sensible of this; you find you are

kept out of hell, but do not see the hand of God in it; but

From *Jonathan Edwards,* ed. Clarence H. Faust and Thomas H. Johnson (New York: American Book Company, 1935), pp. 162–63. Reprinted by permission of the American Book Company.

look at other things, as the good state of your bodily

constitution, your care of your own life, and the means you

use for your own preservation. But indeed these things are   15

nothing; if God should withdraw his hand, they would avail no

more to keep you from falling, than the thin air to hold up a

person that is suspended in it.

Your wickedness makes you as it were heavy as lead, and

to tend downwards with great weight and pressure towards hell;   20

and if God should let you go, you would immediately sink and

swiftly descend and plunge into the bottomless gulf, and your

healthy constitution, and your own care and prudence, and best

contrivance, and all your righteousness, would have no more

influence to uphold you and keep you out of hell, than a   25

spider's web would have to stop a fallen rock. Were it not

for the sovereign pleasure of God, the earth would not bear

you one moment; for you are a burden to it; the creation

groans with you; the creature is made subject to the bondage

of your corruption, not willingly; the sun does not willingly   30 shine upon you to give you light to serve sin and Satan; the

earth does not willingly yield her increase to satisfy your

lusts; nor is it willingly a stage for your wickedness to be

acted upon; the air does not willingly serve you for breath

35 to maintain the flame of life in your vitals, while you

spend your life in the service of God's enemies. God's

creatures are good, and were made for men to serve God with,

and do not willingly subserve to any other purpose, and groan

when they are abused to purposes so directly contrary to their

40 nature and end. And the world would spew you out, were it not

for the sovereign hand of him who hath subjected it in hope.

There are black clouds of God's wrath now hanging directly

over your heads, full of the dreadful storm, and big with

thunder; and were it not for the restraining hand of God,

45 it would immediately burst forth upon you. The sovereign

pleasure of God, for the present, stays his rough wind;

otherwise it would come with fury, and your destruction would

come like a whirlwind, and you would be like the chaff of the

summer threshing floor.

AMOS FARSWORTH'S JOURNAL

Amos Farsworth was born in Groton, Massachusetts on April 28, 1754. He was the son of a farmer and a lineal descendant of Matthias Farsworth, one of the earliest settlers of the town. During the Revolutionary War, Amos joined Captain Farwell's company of Minutemen and kept a diary from April 19, 1775, to May 6, 1779. This diary tells us a great deal about the life and language of an eighteenth-century New England soldier. Amos' education would have consisted of a few weeks of instruction at the town school in the winter. Because of his lack of formal training, his spelling is very phonetic and his syntax close to the spoken language.

Amos' style is colorful and colloquial. There is an effective use of idiom in expressions such as "puled on" (l. 3) and "nothing meterial hapned" (l. 13). A typically American use of hyperbole occurs in "blud was half over shoes" (lines 7-8), and a vivid simile in "the bauls (bullets) sung like bees round our heds" (l. 62). The sentence structure is paratactic or coordinate with frequent ellipsis. Amos often omits the subject pronoun when referring to himself (ll. 1-5, 7, 9, 14, 16). At line 10, he leaves out the subject relative pronoun before "wanted." At line 22, the verb of motion is omitted, a common idiom in colloquial English of the seventeenth and eighteenth centuries. Another syntactic form of colloquial speech is the use of "a" as a prefix before present participles, as in "a strugling" (l. 32), "afiring" (l. 53). Features that depart from what had become standard practice include use of "was" for the third person plural present indicative (ll. 5, 6, 11) and the first person plural (ll. 17, 43); "quiet" as an adverb (l. 20); and "sot" as the past tense of "set" (ll. 40, 56).

Amos' spelling points to many features of his pronunciation. The following spellings indicate an identification of "er" and "ar" sounds: "thare" (ll. 3, 4, 10, etc.), "whare" (ll. 3, 4, 7, etc.), "Genarals" (l. 29), "ordars" (ll. 29, 34), "hart" (l. 64); "er" has become "ur" in "hur" (ll. 56, 57). An "i" appears for "e" in "bin" (l. 3), "intrenching" (l. 11), "rigiment" (ll. 14, 15), "ingagement" (l. 58), "frinds" (l. 69); and an "e" for "i" in "Aprel" (ll. 9, 13, 28, 32). The pronunciation [u] rather than [ju] is suggested by "vewed" (l. 11), "Tusday" (ll. 28, 63). The diphthong [ɔɪ] appears as [aɪ] in "gined" (l. 34). Certain spellings suggest unclear articulation of consonants: [θ] occurs for [ʃ] in "mothon" (l. 16); [ʃ] for [s] in "townshind" (l. 35); [ŋ] for [d] in "townsing" (l. 59); and [tʃ] for [k] in "thitch" (l. 49). The [s] is followed by a "t" in "offist"

(l. 33). In "hoses" (ll. 38, 41) and "mash" (l. 45) the "r" is omitted, a trait that occurred in Southern British, New England, and Southern American speech. The use of "n" for "ng" in "firin" (l. 2) and "liven" (l. 65) suggests a pronunciation of [n] rather than [ŋ]. Syllables are dropped in "larm" (l. 27), "victry" (l. 54), and "parding" (l. 66).

Amos Farsworth's Journal

Wednsday morning. April 19. 1775. was Alarmd with the

news of the Regulars Firin At Our men At Concoord. Marched

killed
and Came thare whare Some had Bin ciled. Puled on and Came to

Lexington whare much hurt was Done to the houses thare by

braking glas And Burning Many Houses: but thay was forsed to   5

retret tho thay was more numerous then we. And I saw many

blood
Ded Regulars by the way. went into a house whare Blud was

half over Shoes.

thursday Aprel 20. Came to Cambridge in the fore noon.

thare was Some men wanted to go to Charlston. I went for one   10

viewed
and Vewed the regulars And found thay was intrenching on

Charlston hill.

From *Three Military Diaries Kept by Groton Soldiers in Different Wars*, ed. Samuel
A. Green (Cambridge, Mass.: John Wilson & Son, 1901), pp. 83–84, 86–87, 89.

happened

Friday Aprel 21. nothing meterial hapned in the fore

noon. About Sun set marched with the rigiment in Compony

with

15   Col. Larnards rigiment to Roxbury.

motion

Saterday April 22. Cept in mothon. mooved from that

hous that we was in to Another. this night was Alarmed by the

isthmus

Regulars firing at our gard on the neck. turned out And

marched towards them but nothing more Ensued. Soon turned

into

20   our barrocks and Slept quiet.

Sunday Aprel 23. lay Stil in the fore noon. in the

Afternoon the Regiment to the meeting hous And herd a fine

Sermon from Timothy 2.3 thou therefore Endure Hardness as a

good Solder of jesus Christ.

25   monday April 24. in the forenoon I went round on the

Marsh below our Gards within about Sixty rods of the Regulars.

alarm

this night the Regulars fired at our gard but thare was no larm.

Tusday Aprel 25. lay Stil in the forenoon. in the

afternoon we went up to the Genarals And receved ordars and

marched to Cambridge Again. oh the goodness of God in

Preserving   30

my life from Danger.

Aprel 26. 27. 28. and 29. Days. Was A Strugling with

office
the offisers which shold be the hiest In offist. Finally

joined
Farwell got ordars to List and listed Some and then gined with

Townsend
townshind Company And made out A Company. I myself Listed   35

with the rest.

the
Saturday May ye 27. went on hog island And Brought of

horses
Six hoses twentyseven hornd Cattel And fore hundred And

Eleven

Sheep. about the midel of the afternoon went From hog island

set
to Noddles island and Sot one Hous and Barn on fiar, kild Some   40

horses
hoses and Cattel Brought of two or thre Cows one horse. I

with five men got of the horse And Before we got from Noddels

island to hog island we was fird upon by a Privatear Schooner

But we Crost the river and about fiften of us Squated Down in

marsh

45   a Ditch on the mash and Stood our ground. And thare Came

A Company of Regulars on the marsh on the other side of the

river And the Schooner: And we had A hot fiar untill the

flew

Regulars retreeted. But notwithstanding the Bulets flue very

thick

thitch yet thare was not A Man of us kild. Suerly God has A

50   faver towards us: And He can Save in one Place as well as

Another. we left the island about Sun-Set and Came to Chelsea:

And on Saturday about ten At night Marchd to Winnisimit ferry

whare thare was A Schooner and Sloop Afiring with grate fury

on us thare. But thanks be unto god that gave vs the Victry

fired

55   at this time for throu his Providence the Schooner that Plad

set   *her*

upon us the day before run Aground and we Sot fiar to hur And

Consumed hur thare And the Sloop receved much dammage. in

this

ingagement we had not A man kild: But fore wounded but we

Townsend

hope all will Recover. one of the fore was A tounsing man

belonging to our Company the bulet went throu his mouth from   60

one Cheek to the other. thanks be unto God that so little hurt

bullets

was Done us. when the Bauls Sung like Bees Round our heds.

the

Monday Tusday Wedensday And Thursday. June ye 12. 13.

14. 15 days. Alas my Backsliding hart: Oh how have I Revolted

living

from the Liven God. Alas Alas when I am left of God I Do Soon   65

pardoning

fall into Sin. Oh that God would Glorify his grace in Parding

my many-Fold Sin and gilt: Althoe I am A grate And very

    wicked

And Vile one.

    on wedensday I Took Leve of Frinds And Rode to

    Cambridge

And my Brother Came home.   70

THOMAS JEFFERSON'S ESSAY TOWARDS

FACILITATING INSTRUCTION

IN THE ANGLO-SAXON

Thomas Jefferson was the first American to advocate the study of Anglo-Saxon as a regular branch of academic education. He became interested in the language when he was a law student and had to refer to it for the explanation of many legal terms. While studying it, he devised a procedure for simplifying its grammar and normalizing its orthography so as to make it more accessible to students. In 1818 a plan was prepared for the establishment of the University of Virginia, and through the influence of Jefferson, Anglo-Saxon was included as part of the curriculum. His *Essay Towards Facilitating Instruction in the Anglo-Saxon* was composed for the use of the University. It was first published in 1851, twenty-five years after Jefferson's death, by order of the Board of Trustees of the University.

Although Jefferson insists that he is not "an Anglo-Saxon scholar," he shows himself to be a sensitive student of the language. He protests against "too exclusive a prejudice in favor of the Greek and Latin" on the part of seventeenth and eighteenth-century grammarians who had analyzed Anglo-Saxon; they had "embarrassed the language with rules and distinctions, in imitation of the grammars of Greek and Latin." Yet he is too quick to deny any resemblance: "The language of the Anglo-Saxons and English is based on principles totally different from those of the Greek and Latin." He erroneously claims that Anglo-Saxon did not have gender or a dual number. He sees words that later underwent metathesis, such as "brid" (bird), "gaers" (grass), "yrnan" (run), as misspellings. He too readily identifies vowels as orthographical symbols rather than as inflectional endings: he believes that a final vowel was used to "give sound to the consonant preceding it, and they used for that purpose any vowel indifferently." Nevertheless, most of his observations about the irregular orthography of Anglo-Saxon are accurate. His proposed method for normalizing texts resembles the one used in many modern editions. He provides the original Anglo-Saxon text, a normalized version, and a literal translation (ll. 69–89). Furthermore, he is aware of the conservatism of dialects; he states that the "common parlance of unlettered people" often has "preserved more of the ancient language than those whose style has been polished by education."

Jefferson wrote in the lucid, precise prose style that had become popular in the eighteenth century, a style suited to the age of reason. Elaborate rhetorical figures of sound and sense were disdained. Not a single metaphor appears in the following passage. The focus was on logical, forceful reasoning. Jefferson employs an impressive array of historical facts and linguistic examples to support his thesis regarding the continuity of English from Anglo-Saxon to modern times.

Thomas Jefferson's Essay Towards Facilitating Instruction in the Anglo-Saxon

The importance of the Anglo-Saxon dialect toward a
perfect understanding of the English language seems not to
have been duly estimated by those charged with the education
of youth; and yet it is unquestionably the basis of our
5   present tongue. It was a full-formed language; its frame and
construction, its declension of nouns and verbs, and its
syntax were peculiar to the Northern languages, and
fundamentally different from those of the South. It was the
language of all England, properly so called, from the Saxon
10   possession of that country in the sixth century to the time
of Henry III. in the thirteenth, and was spoken pure and
unmixed with any other. Although the Romans had been in
possession of that country for nearly five centuries from the
time of Julius Caesar, yet it was a military possession
15   chiefly, by their soldiery alone, and with dispositions
intermutually jealous and unamicable. They seemed to have
aimed at no lasting settlements there, and to have had little
familiar mixture with the native Britons. In this state of
connection there would probably be little incorporation of
20   the Roman into the native language, and on their subsequent
evacuation of the island its traces would soon be lost
altogether. And had it been otherwise, these innovations would
have been carried with the natives themselves when driven into
Wales by the invasion and entire occupation of the rest of
25   the Southern portion of the island by the Anglo-Saxons.

From *The Writings of Thomas Jefferson*, ed. Andrew A. Lipscomb and Albert E. Bergh (Washington, D.C.: Thomas Jefferson Memorial Association, 1903), XVIII, 365–67, 394, 404–5.

The language of these last became that of the country
from that time forth, for nearly seven centuries; and so little
attention was paid among them to the Latin, that it was known
to a few individuals only as a matter of science, and without
any chance of transfusion into the vulgar language. We may   30
safely repeat the affirmation, therefore, that the pure
Anglo-Saxon constitutes at this day the basis of our language.
That it was sufficiently copious for the purposes of society
in the existing condition of arts and manners, reason alone
would satisfy us from the necessity of the case. Its   35
copiousness, too, was much favored by the latitude it allowed
of combining primitive words so as to produce any modification
of idea desired. In this characteristic it was equal to the
Greek, but it is more especially proved by the actual fact of
the books they have left us in the various branches of   40
history, geography, religion, law, and poetry. And although
since the Norman conquest it has received vast additions and
embellishments from the Latin, Greek, French, and Italian
languages, yet these are but engraftments on its idiomatic
stem; its original structure and syntax remain the same, and   45
can be but imperfectly understood by the mere Latin scholar.
Hence the necessity of making the Anglo-Saxon a regular branch
of academic education. . . .

The dissimilitude between Saxon and English is more
in appearance than in reality. It consists chiefly in the   50
difference of character and orthography. Suppress that . . .
represent the sounds by the English character and orthography,
and it is immediately seen to be, not a different language,
but the same in an earlier stage of its progression. And
such editions of the Saxon writers, by removing the   55
obstructions of character and false spelling, enabling us
to give habitual and true, instead of uncouth and false
sounds to words, would promote the study of the English
language, by facilitating its examination in its mother
state, and making us sensible of delicacies and beauties   60
in it, unfelt but by the few who have had the courage,
through piles of rubbish to seek a radical acquaintance
with it. . . .

A Specimen of the Form in Which the Anglo-Saxon
65   Writings Still Extant Might be Advantageously Published, for
Facilitating to the English Student the Knowledge of the
Anglo-Saxon Dialect.

Genesis—Chapter I.

1.   On anginne gesceop God heofenan and eorthan.
70   On angin y-shope God hevenan and earthan.
In beginning shaped God heaven and earth.

2.   Seo eorthe sothlice wæs ydel & æmtig, and thoestru
wæron ofer thære niwelnisse bradnisse & Godes gast was
geferod ofer wæteru.
75   Se earth sothelic was idle and empty, and thestre weron
over there newelness broadness; and God's gost was y-fared
over water.
The earth forsooth was idle and empty, and darkness were
over the abyss's broadness; and God's ghost was fared
80   over water.

3.   God cwæth tha, ge-weorthe leoht; & leoht wearth ge-worht.
God cwoth tha, y-werth liht, and liht werth y-wrought.
God quoth then were light, and light were wrought.

4.   God geseah tha thæt hit god was, and he to dælde that
85   leoht fram tham theostrum.
God y-saw tha that it good was, and he to-dealed that
liht from tham thestrum.
God saw then that it good was, and he dealed that
light from the darkness.

QUESTIONS AND ASSIGNMENTS

1. Read what Richard Hakluyt has to say in *Divers Voyages Touching the Discoverie of America* (p. 254) about the Indians brought to Westminster Palace, and then examine John Smith's discussion of the Indians and their language in his *Generall Historie of Virginia, New England, and the Summer Isles* (pp. 267–70). What do these comments suggest about the different kinds of linguistic interchange that occurs among people in different environments?

2. The selection from John Smith's *Generall Historie* includes a glossary of Indian words. Look them up in the *Dictionary of American English* (if that is not available, use any unabridged dictionary).

   a. How many of these words have survived?
   b. What kinds of words are they (ex.: nouns, verbs)?
   c. Do your findings suggest anything about the type of borrowing that occurred, and the kinds of contacts that existed between the colonists and the Indians?

3. Study the language and tone of the Winthrop letters. What does the language of the writers reflect about their social and religious background?

4. The selection from William Bradford's *History of Plimoth Plantation* (p. 000) describes the Pilgrims' landing at Plymouth and provides a good example of the language they brought with them. How does his language differ from later American English in regard to sentence structure, vocabulary, inflections, and spelling?

5. Compare Jonathan Edwards' *Sinners in the Hands of an Angry God* (p. 292) with Hugh Latimer's *Sermon on the Ploughers* (p. 232), which was written two-hundred years earlier. How has the language changed? What are the resemblances between the styles of the two authors?

6. Jonathan Edwards, a graduate of Yale, was a careful writer who believed in following the standard forms set forth by eighteenth-century grammarians. How does his writing reveal this influence?

7. Go over the American English selections, and make a list of the third person singular verb forms used by the various authors.

   a. Which form is more common, the "s" or "th" inflection?
   b. Does the practice change in the later selections?
   c. Do any words continually appear with one inflection or the other?
   d. Does the use of a "th" inflection seem more frequent in a formal context?

307

8. In the Journal of Amos Farsworth (p. 297), we have the colloquial language of a writer with little formal training.

    a. What features make his writing colloquial?

    b. Are similar ones found in colloquial English today?

9. Jonathan Edwards was born at Windsor, Connecticut, and Amos Farsworth, at Groton, Massachusetts. Are there any characteristics in the writing of either man that would distinguish him as an American? Consider idiomatic expressions, vocabulary, syntax, inflections, pronunciation as revealed by spelling.

10. Compare the language of Amos Farsworth with that of Hosea Biglow in Lowell's *Biglow Papers*. What are some of the similarities and differences?

11. Examine the samples of literary dialect taken from Tyler's *The Contrast* (p. 327), Lowell's *Biglow Papers* (p. 331), and Harris' *Mingo* and *Nights with Uncle Remus* (p. 336). Then take a look at the chart on regional pronunciations of American English.

    a. What features portrayed by Tyler, Lowell, and Harris appear on the chart?

    b. What features are general characteristics of colloquial American speech?

    c. Which unconventional spellings actually represent standard pronunciations and are merely examples of eye dialect?

    d. What is the stylistic level of the selections and the social level of the speakers? Does your answer suggest anything about the correlation between style, social environment, and non-standard forms of the language?

12. Study the selection from Thomas Jefferson's *Essay Towards Facilitating Instruction in the Anglo-Saxon* and the introductory headnote.

    a. What statements by Jefferson show an enlightened attitude toward language?

    b. Which ones show a good understanding of Anglo-Saxon?

    c. Which ones reveal misconceptions?

    d. How do you like his method for normalizing Anglo-Saxon texts so as to make them easier to read? You might wish to compare his with some modern examples of normalization, such as Francis P. Magoun Jr.'s *The Anglo-Saxon Poems in Bright's Anglo-Saxon Reader* (Cambridge: Harvard University Press, 1965), and John C. Pope's *Seven Old English Poems* (Indianapolis: The Bobbs-Merrill Co., 1966).

    e. Do you agree or disagree with Jefferson about the importance of studying Anglo-Saxon?

Literary Representations of Dialect

GEOFFREY CHAUCER'S REEVE'S TALE

Literary dialect first appears in English literature in Chaucer's "Reeve's Tale" in *The Canterbury Tales*. It is used to indicate the social inferiority of the two Cambridge students, Aleyn and John. Chaucer emphasizes their provincial origins and tells us they were born in a town "fer in the north." The fall of the proud, unscrupulous miller Symkyn is made all the more humiliating because he is outwitted by two country bumpkins.

The northern dialect of the students is portrayed in the phonology, morphology, and vocabulary of their speeches. An "a" replaces Chaucer's usual "o" in "na" (lines 5, 6), "ham" (l. 11), "gas" (l. 16), "fra" (l. 18). An "s" appears for "sh" in "sal" (l. 22). The third person singular present indicative ends with "th" and the plural with "en" or "th" in Chaucer's dialect; in that of the students we find "s" for the singular, as in "boes" (l. 6), "has" (l. 6), "gas" (l. 16), "wagges" (l. 18), "falles" (l. 21), and "s" for the plural in "fares" (l. 2), "werkes" (l. 9). Northern words include "boes" (l. 6), a contracted form of "behooves," "swa" (l. 9), "heythen" (l. 12), and "til" (l. 18).

Geoffrey Chaucer's Reeve's Tale

Aleyn spak first, "Al hayl, Symond, y-fayth!

Hou fares thy faire doghter and thy wyf?"

"Aleyn, welcome," quod Symkyn, "by my lyf.

And John also, how now, what do ye heer?"

                                              no

5   "Symond," quod John, "by God, nede has na peer.

   behooves   *no* *servant*

Hym boes serve hymselve that has na swayn,

Or elles he is a fool, as clerkes sayn.

              expect   *dead*

Oure manciple, I hope he wil be deed,

so   *aches*   *molar teeth*

Swa werkes ay the wanges in his heed;

   therefore   *also*

10 And forthy is I come, and eek Alayn,

                      home

To grynde oure corn and carie it ham agayn.

Edited by John H. Fisher from the Ellesmere Manuscript, with corrections from the Hengwrt, and used with his permission.

hence
I pray yow spede us heythen that ye may."

faith
"It shal be doon," quod Symkyn, "by my fay!

What wol ye doon whil that it is in hande?"

"By God, right by the hopur wil I stande,"   15

goes
Quod John, "and se how that the corn gas in.

Yet saugh I nevere, by my fader kyn,

to   fro
How that the hopur wagges til and fra."

will you   so
Aleyn answerde, "John, and wiltow swa?

Thanne wil I be bynethe, by my croun,   20

And se how that the mele falles doun

shall   diversion
Into the trough; that sal be my disport.

For John, y-faith, I may been of youre sort;

bad
I is as ille a millere as ar ye."

THE SECOND SHEPHERDS' PLAY

Literary dialect first occurs in English drama in *The Second Shepherds' Play*. It is part of the cycle of mystery plays known as the *Towneley Plays* (because the one surviving manuscript was owned by the Towneley family of Lancashire) or the *Wakefield Plays* (because they were performed at the village of Wakefield in Yorkshire). *Noah, The First Shepherds' Play, The Second Shepherds' Play, Herod the Great,* and *The Buffeting* were composed in the early fifteenth century by a man known as the Wakefield Master. His name is not known; but his work is identified by a nine-line stanza with internal and end rhyme (aaaa bcccb), and by his style. He has a satirical, unconventional sense of humor and a strong social consciousness. Both of these characteristics are revealed in the scene of the *Second Shepherds' Play* in which he uses dialect. Mak pretends he is an arrogant messenger of the king and assumes a southern accent, which his comrade calls a "sothren tothe" (l. 28).

When Mak first appears on stage, he employs "I" for the first person pronoun (ll. 3, 4, 7). His third person singular present indicative ending for the verb is "s": "tharnys" (l. 2), "moves" (l. 3), "walkys" (l. 8), "has" (l. 9). When he imitates the king's messenger, he uses a "th" ending in "goyth" (l. 15) and "doth" (l. 26), and "ich" for the first person pronoun (ll. 12, 18, 24). "I" is used at lines 12 and 17, which may be an inconsistency or an unstressed form.

The Second Shepherds' Play

Mak. Now lord, for thy naymes sevyn, that made both moyn &   *moon*

    stars
    starnes

        more   *relate*   *lacks*
    Well mo then I can neuen, thi will, lorde, of me tharnys;

            uneven (at odds)   *brains*
    I am all vneuen, that moves oft my harnes,

                                        children
    Now Wold god I were in heuen, for there wepe no barnes

    So styll.   5

Primus Pastor. Who is that pypys so poore?

                        fared
Mak. Wold god ye wyst how I foore!

    lo, a man that walkys on the moore,

    And has not all his wyll!

From *The Towneley Plays,* ed. George England (London: Early English Text Society, 1897), pp. 122–23. Reprinted by permission of The Council of The Early English Text Society.

tidings

10 *Secundus Pastor.*   Mak, where has thou gon? tell vs tythyng.

each one

Tercius Pastor.   Is he commen? then ylkon, take hede to his

thyng.

I

Mak.   What! ich be a yoman, I tell you, of the king;

messenger

The self and the same, sond from a greatt lordyng,

such

And sich.

15   ffy on you! goyth hence

Out of my presence!

I must haue reuerence;

I

why, who be ich?

Primus Pastor.   Why make ye it so qwaynt? Mak, ye do wrang.

desire you to play the saint believe

20 *Secundus Pastor.*   Bot, Mak, lyst ye saynt? I trow that

wish to

ye lang.

believe   rascal   deceive   devil

Tertius Pastor.   I trow the shrew can paynt, the dewyll

myght hym hang!

be flogged

Mak.   Ich shall make complaynt, and make you all to thwang

At a worde,   25

And tell euyn how ye doth.

true

Primus Pastor.   Bot, Mak, is that sothe?

southern   tooth

Now take outt that sothren tothe,

And sett in a torde!

WILLIAM SHAKESPEARE'S
HENRY IV, PART, II AND HENRY V

Shakespeare used social and regional dialects in his plays to provoke laughter, portray character, and create local color. In the *Henry* plays, Mistress Quickly's speech helps to make her a convincing hostess of the Boar's Head Tavern in Eastcheap. In the following passage she lodges a complaint against Falstaff. She uses a lower class dialect that may be considered Elizabethan Cockney English (her language may be compared with that of Henry Machyn). Shakespeare uses her malapropisms, such as "infinitive" (l. 2), and her unconscious punning, as with "bear" (l. 13), for comic effect. Features in her speech that were characteristic of a lower class dialect include raising the vowel in "exion" (l. 7), unvoicing the final "d" in "Lumbert" (l. 6), using the old-fashioned form and dropping the "d" in "Lubber's" (l. 5), confusing consonants in "indited" (l. 5) and "continuantly" (l. 4), dropping a syllable in " 'scape" (l. 3), and using "a" for "he" (l. 3).

Regional dialects are used in the characterization of the Welsh, Scottish, and Irish captains in *Henry V*. Besides being comic, the dialects contribute a historical touch since men of all these nationalities did fight at Harfleur. Captain Fluellen, the Welshman, unvoices his initial consonants in "plow" (l. 24), "falorous" (l. 37); substitutes "th" for "d" in "athversary" (l. 22), and "ch" for "j" in "Cheshu" (l. 24); and greets his comrade with the dialectal form "godden" (l. 44), a contraction of "good afternoon." His use of "a" for "he" (l. 24) is colloquial rather than regional.

In Captain Jamy's Scottish speech, we find "a" for "o" in "bath" (l. 60), "tway" (l. 76); "u" for "o" in "gud" (l. 60); "u" for the diphthong "ou" in "grund" (l. 72); diphthongs instead of monophthongs in "theise" (l. 71), "ay'll" (l. 72); and "s" for "sh" in "sall" (l. 60). A lowered vowel occurs in "vary" (l. 60) and "wad" (l. 75) and a shortened one in "breff" (l. 74). Other northern forms include "mess" for "mass" (l. 71), "de" (l. 72), "lig" (l. 72), and "suerly" (l. 74). Features that are colloquial rather than regional include dropping a syllable in "'tween" (l. 75), and the contracted forms for "in" (l. 72) and "it" (l. 73).

Captain Macmorris is an early representation of the truculent stage Irishman. His blustering is a burlesque of King Henry's "Once more unto the breach, dear friends" speech in the preceding scene (III, i, 1–34). Macmorris employs "sh" for "st" in "Chrish" (l. 47), "sh" for "s" in "ish" (l. 47), and "ch" for "g" in "beseeched" (l. 65). Among the colloquialisms in his speech are the exclamation "la" (l. 47), the contracted form for "it" (l. 47), the omission of "n" on the past participle "given" (l. 47), the analogical weak past tense for the past participle of "blow" (l. 50), and the dropping of "v" in "save" (l. 67).

Colloquialisms in the speech of the English Captain Gower are the contracted form for "in" (l. 28), and "a" for "he" (l. 35). Although the four dialects are individualized, some of the same colloquial features occur in all of them.

William Shakespeare's
Henry IV, Part II and Henry V

HENRY IV, PART II (II, i, 25-45)

Hostess: I am undone by his going. I warrant you, he's an

infinite   *tavern account*
infinitive thing upon my score. Good Master Fang, hold him

                                        escape   *he*
sure. Good Master Snare, let him not 'scape. A' comes

continually
continuantly to Pie Corner—saving your manhoods — to buy a

                  invited   *Libbard's (Leopard's)*
5   saddle, and he is indited to dinner to the Lubber's Head

        Lombard
in Lumbert Street, to Master Smooth's the silkman. I pray ye,

        action
since my exion is entered and my case so openly known to the

world, let him be brought in to his answer. A hundred mark is

a long one for a poor lone woman to bear. And I have borne, and

From *Shakespeare, The Complete Works*, ed. G. B. Harrison (New York: Harcourt Brace Jovanovich, Inc., 1952), pp. 665, 748–49. Reprinted by permission of Harcourt Brace Jovanovich, Inc.

put off

borne, and borne, and have been fubbed off, and fubbed off, and   10

fubbed off, from this day to that day, that it is a shame to be

thought on. There is no honesty in such dealing, unless a

woman should be made an ass and a beast, to bear every knave's

wrong. Yonder he comes, and that arrant malmsey-nose knave

Bardolph with him. Do your offices, do your offices, Master   15

Fang and Master Snare, do me, do me, do me your offices.

HENRY V (*III, ii, 58–128*)

Gower: Captain Fluellen, you must come presently to the mines.

The Duke of Gloucester would speak with you.

Fluellen: To the mines! Tell you the Duke it is not so good

to come to the mines. For look you, the mines is not according   20

to the disciplines of the war. The concavities of it is not

adversary

sufficient. For look you, th'athversary, you may discuss unto

the Duke, look you, is digt himself four yard under the

he   blow

countermines. By Cheshu, I think a' will plow up all if there

is not better directions.   25

Gower: The Duke of Gloucester, to whom the order of the siege

is given, is altogether directed by an Irishman, a very valiant

gentleman, i' faith.

Fluellen: It is Captain Macmorris, is it not?

30   *Gower:*   I think it be.

Fluellen: By Cheshu, he is an ass, as in the world. I will verify

as much in his beard. He has no more directions in the true

disciplines of the wars, look you, of the Roman disciplines,

than is a puppy dog.

                    he
35   *Gower:*   Here a' comes, and the Scots captain, Captain Jamy,

with him.

                              valorous
Fluellen: Captain Jamy is a marvelous falorous gentleman, that is

certain, and of great expedition and knowledge in th'aunchient

wars, upon my particular knowledge of his directions. By

40   Cheshu, he will maintain his argument as well as any military

man in the world, in the disciplines of the pristine wars

of the Romans.

Jamy: I say gud day, Captain Fluellen.

good afternoon

Fluellen: Godden to your Worship, good Captain James.

Gower: How now, Captain Macmorris! Have you quit the

mines?   45

diggers

Have the pioners given o'er?

it is

Macmorris: By Chrish, la! Tish ill done. The work ish give

over, the trompet sound the retreat. By my hand, I swear, and

my father's soul, the work ish ill done, it ish give over.

I would have blowed up the town, so Chrish save me, la! in an   50

hour. Oh, tish ill done, tish ill done, by my hand, tish

ill done!

Fluellen: Captain Macmorris, I beseech you now will you

vouchsafe

me, look you, a few disputations with you, as partly touching

or concerning the disciplines of the war, the Roman wars, in   55

the way of argument, look you, and friendly communication —

partly to satisfy my opinion, and partly for the satisfaction, look you, of my mind, as touching the direction of the military

discipline. That is the point.

shall   very   both

60 *Jamy:*   It sall be vary gud, gud feith, gud Captains bath.

shall

And I sall quit you with gud leve, as I may pick occasion.

shall

That sall I, marry.

Macmorris: It is no time to discourse, so Chrish save me. The

day

is hot, and the weather, and the wars, and the King, and the

besieged

65 Dukes. It is no time to discourse. The town is beseeched,

and the trumpet call us to the breach, and we talk and, be

save

Chrish, do nothing. 'Tis shame for us all. So God sa' me,

'tis shame to stand still. It is shame, by my hand. And

there is throats to be cut, and works to be done, and there

save

70 ish nothing done, so Chrish sa' me, la!

mass

Jamy: By the mess, ere theise eyes of mine take themselves

I'll   *do*   *lie*   *ground*

to slomber, ay'll de gud service, or ay'll lig i' the grund

                       I'll

for it — aye, or go to death. And ay'll pay't as valorously

        shall   *surely*   *brief*

as I may, that sall I suerly do, that is the breff and the

        would

long. Marry, I wad full fain hear some question 'tween   75

    two

you tway.

ROYALL TYLER'S THE CONTRAST

The humorous dialect character of the rustic Yankee made his first appearance in drama in Royall Tyler's *The Contrast*. Tyler was born into one of the wealthiest families of Boston in 1758, graduated from Harvard, and served as a Major during the Revolutionary War and in Shays' Rebellion. When he visited New York, he became interested in the theater and within a three-week period composed *The Contrast*. It was performed at the John Street Theater in New York City on April 16, 1787, and was the first American play to be performed in public by a company of professional actors.

The theater had a bad reputation in America. The Puritans had established prohibitory laws against theatrical amusements in New England, and in 1778 the Continental Congress had ruled that any government official who attended a play should be dismissed from office. But the success of *The Contrast* helped to bring about a change in sentiment. George Washington, President of the United States, appears at the top of the list of subscribers. The play contrasts individuals who have remained true to simple, honest American ideals with those who have been corrupted by the doctrines of Lord Chesterfield and the fashions of Paris. Colonel Manly is the serious spokesman for American ideals, whereas Jonathan supports them in a naive, comic way.

In the following scene Jonathan tells two fellow servants, Jenny and Jessamy, of having gone to a place where he expected to see a magician, but "they lifted up a great green cloth and let us look right into the next neighbor's house." He is horrified to discover that he has seen a play. Jonathan's speech helps to make him a convincing rustic Yankee. It is filled with colloquial, idiomatic expressions, such as "they came on as thick as mustard" (l. 1), "jocky me out of my money" (l. 34), "dogs a bit of a sight" (l. 35), and "jogged off" (l. 40). "Shooting irons" (l. 17), "mayhap" (l. 25), and "think on't" (l. 27) contribute an archaic flavor. Dialect words include "sling" (l. 11), an American drink made of brandy or rum and water, and "tarnally" (l. 28), an aphetic form of "eternally." Dialectal features of pronunciation are the dropping of "h" in "here" (ll. 17, 25), "a" for "o" in "drap" (l. 12), and possibly the "ar" in "Darby" (l. 9).

Royall Tyler's The Contrast

Jonathan: Why, they came on as thick as mustard. For my

part, I thought the house was haunted. There was a soldier

fellow, who talked about his row de dow, dow, and courted a

young woman; but, of all the cute folk I saw, I liked one

little fellow —   5

Jenny: Aye! who was he?

Jonathan: Why, he had red hair, and a little round plump

face like mine, only not altogether so handsome. His name was —

Darby; —that was his baptizing name; his other name I forgot.

Oh! it was Wig—Wag—Wag-all, Darby Wag-all, — pray, do   10

drink
you know him? I should like to take a sling with him, or a

drop
drap of cyder with a pepper-pod in it, to make it warm and

comfortable.

From *The Contrast* (New York: Burt Franklin, 1970), pp. 56–58. Reprint of 1787
edition.

Jenny: I can't say I have that pleasure.

15   *Jonathan:*   I wish you did; he is a cute fellow. But there was

one thing I didn't like in that Mr. Darby; and that was, he was

afraid of some of them 'ere shooting irons, such as your

troopers wear on training days. Now, I'm a true born Yankee

American son of liberty, and I never was afraid of a gun yet

20   in all my life.

Jenny: Well, Mr. Jonathan, you were certainly at the playhouse.

Jonathan: I at the play-house! Why didn't I see the play then?

Jenny: Why, the people you saw were players.

Jonathan: Mercy on my soul! did I see the wicked players?

perhaps
25   Mayhap that 'ere Darby that I liked so was the old serpent

himself, and had his cloven foot in his pocket. Why, I vow,

now I come to think on't, the candles seemed to burn blue, and

I am sure where I sat it smelt tarnally of brimstone.

Jessamy: Well, Mr. Jonathan, from your account, which I

30   confess is very accurate, you must have been at the play-house.

Jonathan: Why, I vow, I began to smell a rat. When I came

away, I went to the man for my money again; you want your

money?

says he; yes, says I, for what? says he; why, says I, no man

shall jocky me out of my money; I paid my money to see sights,

and the dogs a bit of a sight have I seen, unless you call   35

listening to people's private business a sight. Why, says

he, it is the School for Scandalization. — The School for

Scandalization! — Oh! ho! no wonder you New-York folks

are so cute at it, when you go to school to learn it;

and so I jogged off.   40

JAMES RUSSELL LOWELL'S BIGLOW PAPERS

The rustic Yankee is realized most fully as a literary device in Lowell's *Biglow Papers*. The First Series (1848) concerned the Mexican War, and the Second (1866) was written during the Civil War. Lowell states that in creating the character of Hosea Biglow, "I imagined to myself such an upcountry man as I had often seen at antislavery gatherings, capable of district-school English, but always instinctively falling back into the natural stronghold of his homely dialect when heated to the point of self-forgetfulness." He used the Yankee dialect because he believed it was "racy with life and vigor and originality," particularly in its humor and metaphor.

Lowell's comments in his Preface to the Second Series show a strong awareness of the conservatism of dialects in preserving old forms and pronunciations. Through the analysis of spellings and rhymes, he traces many features of the New England dialect back to English literature of the Middle English and Early Modern periods. Pronunciations that he identifies as typical of New England are use of [ɛ] for [æ], as in "ken" (l. 13), "hev" (l. 20), "thet" (l. 22), "hed" (l. 26), "metch" (l. 30), "helves" (l. 31), "hetchet" (l. 32); [ɪ] for [ɛ], as in "agin" (l. 7), "git" (l. 21), "yit" (l. 25); [ɛ] for [ɪ], as in "ef" (l. 13), "sence" (l. 17), "ben" (l. 18); [ɛ] for [ʌ] in "resh" (l. 38); [ʊ] for [o] in "druv" (l. 36); [ʌ] for [ɑ] and [w] for [hw] in "wut" (l. 4); dropping of "r," as in "wuth" (l. 36).

Features identified as characteristic of New England which also appear in the colloquial speech of other regions include omitting the first syllable in "without" (l. 8) and the "w" in "would" (l. 11); dropping a final "d," as in "han" (l. 1), "an" (l. 7), "kin" (l. 10); using [n] for [ŋ] as in "requestin" (l. 2), "comin" (l. 4), "sunthin" (l. 9), "rattlin" (l. 10). Other general colloquial features are the use of contractions for "is" (l. 4), "in" (l. 9), "of" (l. 9), "the" (l. 23); and dropping "th" in "them" (l. 6). Among the non-standard forms are the contraction "ain't" (l. 3), which appears with an intrusive "h" at line 18; omission of "has" before "come" (l. 1); "begun" as the preterit of "begin" (l. 17); "took" as the past participle of "take" (l. 20). Use of "a" as a prefix of the present participle, as in "a-wheelin" (l. 40), was common in colloquial speech until the early twentieth century, and this form often appears in literary dialect.

James Russell Lowell's
Biglow Papers

Mr. Hosea Biglow to the Editor of the Atlantic Monthly:

> Dear Sir, Your letter come to han',
>
> Requestin' me to please be funny;
>
> But I ain't made upon a plan
>
> Thet knows wut's comin', gall or honey:
>
> Ther's times the world doos look so queer,   5
>
> Odd fancies come afore I call 'em;
>
> An' then agin, for half a year,
>
> <small>*without*</small>
> No preacher 'thout a call's more solemn.
>
> You're 'n want o'sunthin' light an' cute,
>
> Rattlin' an' shrewd an' kin' o' jingleish,   10

From *The Biglow Papers, Second Series* (Boston: Ticknor and Fields, 1867), pp. 212–14.

would
An' wish, pervidin' it 'ould suit,

I'd take an' citify my English.

I ken write long-tailed, ef I please,

But when I'm jokin', no, I thankee;

15   Then, 'fore I know it, my idees

Run helter-skelter into Yankee.

Sence I begun to scribble rhyme,

I tell ye wut, I hain't ben foolin';

The parson's books, life, death, an' time

20   Hev took some trouble with my schoolin';

earth
Nor th'airth don't git put out with me,

as
Thet love her 'z though she wuz a woman;

Why, th'ain't a bird upon the tree

But half forgives my bein' human.

25   An' yit I love th'unhighschooled way

had
Ol' farmers hed when I wuz younger;

Their talk wuz meatier, an' 'ould stay,

    While book-froth seems to whet your hunger;

For puttin' in a downright lick

    'Twixt Humbug's eyes, ther's few can metch it,   30

An' then it helves my thoughts ez slick

    Ez stret-grained hickory doos a hetchet.

But when I can't, I can't, thet's all,

                          fooling
    For Natur' won't put up with gullin';

Idees you hev to shove an' haul   35

        drove   *worth*   *herbaceous plant*
    Like a druv pig ain't wuth a mullein;

Live thoughts ain't sent for; thru all rifts

                   rush
    O' sense they pour an' resh ye onwards,

Like rivers when south-lyin' drifts

              earth
    Feel thet th' old airth's a-wheelin' sunwards.   40

JOEL CHANDLER HARRIS'S MINGO
AND NIGHTS WITH UNCLE REMUS

Many nineteenth-century American authors tried to capture the atmosphere of their native regions in literary works. Dialect was one of the tools they used. Joel Chandler Harris was one of the most skillful literary transcribers of Southern speech. He tried to make his representations phonetically genuine, for he believed that the dialect was "a part of the legends themselves, and to present them in any other way would be to rob them of everything that gives them vitality."

In *Mingo*, a story set in the village of Rockville in Middle Georgia, Harris portrays the dialects of Mrs. Feratia Bivins, a middle-class white woman, and Mingo, a black man who works for her. Their dialects are very similar. Southern features that would be shared by both speakers are omission of "r" with resultant lengthening of the preceding vowel, as in "yo" (l. 3), "po" (l. 3), "wa'n't" (l. 20); a lowered vowel in "thar" (l. 12); use of "allow" to mean "think" or "say" (l. 10). General colloquial forms that would be shared by both include use of the schwa sound [ə] for "of," which Harris spells "er" (ll. 2, 12); dropping final or initial consonants, as in "en'" (l. 2), "cole" (l. 3) "an'" (l. 11), "'im" (l. 13), "'em" (l. 17), "mus'" (l. 26); omitting syllables, as in "'members" (l. 1), "'lowed" (l. 10), "'bout" (l. 16), "gener'ly" (l. 16), "'fore" (l. 21), "'way" (l. 22); the contraction "ain't" (l. 14; Mingo uses it in a later passage).

Mrs. Bivins confuses her consonants in "ast" (l. 10) and "thes" (l. 22), and uses intrusive ones in "betweenst" (l. 19), "hit" (l. 22), "hain't" (l. 14). She uses an "s" inflection for the first person singular (ll. 11, 13–14) and often begins her present participles with "a" and ends them with [n] rather than [ŋ] (ll. 11, 13). A feature that appears in Mingo's dialect but not in that of Mrs. Bivins is the use of "d" for "th," as in "wid" (l. 3).

In *African Jack*, Harris presents two black dialects, the Gullah dialect of Daddy Jack and the Middle Georgia dialect of Uncle Remus. The Gullah dialect is spoken along the coast of South Carolina and Georgia. It is a creole or pidgin language that employs a large part of the vocabulary and phonology of English but simplifies its syntax. It has no plural number: "dem" can refer to one thing or many (l. 33). It does not recognize gender: "e" can stand for "he," "she," or "it" (l. 34); "him," which can be masculine or feminine, is here used for "she" (l. 34). Word endings are often reduced to "y," as in "lilly" (l. 33), "t'anky" (l. 34), "eaty" (l. 34), "taty" (l. 35). The dialect makes greater use of auxiliaries but simplifies tense forms, as in "is bin tek" (l. 33), "is bin say" (l. 34), "is bin ris" (l. 36). "Do" appears as an auxiliary in declarative sentences (lines 35, 37, 40). Pronunciations that occur in the Gullah dialect and in the Middle Georgia dialect of Uncle Remus are "d" for "th," as in "da" (l. 33), "dem" (l. 33), "dis" (l. 39); dropping of "r," as in "pop-co'n" (l. 35); omission of "d" in "an'" (l. 37), "ole" (l. 39); and "gwan" for the present participle of "go" (lines 38, 39). This last form, common in black dialect, was formerly current in colonial Southern and New England speech.

In the Middle Georgia dialect of Uncle Remus, we find "d" for "th" in "dat" (l. 43), "de" (l. 44), "dar" (l. 46), "dey" (l. 46), "den" (l. 47), "wid" (l. 56); "d" for "j" in "des" (l. 45); "f" for "th" in "mouf" (l. 47), "bofe" (l. 57); an intrusive "h" on "it" (l. 45); dropping of "r" plus lengthening of the vowel in "mo" (l. 44); omission of "d" in "en'" (l. 44), "hol'" (l. 57), "han's" (l. 57), of "h" in "'im" (l. 44), of "th" in "'em" (l. 45); [ɪ] for [ɛ] in "yit" (l. 53), "gits" (l. 62); a lowered vowel in "dar" (l. 46); an intrusive "y" in "yer" (l. 48), "yuther" (l. 51). Syllables are dropped in "'simmons" (l. 44), "nat'ally" (l. 45), "und'" (l. 52), "br'er" (l. 56), "'bout" (l. 56). The spelling of "obliged" (l. 45) indicates the old pronunciation with [i], which persisted in the South into the nineteenth and early twentieth centuries. An "a" prefix appears on the present participle of "a-tellin" (l. 65), and "gwine" is used for "going" (l. 55); present participles end with [n] rather than [ŋ] as in "marryin" (l. 56), "squallin" (l. 60). An analogical weak past tense is used for "know" (l. 42). The verb "is" occurs with "I" (l. 63) and "they" (l. 46). An "s" inflection appears on the verb for the first person singular in "knows" (l. 61), the first person plural in "goes," "shakes" (l. 49), and the third person plural in "comes," "stays" (l. 50). There is omission of "s" for the third person singular in Uncle Remus' narration of his anecdote (ll. 45, 46, 47, 52), which may be a special form for the historic present, and in his description of Daddy Jack's behavior (l. 57), where it indicates habitual action.

Joel Chandler Harris's Mingo
and Nights with Uncle Remus

MINGO

"Miss F'raishy 'members you, boss," he said [Mingo],

of

bowing and smiling, "en she up 'n say she be mighty glad er

                   cold   *poor*

yo' comp'ny ef you kin put up wid cole vittles an' po'

far'; en ef you come," he added on his own account, "we like

5   it mighty well."

Accepting the invitation, I presently found myself

dining with Mrs. Bivins, and listening to her remarkable flow

of small talk, while Mingo hovered around, the embodiment of

active hospitality.

         allowed   *ask*

10   "Mingo 'lowed he'd ast you up," said Mrs. Bivins,

From *Mingo and Other Sketches in Black and White* (New York: Houghton Mifflin Company, 1896), pp. 10–12.

"an' I says, says I, 'Don't you be a-pesterin' the gentulmun,

of

when you know thar's plenty er the new-issue quality ready

an' a-waitin' to pull an' haul at 'im,' says I. Not that I

begrudges the vittles, — not by no means; I hope I hain't

got to that yit. But somehow er 'nother folks what hain't   15

got no great shakes to brag 'bout gener'ly feels sorter

skittish when strange folks draps in on 'em. Goodness knows,

I hain't come to that pass wher' I begrudges the vittles

that folks eats, bekaze anybody betweenst this an' Clinton,

Jones County, Georgy, 'll tell you the Sanderses wa'n't the   20

set to stint the'r stomachs. I was a Sanders 'fore I married,

just

an' when I come 'way frum pa's house hit was thes like

turnin' my back on a barbecue. Not by no means was I

begrudgin' of the vittles. Says I, 'Mingo,' says I, 'ef the

gentulmun is a teetotal stranger, an' nobody else hain't got   25

ask

the common perliteness to ast 'im, shorely you mus' ast 'im,'

says I; 'but don't go an' make no great to-do,' says I,

'bekaze the little we got mightent be satisfactual to the

gentulmun,' says I. What we got may be little enough, an'

30   it may be too much, but hit's welcome."

AFRICAN JACK

Daddy Jack shut his shrewd little eyes tightly and held

them so, as if by that means to recall all the details of the

that   little   took   those

flirtation. Then he said: "Da' lilly gal is bin tek dem

things   she   said   thank you   she

t'ing. 'E is bin say, 'T'anky, t'anky.' Him eaty da' possum,

potato   she did

35   him eaty da' pop-co'n, him roas'n da' taty. 'E do say,

talked about marrying   raised   voice

'T'anky, t'anky!' Wun I talk marry, 'e is bin ris 'e v'ice

and   little

un squeal lak lilly pig stuck in 'e t'roat. 'E do holler:

young   going

'Hi, Daddy Jack! wut is noung gal gwan do wit' so ole man

said

lak dis?' Un I is bin say: 'Wut noung gal gwan do wit' ole

except   enjoy   herself

40   Chris'mus' cep' 'e do 'joy 'ese'f?' Un da' lil gal 'e

From *Nights with Uncle Remus* (New York: McKinley, Stone & MacKenzie, 1911), pp. 136–37.

flutter herself   away   here

do lahff un flut 'ese'f way fum dey-dey."

"I know'd a nigger one time," said Uncle Remus, after

of

pondering a moment, "w'at tuck a notion dat he want a bait er

persimmons   him

'simmons, en de mo' w'at de notion tuck 'im de mo' w'at he

them   by and by   just   obliged

want um, en bimeby, hit look lak he des nat'ally erbleedz   45

there

ter have um. He want de 'simmons, en dar dey is in de tree.

He mouf water, en dar hang de 'simmons. Now, den, w'at do dat

this   here

nigger do? W'en you en me en dish yer chile yer wants 'simmons,

they're

we goes out en shakes de tree, en ef deyer good en ripe, down

this

dey comes, en ef deyer good en green, dar dey stays. But dish   50

here other   just

yer yuther nigger, he too smart fer dat. He des tuck'n tuck

he stan' und' de tree, en he open he mouf, he did, en wait fer

de 'simmons fer ter drap in dar. Dey aint none drap in yit,"

continued Uncle Remus, gently knocking the cold ashes out of

going

55   his pipe; "en w'at's mo', dey aint none gwine ter drap in dar.

      just exactly   *brother*   *here*

Dat des 'zackly de way wid Brer Jack yer, 'bout marryin'; he

stan' dar, he do, en he hol' bofe han's wide open en he 'speck

de gal gwine ter drap right spang in um. Man want gal, he

just

des got ter grab 'er—dat's w'at. Dey may squall en dey

60   may flutter, but flutter'n' en squallin' aint done no damage

yit ez I knows un, en 't aint gwine ter. Young chaps kin

make great 'miration 'bout gals, but w'en dey gits ole ez

I is, dey ull know dat folks is folks, en w'en it come ter

bein' folks, de wimmen ain gut none de 'vantage er de men.

         just

65   Now dat's des de plain up en down tale I'm a-tellin' un you."

Appendix

BIBLIOGRAPHY

The way in which the authors have used the foregoing selections with their students has been to have them trace the Old English forms and sentences to Modern English; the Middle English back to Old English and forward to Modern; and the Modern back to Middle and Old. The following charts are intended to assist in this and other such linguistic analyses. They make no pretense at providing complete grammars of Old and Middle English or complete accounts of the historical developments. However, they list the most common patterns and changes, and can be used to describe most of the orthographic, phonetic, inflectional, and syntactic details in the selections. A list of reference books to supplement these charts would include the following:

OLD ENGLISH

Brunner, K., *Altenglische Grammatik nach der Angelsachsischen Grammatik von Eduard Sievers*. Halle: Niemeyer, 1951.

Campbell, A., *Old English Grammar*. Oxford: Oxford University Press, 1959.

Cassidy, F. G., and R. Ringler, *Bright's Old English Grammar and Reader*. New York: Holt, Rinehart and Winston, Inc., 1971.

Davis, N., ed., *Sweet's Anglo Saxon Primer*. Oxford: Oxford University Press, 1970.

Marckwardt, A. H., and J. Rosier, *Old English Language and Literature*. New York: W. W. Norton & Company, Inc., 1972.

Quirk, R., and C. L. Wrenn, *An Old English Grammar*. New York: Holt, Rinehart and Winston, Inc., 1957.

MIDDLE ENGLISH

Brunner, K., *An Outline of Middle English Grammar*, trans. G. Johnston. Oxford: Oxford University Press, 1963.

Jones, C., *An Introduction to Middle English*. New York: Holt, Rinehart and Winston, Inc., 1972.

Kaluza, M., *Historische Grammatik der mittelenglischen Sprache*, 2 vols. Berlin: Felber, 1900–01.

Mossé, F., *A Handbook of Middle English*, trans. J. Walker. Baltimore: Johns Hopkins University Press, 1952.

Roseborough, Margaret M., *An Outline of Middle English Grammar*. New York: The Macmillan Company, 1938.

AMERICAN ENGLISH

Krapp, G. P., *The English Language in America*, 2 vols. New York: Century, 1925.

Kurath, H., *A Word Geography of the Eastern United States*. Ann Arbor: University of Michigan Press, 1949.

Kurath, H., and R. I. McDavid, *The Pronunciation of English in the Atlantic States*. Ann Arbor: University of Michigan Press, 1961.

Mencken, H. L., *The American Language*, rev. by R. I. McDavid. New York: Alfred A. Knopf, Inc., 1963.

HISTORICAL GRAMMARS

Brunner, K., *Die englische Sprache*. Halle: Niemeyer, 1950–51.

Jespersen, O., *A Modern English Grammar on Historical Principles*, 7 vols. Copenhagen: Munksgaard, 1909–49.

Luick, K., *Historische Grammatik der englischen Sprache*. Published in parts. Leipzig: Tauchnitz, 1913–40.

Sweet, H., *A New English Grammar*, 2 vols. Oxford: Oxford University Press, 1900–03.

Wyld, H. C., *A History of Modern Colloquial English*, 3rd ed. Oxford: Oxford Univesity Press, 1936.

Wyld, H. C., *A Short History of English*, 3 ed. New York: Dutton, 1927.

DICTIONARIES

A Dictionary of American English on Historical Principles, 4 vols. Chicago: University of Chicago Press, 1938–44.

Hall, J. R. Clark, *A Concise Anglo-Saxon Dictionary*, 4th ed. with Supplement by H. D. Merritt. Cambridge: Cambridge University Press, 1960.

Holthausen, F., *Altenglisches etymologisches Wörterbuch*, 2nd ed. Heidelberg: Winter, 1963.

Kurath, H., and S. Kuhn, *Middle English Dictionary*. Ann Arbor: University of Michigan Press, 1956 —

Mathews, M. M., *A Dictionary of Americanisms on Historical Principles*. Chicago: University of Chicago Press, 1951.

The Oxford English Dictionary, 13 vols. Oxford: Oxford University Press, 1933. Supplement, 1972.

Skeat, W. W., *An Etymological Dictionary of the English Language*, 4th ed. Oxford: Oxford University Press, 1910.

Stratmann, F. A., *A Middle English Dictionary*, ed. H. Bradley. Oxford: Oxford University Press, 1891.

SPECIAL STUDIES

Andrew, S. O., *Syntax and Style in Old English*. Cambridge: Cambridge University Press, 1940.

Bacquet, Paul, *La structure de la phrase verbale à l'epoque alfrédienne*. Paris: Les Belles Lettres, 1962.

Bailey, Richard W., and Dolores M. Burton, *English Stylistics: a Bibliography*. Cambridge, Mass.: M. I. T. Press, 1968.

Brook, G. L., *English Dialects*. London: André Deutsch, 1963.

Chambers, Raymond W., *On the Continuity of English Prose from Alfred to More and His School*. London: Oxford University Press, 1932.

Craigie, W. A., *English Spelling: Its Rules and Reasons*. New York: Crofts, 1927.

Davis, Norman, "Styles in English Prose of the Late Middle and Early Modern Period," *Langue et littératures: Actes du VIIIe congrès de la Fédération Internationale des Langues et Littératures*. Paris, 1961.

Decamp, David, "The Genesis of the Old English Dialects: a New Hypothesis," in *Readings for the History of the English Language*, ed. C. T. Scott and J. L. Erickson. Boston: Allyn & Bacon, Inc., 1968.

Denholm-Young, N., *Handwriting in England and Wales*. Cardiff: University of Wales Press, 1964.

Fillmore, Charles J., "The Case for Case," in E. Bach and R. T. Harms, eds., *Universals in Linguistic Theory*. New York: Holt, Rinehart, and Winston, Inc., 1968.

Fisiak, Jacek, *Morphemic Structure of Chaucer's English*. Alabama: University of Alabama Press, 1965.

Fridén, Georg, *Studies on the Tenses of the English Verb from Chaucer to Shakespeare with Special Reference to the Late Sixteenth Century*. Cambridge, Mass.: Harvard University Press, 1948.

Fries, Charles C., "On the Development of the Structural Use of Word Order in Modern English," in *Readings for the History of the English Language*, ed. C. T. Scott and J. L. Erickson. Boston: Allyn & Bacon, 1968.

Gordon, Ian A., *The Movement of English Prose*. Bloomington and London: University of Indiana Press, 1966.

Hulme, Hilda, *Explorations in Shakespeare's Language: Some Problems of Lexical Meaning in the Dramatic Text*. London: Longmans, Green & Co. Ltd., 1962.

Jones, Charles, "The Grammatical Category of Gender in Early Middle English," *English Studies*, 48 (1967), 289–305.

Jones, Richard F., *The Triumph of the English Language: A Survey of Opinions Concerning the Vernacular from the Introduction of Printing to the Restoration*. Stanford: Stanford University Press, 1953.

Kiparsky, Paul, "Linguistic Universals and Linguistic Change," in *Universals in Linguistic Theory*, ed. E. Bach and R. T. Harms. New York: Holt, Rinehart and Winston, Inc., 1968.

Klima, Edward S., "Negation in English," in *The Structure of Language: Readings in the Philosophy of Language*, ed. J. A. Fodor and J. J. Katz. Englewood Cliffs, N. J.: Prentice-Hall, Inc., 1964.

Kokeritz, Helge, *A Guide to Chaucer's Pronunciation*. New York: Holt, Rinehart and Winston, Inc., 1962.

———, *Shakespeare's Pronunciation*. New Haven: Yale University Press, 1953.

Labov, William, "The Social Motivation of a Sound Change," in *Readings for the History of the English Language*, ed. C. T. Scott and J. L. Erickson. Boston: Allyn & Bacon, Inc., 1968.

———, "Phonological Correlates of Social Stratification," *Ethnography*, 66 (1964), 164–76.

McIntosh, Angus, *An Introduction to a Survey of Scottish Dialects*. London and New York: Thomas Nelson and Sons, 1952.

———, "A New Approach to Middle English Dialectology," *English Studies*, 44 (1963), 1–11.

———, "The Relative Pronouns þe and þat in Early Middle English," *English and Germanic Studies*, 1 (1947–48), 73–87.

Mendenhall, John C., *Aureate Terms: A Study in the Literary Diction of the Fifteenth Century*. Lancaster, Pa.: Wickersham Printing Co., 1919.

Mitchell, Bruce, "Syntax and Word Order in *The Peterborough Chronicle* 1122–1154," *Neuphilologische Mitteilungen*, 65 (1964), 113–44.

Moore, Samuel, "Earliest Morphological Changes in Middle English," in *Readings for the History of the English Language*, ed. C. T. Scott and J. L. Erickson. Boston: Allyn & Bacon, Inc., 1968.

Palmer, Frank R., *A Linguistic Study of the English Verb*. London: Longmans, Green & Co. Ltd., 1965.

Partridge, Eric, *Shakespeare's Bawdy: A Literary and Psychological Essay and a Comprehensive Glossary*. New York: E. P. Dutton & Co., Inc., 1948.

Prins, Anton A., *French Influence in English Phrasing*. Leiden: Universitaire pers Leiden, 1952.

Reed, Carroll E., *Dialects of American English*. Cleveland and New York: World Publishing Company, 1967.

Reskiewicz, Alfred, "Split Constructions in Old English," in *Studies in Language and Literature in Honor of Margaret Schlauch*. Warsaw: Polish Scientific Publishers, 1966.

Salmon, Vivian, "Sentence Structures in Colloquial Shakespearian English," *Transactions of the Philological Society* (1965), 105–40.

Serjeantson, M. S., *A History of Foreign Words in English*. London: Paul, Trench, 1935.

Stockwell, Robert P., "On the Utility of an Overall Pattern in Historical English Phonology," in *Readings for the History of the English Language*, ed. C. T. Scott and J. L. Erickson. Boston: Allyn & Bacon, Inc., 1968.

Traugott, Elizabeth C., "Diachronic Syntax and Generative Grammar," in *Modern Studies in English*, ed. D. Riebel and S. Schane. Englewood Cliffs, N. J.: Prentice-Hall, 1969.

———, *The History of English Syntax: A Transformational Approach to the History of English Sentence Structure*. New York: Holt, Rinehart, and Winston, Inc., 1972.

————, "Toward a Theory of Syntactic Change," *Lingua*, 23 (1969), 1–27.

Tucker, Susie I., *English Examined*: *Two Centuries of Comment on the Mother Tongue*. Cambridge: Cambridge University Press, 1961.

————, *Protean Shape*: *A Study in Eighteenth-Century Vocabulary and Usage*. London: The Athlone Press of the University of London, 1967.

Visser, F. T., *An Historical Syntax of the English Language*, 3 vols. Leiden: Brill, 1963, 1966, 1969.

Workman, Samuel K., *Fifteenth-Century Translation as an Influence on English Prose*. Princeton: Princeton University Press, 1940.

Wright, Joseph, *The English Dialect Grammar*. Oxford: The Clarendon Press, 1905; reprinted 1968.

BRITISH DIALECT AREAS

OLD ENGLISH

NORTHUMBRIAN

Northumbria

Humber
River

Welsh

Mercia

MERCIAN

East
Anglia

Essex

Thames
River

KENTISH

Kent

WEST SAXON

Wessex

Sussex

Welsh

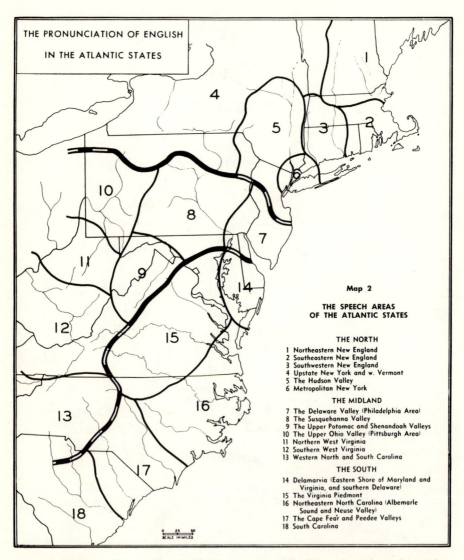

THE PRONUNCIATION OF ENGLISH

IN THE ATLANTIC STATES

Map 2

**THE SPEECH AREAS
OF THE ATLANTIC STATES**

THE NORTH

1 Northeastern New England
2 Southeastern New England
3 Southwestern New England
4 Upstate New York and w. Vermont
5 The Hudson Valley
6 Metropolitan New York

THE MIDLAND

7 The Delaware Valley (Philadelphia Area)
8 The Susquehanna Valley
9 The Upper Potomac and Shenandoah Valleys
10 The Upper Ohio Valley (Pittsburgh Area)
11 Northern West Virginia
12 Southern West Virginia
13 Western North and South Carolina

THE SOUTH

14 Delamarvia (Eastern Shore of Maryland and
   Virginia, and southern Delaware)
15 The Virginia Piedmont
16 Northeastern North Carolina (Albemarle
   Sound and Neuse Valley)
17 The Cape Fear and Peedee Valleys
18 South Carolina

From H. Kurath and R. McDavid, *The Pronunciation of English in the Atlantic States* (Ann Arbor: The University of Michigan Press, 1961), Map 2. Copyright © by The University of Michigan, 1961. Reprinted by permission.

THE PHONETIC ALPHABET

PHONETIC SYMBOLS	SAMPLE WORDS (Old English and Modern English spelling)	
Consonants-Stops	*Old English*	*Modern English*
b	*b*āt	*b*oat
p	*p*ytt	*p*it
d	*d*ocga	*d*og
t	*t*ōþ	*t*ooth
g	*g*old	*g*old
k	*c*yning, *c*orn	*k*ing, *c*orn
Consonants-Fricatives		
v	lu*f*u	lo*v*e
f	*f*lōd	*f*lood
ð	brō*ð*or	bro*th*er
θ	*þ*ing	*th*ing
z	freo*s*an	free*z*e
s	*s*āwan	*s*aw
ʒ	—	vi*s*ion
ʃ	*sc*ip	*sh*ip
h	*h*āt	*h*ot
Consonants-Affricates		
dʒ	bry*cg*	bri*dg*e, *j*udge
tʃ	*c*ild	*ch*ild
Consonants-Nasals		
m	*m*ete	*m*eat
n	*n*ama	*n*ame
ŋ	þi*ng*	thi*ng*
Consonants-Liquids		
l	*l*īf	*l*ife
r	*r*ēn	*r*ain
Semivowels or Glides		
w	*w*īs	*w*ise
j	*g*ēar	*y*ear

Front Vowels	Old English	Modern English
i	mīn (mine)	feet, machine
ɪ	hit	it
e	hē	name, obey
ɛ	settan	set
æ	æt	at

Central Vowels		
ɨ	—	children
ɕ	—	further
ə (schwa)	—	above, sofa
ʌ	—	hut, son
a	stān, nama	hot, father
ȧ	—	past (New England)

Back Vowels		
u	hūs (house)	too, flute
ʊ	full	full
o	tō, mōna (moon)	go, boat
ɔ	—	law, sought

Diphthongs		
aɪ	—	ride
aʊ	—	house
ɔɪ	—	boy
iə	hīe (she), hiera (their)	—
eə	nēod (need), eom (am)	—
æə	ēage (eye), ealde (old)	—

Other Old English sounds not found in Modern English		
ç	riht (right)	Mod. German ich
x	þohte (thought)	Mod. German ach
y	synn (sin)	Mod. French lune

SOME OLD ENGLISH INFLECTIONAL FORMS

MAIN FUNCTIONS OF CASES

Nominative: subject of sentence

Accusative: direct object, extent of space or time, prepositions implying movement or destination in space or time

Genitive: possessive, measure, partitive, object of verbs of depriving or denying

Dative: indirect object, object of impersonal verbs, place, time, instrumental or means of an action, chief case used with prepositions

Instrumental: means or manner of an action

SAMPLE PARADIGMS

NOUNS

Masculine: bāt (*boat*)

Singular			Plural	
	N.	bāt		bātas
	G.	bātes		bāta
	D.	bāte		bātum
	A.	bāt		bātas

Neuter short stem: scip (*ship*)

Singular			Plural	
	N.	scip		scipu
	G.	scipes		scipa
	D.	scipe		scipum
	A.	scip		scipu

Neuter long stem: scēap (*sheep*)

Singular			Plural	
	N.	scēap		scēap
	G.	scēapes		scēapa
	D.	scēape		scēapum
	A.	scēap		scēap

Feminine: talu (*tale*)

Singular			Plural	
	N.	talu		tala
	G.	tale		tala

353

D.	tale		talum	
A.	tale		tala	

Mutation: fōt (*foot, masculine*)

Singular N.	fōt	Plural	fet	
G.	fōtes		fōta	
D.	fēt		fōtum	
A.	fōt		fet	

The -an Declension: oxa (*ox, masculine*)

Singular N.	oxa	Plural	oxan	
G.	oxan		oxena	
D.	oxan		oxum	
A.	oxan		oxan	

ADJECTIVES

Strong or Indefinite Declension (without demonstrative)

wīs (*wise*)	Masc.	Neuter	Fem.
Singular N.	wīs	wīs	wīs
G.	wīses	wīses	wīsre
D.	wīsum	wīsum	wīsre
A.	wīsne	wīs	wīse
I.	wīse	wīse	wīsre
Plural N.	wīse	wīs	wīsa, -e
G.	wīsra	wīsra	wīsra
D.	wīsum	wīsum	wīsum
A.	wīse	wīs	wīsa, -e
I.	wīsum	wīsum	wīsum

Weak or Definite Declension (with demonstrative)

	Masc.	Neuter	Fem.
Singular N.	wīsa	wīse	wīse
G.	wīsan	wīsan	wīsan
D.	wīsan	wīsan	wīsan
A.	wīsan	wīse	wīsan
I.	wīsan	wīsan	wīsan
Plural N.	wīsan	wīsan	wīsan
G.	wīsena	wīsena	wīsena
D., I.	wīsum	wīsum	wīsum
A.	wīsan	wīsan	wīsan

DEMONSTRATIVE

	Masc.	Neuter	Fem.
Singular N.	sē	þæt	sēo
G.	þæs	þæs	þǣre

	D.	þǣm	þǣm	þǣre
	A.	þone	þæt	þā
	I.	þȳ	þȳ	þǣre
Plural	N.	þā	þā	þā
	G.	þāra	þāra	þāra
D., I.		þǣm	þǣm	þǣm
	A.	þā	þā	þā

PERSONAL PRONOUNS

		Singular	*Dual*	*Plural*
First	N.	ic	wit	wē
Person	G.	mīn	uncer	ūre
	D.	mē	unc	ūs
	A.	mē	unc	ūs
		Singular	*Dual*	*Plural*
Second	N.	þū	git	gē
Person	G.	þīn	incer	ēower
	D.	þē	inc	ēow
	A.	þē	inc	ēow
		Masc.	*Neuter*	*Fem.*
Third	N.	hē	hit	hēo
Person	G.	his	his	hiere
Singular	D.	him	him	hiere
	A.	hine	hit	hīe

Third Person Plural	N.	hīe
All Genders	G.	hiera
	D.	him
	A.	hīe

VERBS—SAMPLE CONJUGATIONS

WEAK VERBS (*dental preterit—d or t ending*)

		Class I fēran (*travel*)	*Class II* lufian (*love*)	*Class II* (*mutation*) þencan (*think*)
Present Indicative Singular	1	fēre	lufie	þence
	2	fērest	lufast	þencest
	3	fēr(e)þ	lufaþ	þencþ
Plural		fēraþ	lufiaþ	þencaþ
Present Subjunctive Singular		fēre	lufie	þence
Plural		fēren	lufien	þencen
Present Imperative Singular		fēre	lufa	þence
Plural		fēraþ	lufiaþ	þencaþ
Preterit Indicative Singular	1	fēr(e)de	lufode	þohte
	2	fēr(e)dest	lufodest	þohtest

3	fēr(e)de	lufode	þohte
Plural	fēr(e)don	lufodon	þohton
Preterit Subjunctive Singular	fēr(e)de	lufode	þohte
Plural	fēr(e)den	lufoden	þohten
Present Participle	fērende	lufiende	þencende
Past Participle	(ge)fēred	(ge)lufod	(ge)þoht

STRONG VERBS (*gradation or vowel change for preterit*)

rīdan (*ride*)

Present Indicative Singular	1	rīde
	2	rīdest, rītst
	3	rīdeþ, rītt
Plural		rīdaþ
Present Subjunctive Singular		rīde
Plural		rīden
Present Imperative Singular		rīd
Plural		rīdaþ
Preterit Indicative Singular	1	rād
	2	ride
	3	rād
Plural		ridon
Preterit Subjunctive Singular		ride
Plural		riden
Present Participle		rīdende
Past Participle		(ge)riden

Bēon (*to be*)

Present Indicative Singular	1	eom (W.S.), eam (Merc.), bēo
	2	eart, bist
	3	is, biþ
Plural		sindon, earon (Merc.), bēoþ
Present Subjunctive Singular		sīe, bēo
Plural		sīen, bēon
Present Imperative Singular		bēo
Plural		bēoþ
Preterit Indicative Singular	1	wæs
	2	wǣre (W.S.), wēre (Merc.)
	3	wæs
Plural		wǣron (W.S.), wēron (Merc.)
Preterit Subjunctive Singular		wǣre (W.S.), wēre (Merc.)
Plural		wǣren (W.S.), wēren (Merc.)
Present Participle		bēonde
Past Participle		(ge)bēon

SOME OLD ENGLISH SENTENCE PATTERNS*

Affirmative declarative sentences, main clauses:

    subject + (auxiliary) + verb + (object) . . .

           merchants   brought   their   merchandise Rome
    Englisce cypmenn brohton heora ware to Romanabyrig.
    (Aelfric's *Homily*, l. 23)

       I grant to Athelflede   daughter
    And ic an Athelflede mine douhter þe lond at Cokefield.
    (Aelfgar's Will, lines 8-9)

    and   yielded   gold
    7 menn guldon him gyld.
    (*Anglo-Saxon Chronicle*, l. 47)

Affirmative declarative sentences with an object pronoun:

    subject + (auxiliary) + object pronoun + verb . . .

    they loved   through it   they obtained   wealth to us left
    hie lufedon wisdom & ðurh ðone hi begeaton welan & us læfdon.
    (Alfred's Preface, *Pastoral Care*, lines 34-35)

    and the sailors (boatmen) him deserted
    7 þa butse carlas hine for socan.
    (*Anglo-Saxon Chronicle*, lines 33-34)

    Exception (also indirect object in above example, *Chronicle*, l. 47)

      king   Vortigern   gave them   south   this
    Se cyning Wyrtgeorn gef heom land on suðan eastan ðissum lande.
    (*Anglo-Saxon Chronicle*, lines 4-5)

Negative declarative sentences, main clauses:

$$\text{Ne} + \left\{ \begin{array}{l} \text{verb} \\ \text{auxiliary} \end{array} \right\} + \text{subject} \ldots$$

   * Parentheses indicate optional items, braces, a choice. Line numbers refer to those used in this anthology.

and not lead   you   temptation
7 ne gelæd þu us on costnunge.
(The Lord's Prayer, l. 11)

not were   never   no   so .tortured   they were
for ne uuæren næure nan martyrs swa pined alse hi wæron.
(*Anglo-Saxon Chronicle*, ll. 68-69)

Multiple negatives such as the above were common in Old English and Middle English.

Exception (subject precedes negative particle and verb)

they didn't expect   ever   should   so   careless   become
Hie ne wendon þætte æfre men sceoldon swa reccelease weorðan.
(Alfred's Preface, *Pastoral Care*, ll. 43-44)

Main clauses beginning with adverb of time or place:

$$\text{adverb} + \begin{Bmatrix} \text{verb} \\ \text{auxiliary} \end{Bmatrix} + \text{subject} \ldots$$

this   year   succeeded   English people's kingdom
Her on þisum geare feng Cnut cyning to eall Angel cynnes rice.
(*Anglo-Saxon Chronicle*, ll. 20-21)

and   came   with   ships
7 þa while com Tostig eorl into Humbran mid 1x scipum.
(*Anglo-Saxon Chronicle*, l. 32)

year   went
Þis geare for þe King Stephne ofer sæ to Normandi.
(*Anglo-Saxon Chronicle*, l. 49)

Interrogative sentences:

$$\text{interrogative} \atop \text{pronoun} + \begin{Bmatrix} \text{verb} \\ \text{auxiliary} \end{Bmatrix} + \text{subject} \ldots$$

have   you
Hwæt hæfst þu weorkes?
(*Aelfric's Colloquy*, l. 2)

know   these your companions
Hwæt cunnon þas þine ӡeferan?
(*Aelfric's Colloquy*, l. 7)

perform you
Hu beӡæst þu weorc þin?
(Aelfric's *Colloquy*, l. 12)

Subordinate clauses:

subject + (object) + . . . verb

because   wouldn't   the   track   with our spirit incline
forðamþe we noldon to ðæm spore mid ure mode onlutan.

(Alfred's Preface, *Pastoral Care*, ll. 38–39)

*   kings   who the   power   had   over the people   ministers*
hu þa kyningas þe ðone anwald hæfdon ðaes folces Gode & his ærendwre-

obeyed
cum hirsumedon.

(Alfred's Preface, *Pastoral Care*, ll. 5–6)

although   it   is translated
þeah ðe heo on Englisc awend.

(Aelfric's *Homily*, l. 11)

SOME MIDDLE ENGLISH INFLECTIONAL FORMS

SAMPLE PARADIGMS*

NOUNS

dom (*judgment*)

Singular			Plural	
	N.	dom		domes
	G.	domes		domes
	D.	dom		domes
	A.	dom		domes

The -n Declension: oxe

Singular			Plural	
	N.	oxe		oxen
	G.	oxes		oxen
	D.	oxe		oxen
	A.	oxe		oxen

ADJECTIVES

Strong or Indefinite Declension (without demonstrative)

Singular	good
Plural	goode

Weak or Definite Declension (with demonstrative)

Singular	goode
Plural	goode

DEMONSTRATIVE

Singular	that
Plural	tho

DEFINITE ARTICLE (*from the demonstrative*)

Singular	the
Plural	the

* For dialectal variations, see pp. 371–72.

PERSONAL PRONOUNS

		First Person	*Second Person*
Singular	N.	I, ich, ik	thou, thu
	G.	my, myn	thy, thyn
	D.	me	the
	A.	me	the
Plural	N.	we	ye
	G.	our	your, eower
	D.	us, ous	you, eow
	A.	us, ous	you, eow

Third Person

		Masc.	Neuter	Fem.
Singular	N.	he	hit, it	sche, scho, heo, hi, he
	G.	his	his	hire, her
	D.	him	hit, it	hire, her
	A.	him, hine	hit, it	hire, her, hi

Plural, All Genders	N.	heo, hie, he, hi, they, thai
	G.	hire, here, their, thair
	D.	hem, heom, them, thaim
	A.	hem, heom, them, thaim

VERBS

Weak Verbs (dental preterit): love(n)

Present Indicative Singular	1	love
	2	lovest, love(s)
	3	loveth, loves
Plural		love(n), loveth, love(s)
Present Subjunctive Singular		love
Plural		love(n)
Present Imperative Singular		lov(e)
Plural		love(n), loveth, love(s)
Preterit Indicative Singular	1	lovede, loved
	2	lovedest, lovede(s)
	3	lovede, loved
Plural		lovede(n), loved
Preterit Subjunctive Singular		lovede, loved
Plural		lovede(n), loved
Present Participle		loving, lovinde, lovende, lovand
Past Participle		loved, yloved

Strong Verbs (ablaut or vowel change for preterit): ride(n)

Present Indicative Singular	1	ride
	2	ridest, ride(s)

	3	rideth, rit, rides
Plural		ride(n), rideth, ride(s)

Present Subjunctive Singular		ride
Plural		ride(n)

Present Imperative Singular		rid(e)
Plural		ride(n), rideth, ride(s)

Preterit Indicative Singular	1	rood
	2	ride, rood
	3	rood
Plural		ride(n)

Preterit Subjunctive Singular		ride
Plural		ride(n)

Present Participle		riding, ridende, ridinde, ridand
Past Participle		ride(n), yride(n)

Be, be(n)

Present Indicative Singular	1	am, em, be
	2	art, ert, bist, es
	3	is, biþ, beþ, beis
Plural		are(n), be(n), beoþ, beþ, sinde(n), es

Present Subjunctive Singular		si, be
Plural		si(n), be(e)(n)

Present Imperative Singular		be
Plural		beeþ, be

Preterit Indicative Singular	1	was, wes
	2	were, was
	3	was, wes
Plural		were(n)

Preterit Subjunctive Singular		were
Plural		were(n)

Present Participle		being, beand
Past Participle		bee(n), be, ybe(n)

SOME MIDDLE ENGLISH SENTENCE PATTERNS

Affirmative declarative sentences:

subject + (auxiliary) + verb + (object) . . .

saw   tower   hill excellently made
I saiȝ a tour on a toft triȝely imakid.
(*Piers Plowman*, l. 14)

fighting   *their*
Arestotill sais þat þe bees are feghtande agaynes hym þat will drawe þaire

from
hony fra thaym.
(Rolle's *Bee and the Stork*, ll. 17–18)

their power
Thenne they put alle hyr pouer unto the man that namyd hym captayne

their army
of alle hyr oste.
(Gregory's *Chronicle*, ll. 11–13)

Declarative sentences with impersonal verbs and pronoun objects:

pronoun + verb . . .
object

to me seems   *twice   good*
Me semeth betre to wryten unto a child twies a good sentence than he

once
forgete it ones.
(Chaucer's *Treatise on the Astrolabe*, ll. 38–39)

wonder   fairie origin to me seemed
Me befel a ferly, of fairie   me þouȝte.
(*Piers Plowman*, l. 6)

seems
Me thynketh it acordaunt to resoun

situation in life
To telle yow al the condicioun

them
Of ech of hem, so as it semed me.
(Chaucer's *Canterbury Tales*, ll. 37–39)

Negative declarative sentences:

$$\text{subject} + \text{ne} + \begin{Bmatrix} \text{auxiliary} \\ \text{verb} \end{Bmatrix} \ldots$$

for   she   not was   worthy   for to   be   servant
vor heo nes neuer wurðe vorte beon his schelchine.
(*Ancrene Riwle*, l. 18)

$$*\text{subject} + \begin{Bmatrix} \text{auxiliary} \\ \text{verb} \end{Bmatrix} + \text{not} + (\text{verb}) \ldots$$

saw
I saugh nat this yeer so myrie a compaignye

at once   inn
Atones in this herberwe as is now.
(Chaucer's *Canterbury Tales*, ll. 764–765)

But all myght nat prevayle, for quene Gwenyver wolde never, for fayre

speache nother for foule, never to truste unto sir Mordred to com in hys

hondes agayne.
(Malory, ll. 24–26)

Interrogative sentences:

$$**\begin{pmatrix} \text{interrogative} \\ \text{pronoun} \end{pmatrix} + \begin{Bmatrix} \text{auxiliary} \\ \text{verb} \end{Bmatrix} + \text{subject} + (\text{verb}) \ldots$$

will   you
Hwat wult tu more?
(*Ancrene Riwle*, l. 10)

Why shulden not men do nou so?
(Wyclif's *De Officio Pastorali*, ll. 19–20)

Lo ye all Englysshemen, se ye nat what a myschyff here was?
(Malory, ll. 66–67)

Subordinate clauses:

$$\text{subject} + (\text{auxiliary}) + \text{verb} + (\text{object}) \ldots$$

---

* If the auxiliary is chosen for the second position, the verb follows "not."
** If the auxiliary is chosen for the second position, the verb follows the subject.

                     taught   *people*   *language*

& þus crist & his apostlis tauȝten þe puple in þat tunge

þat was moost knowun to þe puple.

(Wyclif's *De Officio Pastorali*, ll. 18–19)

Some are þat kan noghte flyghe fra þis lande.

(Rolle's *Bee and the Stork*, ll. 38–39)

And whan I sawe the fayr & straunge termes therin, I

feared
doubted that it sholde not please some gentylmen whiche

late blamed me, sayeng that in my tranlacyons I had ouer

erudite
curious termes whiche coude not be vnderstande of

comyn peple.

(Caxton's Prologue to *Eneydos*, ll. 10–14)

VOWEL CHANGES

OLD ENGLISH TO MODERN ENGLISH

I. CHANGES IN QUANTITY

A. *Lengthening*

1. Before end of ninth century, all short vowels and diphthongs were lengthened before homorganic consonant clusters such as ld, rd, mb, nd, ng, rl, rn, rth (voiced). Examples: cīld, fēld, ēald; wōrd, hīerd, swēord; clīmban, cāmb, dūmb; behīndan, bīndan, hūnd; sīngan, tūnge, lāng; ēorl, stīorne, bēarn; ēorthe, fūrther.

Did not occur when consonant group was immediately followed by a third consonant: cildru, cīld; hundred, hūnd; heardra, hēard.

Did not occur in words used frequently in unstressed sentence positions (see below): and, under, sceolde, wolde.

Note shortenings before group lengtheners in thirteenth century (below).

2. Before 1250 (earlier in the North) short vowels a, e, o, in open syllables of words of two syllables became long. Examples: bacan, bāken; caru, cāre; nacod, nāked; beran, bēren; mete, mēte; etan, ēten; flotian, flōten; smoca, smōke; nosu, nōse.

Again frequently prevented by weak sentence stress: have, behāve.

3. Compensatory lengthening occurred in Old English through disappearance of medial h or g: mearh, mēares; seolh, sēoles; brigdels, brīdels; sægde, sæde.

In Middle English, through loss of voiced th or k: other, ōr; siþþan, sīn; makede, māde.

In Middle English, through vocalization of g, c, v, and h: ich, Ī; nigon, nīne; hlæfdige, lāde; niht, nīt; liht, līt.

B. *Shortening*

1. Before consonant groups:

In tenth-eleventh centuries before two consonants other than group lengtheners (above): kepte, softe, brohte, fifta. Did not occur in open syllables: nēdle, ēastan, prēostas.

In thirteenth-fourteenth centuries before group lengtheners: lamb (cf.

lambren, pl.), frend (cf. frendshipe; fēnd, fiend); in weak verbs, wenden, shenden, blenden; frequent before ng, thing, singen, ringen, tunge; before nd, hond, lond, wind.

2.   Before a single consonant in three-syllable words, through weakening of secondary stress or development of parasitic vowel: hāligdōm, halidom; sǣligness, seliness, siliness; brēthren, bretheren; wēpnes, wēpenes, wepenes.

3.   In unstressed syllables. In Modern English a long vowel rarely occurs in an unstressed syllable. This was not the case in Old English; hence, when a vowel came to stand in an unstressed position, it usually became short. Examples: cnāwlǣcan, knowleschen; wīsdōm, wisdom; -hām, -dūn, Durham, Maldon.

4.   In one or two syllable words that occurred frequently with weak sentence stress: an, theah, lǣt, buton.

II. CHANGES IN QUALITY (in IPA notation)

Original Spelling	OE	ME	16c.	17c.	18c.	Eng.	Am.	Modern Spelling
The Long Vowels								
ā, hām	a:	ɔ:	ɔː/oː	oː	oː	oᵁ	oᵁ	home
ǣ, ē̆, ēa, hǣte, lēaf	æ:	ɛ:	ɛː/eː	eː	iː	iː	i¹	heat, leaf
ē, ēo, fēlan, þēof	e:	e:	eː/iː	iː	iː	iː	i¹	feel, thief
ī, ȳ, hwīle, mȳs	i:	i:	əɪ	əɪ	aɪ	aɪ	aɪ	while, mice
ō, dōm	o:	o:	oː/uː	uː	uː	uᵁ	uᵁ	doom
ū, hūs	u:	u:	ou	ou	au	au	au	house
a, nama (orig. short)	a	a:	ɛː	eː	eː	eᶦ	eᶦ	name
The Short Vowels								
a, stagga	a	a	æ	æ	æ	æ	æ	stag
e + r + cons., earm	ɛ	ɛ/a	a	a	a	a	a	arm
æ, hæt, þæt	æ	æ/a	æ	æ	æ	æ	æ	hat, that
e, helm	ɛ	ɛ	ɛ	ɛ	ɛ	ɛ	ɛ	helm
i, y, sittan, pyt	ɪ	ɪ	ɪ	ɪ	ɪ	ɪ	ɪ	sit, pit
o, oxa	ɔ	ɔ	ɔ	ɒ/a	ɒ/a	ɒ/a	a	ox
u, sunne	ʊ	ʊ	ʌ	ʌ	ʌ	ʌ	ʌ	sun
e, i, o, u, + r + cons. heord, brid, word, turf	original sound + r (OE and ME)		ɞ	ɞ	ɞ	ɞ	ɞ	herd, bird, word, turf
The New Diphthongs								
æ, ǣ, e, e + g(h), dæg fæge, weg, twegen	æɪ	æɪ	ɛɪ	eː	eᶦ	eᶦ	eᶦ	day, fay, way, twain
æ, ea, eo, i + w lǣwede, fēawe	orig. sound + w	eu	ɪu	ru/iu	ru/iu	ru/iu	ru/iu	lewd, few
a + g(h), a, o + ht dragan, tahte, bohte	ax, ox	ax, au	ɔᵁ	ɔː	ɔː	ɔː	ɔː	draw, taught, bought
o, u + g(h), bog	ox	ox, ou	ou	ou	au	au	au	bough
a, o, o + w, g(h) cnawan, growan, agan, boga	orig. sound + w, x	ɔu	ɔᵁ	oː	oᵁ	oᵁ	oᵁ	know, grow, own, bow

CONSONANT CHANGES,

OLD ENGLISH TO MODERN ENGLISH

Many of these changes are only orthographic.

C

Preserved as a stop before back vowels: come, cot.

Preserved in combination [ks]: sex, six (spelled *x*). *cw*: spelled *qu* by French scribes: cwen, queen.

Found as hard *k* in *Norman French* words or learned importations: case, catch.

(Palatalized in *Central French* words: charity, chase.)

Found in combination *sk* in borrowed words: *Norse*: skirt, scrub, scoot; *French*: scorn, scour, scout.

Preserved before front vowels resulting from mutation, spelled *k* to distinguish it from *French c*: cyning, king; cempa, kempe; cf. cinque, cent.

Found before front vowels in borrowed words: *OF* kennel, kitten.

Palatalized before and after front vowels, spelled *ch, tch, cch* medially: cirice, church; cild, child; ceorl, churl; wrecan, wretch; specan, speech.

(Palatal *c* from *Central French* fell in with this.)

F

Preserved initially and with voiceless stops: folk, oft. (In *Southern English* shifted to *v* initially: fana, fan, vane; fæt, vat; fyxen, vixen.)

Medially spelled *v* (or *u*) by French scribes to indicate its original sound.

G

Preserved as a stop before back vowels and consonants: gold, green.

Found as hard *g* before *i* by mutation: gylden, gild; gylt, guilt.

In *OF* words where *g* represents *gu*: *ME* gile, guile; giterne, guitar.

ON gil, gill; gest, guest.

Medial and final *g* vocalized to become diphthongs (see vowel chart).

In *Central French*, *Teutonic w* became *gu*: war-guerre, ward-guard. *Middle English* sometimes preserved or borrowed the *Teutonic* as well as borrowing the *French*.

Hard *g* medially or finally usually implies borrowing: *Norse*: egg, big, leg (but cf. dog, stag).

Before front vowels, initial *g* became a semivowel: ger, year; gerd, yard; gedon, idon.

The combination *cg* (seldom found initially in *OE*) palatalized to [dʒ]: hecg, hedge; brycg, bridge. (cf. *Anglo-Norman* just, join, judge, and *Central French* rouge, garage).

H

Lost initially before consonants and elsewhere in unstressed syllables: hlaf, loaf.

hw was respelled *wh*, preserved but softened: hwā-who, hwæt-what.

Medially and finally preserved as aspirate until end of Middle English period, especially in combination with *t*; spelled *ht*, *ght*: right, thought. Later vocalized (see vowel chart).

S

Preserved as voiceless initially and with consonants.

Became [z] intervocalically.

Became [z] in unstressed final syllables, except with voiceless stops: fishes, nets.

The combination sc became sh (both pronounced [ʃ]): fisc, fish; sceal, shall. (cf. OF: iss, perish, finish).

TH

Voiceless except intervocalically through Middle English period, then voiced in pronouns, adverbs, and some other words: this, that, then.

SUMMARY OF MIDDLE ENGLISH
DIALECT CHARACTERISTICS

SOUTHWESTERN

Phonology and Spelling

OE f, s, hw, þ are voiced initially to v, z, w, and voiced th(vox, zit).

OE æ becomes e in early texts (þet, epple; when, then); a by 1300.

OE y becomes u (dude, did; sunne, sin; put, pit; cudgel, rush; cf. busy).

OE eo becomes rounded o, spelled eo, o, ue, u (tro, bleo, ʒung, wurth).

WS ea frequently appears as e (yerd, herm).

a is frequently rounded to o before nasal (man, mon; can, con).

Morphology

Noun: frequent plurals in -en; genitive plural -e or -ene.

Pronoun: ich; genitive and accusative second person plural without y (eow, eower); hine beside him; heo becomes hi, he; h forms for third person plural (hi, here, heom).

Verb: Infinitive -en; third person present singular -eþ, plural -eþ; present participle -inde; past participle y- prefix, strong verbs drop final -n (ybounde); plural of to be, ben.

KENTISH

Phonology and Spelling

f, s, hw, þ are voiced initially to v, z, w, voiced th.

æ becomes e.

OE y becomes e (here, hire; senne, sin; dede, did; merry, knell, cf. bury).

OE eo appears initially, after a dental, and finally as i, y (dyepe, deep; vly, flee).

ea appears as e.

OE ea becomes a rising diphthong spelled ea, ia, yea (dyead, dead; heaued, head).

Morphology

Same as Southwest.

WEST MIDLAND

Phonology and Spelling

f, s, hw, þ not voiced.
æ becomes e.
y becomes u.
eo becomes rounded o.
ea appears as e.
a rounded before nasal to o.

Morphology

Same as East Midland.

EAST MIDLAND

Phonology and Spelling

Old English to Modern English—see vowel and consonant charts.

Morphology (again in the direction of Modern English)

Noun: genitive and plural in -es.

Pronoun: I; scae, þeȝȝre, þeȝȝm appear early; they is regular for nom.

Verb: Infinitive -en; third person present singular -eþ, -es; plural -en; present participle -ende, -ing; y- prefix on past participle lost, but -en retained for strong verbs (bounden).

NORTHERN

Phonology and Spelling

OE c(k), g(h) remain guttural.

OE hw is strongly aspirated, spelled qu, quh (quhat, what).

OE sc (sh) becomes simple s in lightly stressed positions (sal, shall). (The spelling *s* or *ss* may appear in the Southeast but there is purely orthographic; cf. Fr.-iss).

OE ā remains a.

OE ō raised to u [y] or [u] (flude, flood; buik, book).

Morphology

Noun: most plurals in -es; genitive without ending frequent.

Pronoun: ik appears; scho appears regularly; þ forms regular for third person plural (þai, þair, þaim).

Verb: Infinitive without ending; third person present singular -is, -es, plural -e, -is; present participle -and; past participle -en; plural of to be, aren.

SOME CHARACTERISTIC REGIONAL
PRONUNCIATIONS OF AMERICAN ENGLISH

EASTERN NEW ENGLAND

[ȧ]	inconsistently in *afternoon, bath, grass*; consistently in *yard, barn, calm*
[e]	in *dairy,* Mary
[i]	in *beard, ear*
[ɨ]	in the stressed syllable of *sister*; in the unstressed syllables of *haunted, careless*
[u]	after *t, d, n,* as in *Tuesday, due, new*
[ɑ]	in *orange, foreign*; no contrast between *cot-caught, horse-hoarse*
[r]	lost postvocalic, *car, there*; sometimes intrusive, *idea*
[w]	in *what, why*

INLAND NORTH

[e]	in *dairy,* Mary
[æ]	in *stairs, care*
[ɨ]	in unstressed syllables of *haunted, careless*
[u]	in *Tuesday, due, new*
[ɔ]	in *orange, foreign*; contrast between *cot-caught; horse-hoarse*
[r]	retained postvocalic
[ð]	regular in *with*
[s]	regular in *grease* (verb), *greasy*
[w]	in *what, why*

NEW YORK CITY

[e]	in *dairy,* Mary
[a]	in *orange, foreign*
[ɔ]	raised and lengthened in *dog, law*; no contrast between *hoarse-horse, mourning-morning*; contrast between *cot-caught.*
[r]	often lost or weak postvocalic

373

[w]	in *what, why*
[ŋg]	for [ŋ] in *thinking, saying*
[ʔ]	glottal stop in *bottle, mountain*

NORTH MIDLAND

[ɛ]	in *dairy, Mary*
[u]	in *Tuesday, due, new*
[ɔ]	raised and lengthened in *dog, law*; contrast between *cot-caught;* no contrast between *hoarse-horse*; in Western Pennsylvania no contrast between *cot-caught*
[ə]	in unstressed syllables of *haunted, careless*
[ɑ]	for [aɪ] in Appalachian dialect when final and before stops and voiced consonants, *my, night, time*
[r]	retained postvocalic; sometimes intrusive, *wash, judge*
[θ]	regular in *with*
[s]	regular in *grease, greasy,* Mrs.
[hw]	in *what, why*

SOUTH MIDLAND (*Appalachian*)

[ɛ]	in *dairy, Mary*
[ʊ]	in *coop, cooper*
[ju]	in *Tuesday, due, new*
[o]	in *poor, your*
[ɑ]	in *my, night, time*
[ʌ]	in *put*
[r]	preserved postvocalic
[z]	in *grease, greasy,* Mrs.
[hw]	in *what, why*

PLANTATION SOUTH

[ɛ]	in *dairy, Mary, ear, fear*; also in Tidewater dialect, *afraid, date*
[ju]	in *Tuesday, due, new*
[ɔ]	lowered and rounded in *dog, law*; contrast between *cot-caught, horse-hoarse*
[æ]	in *stairs, care*
[ɔ]	for [ɔɪ] in *oil, boil, spoil*
[ɑ]	for [aɪ] when final and before stops and voiced consonants, *my, night, time*
[ɨ]	in stressed syllables, *dinner, sister*; unstressed syllables, *haunted, careless*

[æʊ]	for [aʊ] in Tidewater dialect, before voiceless consonants only, *house, out*
[oͻ], [eͻ]	in Tidewater dialect, centering diphthongs in *road, post, eight, drain*
[r]	lost postvocalic
[z]	in *grease, greasy, Mrs.*
[hw]	in *what, why*